HISPANO FOLKLIFE OF NEW MEXICO

Photograph by Charles L. Briggs

Lorin W. Brown (1900–1978)

HISPANO FOLKLIFE OF NEW MEXICO

The Lorin W. Brown Federal Writers'
Project Manuscripts

by
Lorin W. Brown

with
Charles L. Briggs

and
Marta Weigle

UNIVERSITY OF NEW MEXICO PRESS

Albuquerque

Library of Congress Cataloging in Publication Data

Brown, Lorin W., 1900-1978
  Hispano folklife of New Mexico.

  Bibliography: p. 259
  Includes index.
  1. Mexican American folklore—New Mexico. 2. Mexican Americans—New Mexico—
Social life and customs. 3. Brown, Lorin W., 1900-1978 4. Federal Writers, Projects.
I. Briggs, Charles L., 1953-   joint author. II. Weigle, Marta, joint author. III. Title.
GR104.B76   790'.09789   78-4932
ISBN 0-8263-0475-3

Manufactured in the United States of America
Library of Congress Catalog Card Number 78-51578
International Standard Book Number 0-8263-0475-3
First Edition

To
los viejitos de antes,
the first settlers of the Pueblo Quemado
and their descendants.
L.W.B.
12-77

In memoriam

Lorenzo
friend and mentor

Born November 22, 1900, Elizabethtown, New Mexico
Died January 17, 1978, Oakland, California
Buried January 21, 1978, Cordova, New Mexico

Que en paz descanse.

C.L.B.
M.W.
2-78

CONTENTS

FOREWORD

The following lines bear witness to the rekindling of an old flame. More than thirty years ago I found myself in the employ of the Works Progress Administration's Federal Writers' Project in Santa Fe, New Mexico, and I labored on their behalf for more than half a decade. This opportunity allowed me to amass over four hundred pages on various facets of Hispano or Spanish-American culture. The tumultuous events that transpired in 1941 and the succeeding years halted work on the Writers' Project and led me far away from my native New Mexico. It is no small wonder that the embers of my work were still aglow when I sought to fan them in the early 1970s, and I must say their waxings and wanings have been numerous in the ensuing years.

I happened to arrive in Santa Fe in December of 1972, upon the occasion of the publication of a *Bibliography of Unpublished Materials Pertaining to Hispanic Culture in the New Mexico WPA Writers' Files*. In this work Gilberto Benito Córdova listed 581 manuscripts together with contributors and informants. The ethnic variety of the workers on this project and the diverse corners of New Mexico represented in the papers assured the representation of a substantial cross section of the state's history, folklore, customs, and typical activities. I was made aware of the existence of this bibliography by many of my friends, who were also quite anxious to know what I was going to do with all the manuscripts I had written.

I had given little thought to that phase of my life in the thirty years I was absent. I had lost my copies of my work in a fire in Idaho, so these no longer served to remind me of the WPA days. It was all such old hat to me that I could think of the project only as piles of old, musty papers.

Then I began to see excerpts from some of my writings included in others' sketches on the Southwest, acknowledgments having been granted to the WPA files alone. I became interested enough to endeavor to collect copies of my manuscripts, and I succeeded in doing so with very few exceptions. In reading these over I became imbued with their possibilities and potential, with the idea of enlarging on some of the more meritorious, researching historical background, and increasing the number of characters and expanding the depth of their portrayals.

The flame I had begun to rekindle from some of my embers lasted only for a short while. It was dissipated when I revisited the villages where I had gleaned my information. Los Alamos, with its opportunities for employment, had changed the whole picture in the *plazas;* their atmosphere had altered and the simplicity of village life was gone. The younger generation was living in the modern era of rock and roll, new cars, and a fast pace unknown thirty years back. And all of my narrators had passed on; the wise and ancient *viejos* and *viejitas* of fond recollection were no longer around to help me fan into flames the embers of my typewritten pages of years gone by.

So, greatly disheartened, I forgot my enthusiasm until my good friends and collaborators, Marta Weigle and Chuck Briggs, awoke me from my lethargy and urged me to ready my Federal Writers' Project contributions for publication. I sincerely hope that the resulting volume will interest the reader.

With the onslaught of World War II there was a great hegira of people from the South to the North, to the West Coast, to the munitions factories, the shipyards, a scattering which resulted in the dispersal of many ethnic groups and a greater assimilation into the mainstream of American industrial life. In many cases, the WPA stories are all that remain of their previous life styles, so, hopefully, these embers will be rekindled into living, pulsing volumes for posterity. The three of us are dedicated to this task, and the work which has culminated in this publication has been undertaken in order to add just a bit more fuel to this fire.

So here we submit these embers for your critical appreciation, or, perhaps, delectation, with a reminder that if you are caught out in the woods on a cold day and you run across an abandoned campfire, you have it made. A careful search in the ashes will undoubtedly uncover several embers, and will serve to warm your hands as well. Segregate the embers in a heap; you will find that they will start to glow at just the proximity of one to the other; they love "togetherness." Careful nurture with cautious fanning and the addition of dry grass, twigs, or dried bark will soon reward you with a bright blaze, a cheerful and warming flame for your enjoyment.

Albuquerque, New Mexico   Lorin W. Brown
June 1, 1977

PREFACE

The 1930s witnessed a florescence of serious interest in Hispano New Mexico. Various government agencies sponsored studies and surveys to ascertain how better to administer the desperately needed relief programs. Sociologists and folklorists began to investigate traditional Hispano culture, especially in the northern villages. Literary and artistic individuals, many of whom had earlier championed the state's Indian groups, began more and more to appreciate and defend Hispano customs and crafts. As a result, documentation from this period provides a rich and valuable resource for anyone concerned with Southwestern Hispanic culture.

The Federal Writers' Project in New Mexico initiated and supported some of the most fruitful studies during the late 1930s. Unfortunately, the astonishing amount of ethnohistorical, folklore, and folklife data gathered by workers on the Federal Writers' Project remain largely uncatalogued and unexplored. This book is a step toward the organization and presentation of these important materials.

Lorin W. Brown was one of the most prolific, sensitive, and intuitively skilled field workers on the New Mexico Writers' Project. Today, anyone with a scholarly, professional, or personal interest in New Mexican Hispano culture almost inevitably discovers useful and delightful information in his extant manuscripts, which have, however, remained rather difficult to obtain. Brown's important contributions to the understanding and appreciation of Hispano folklife in New Mexico deserve a wider audience, and this volume results from that conviction.

Part I provides a biographical background on Lorin Brown and ethnohistorical data on Cordova, New Mexico, where he gathered much of his Federal Writers' Project material. The biography is based on numerous conversations with Brown, two taped interviews in 1976, taped reminiscences he made on his own, and xii

correspondence received by Weigle between 1970 and 1977, and by Briggs since 1973. Brown read and approved this final version, which includes extensive, direct quotations from his letters and tapes. The sketch on Cordova derives from Briggs's archival research and his field work in that community from 1972 to the present.

Throughout, numbers in parentheses refer to entries in the first part of the bibliography, which details the "basic corpus" of Lorin W. Brown's extant Federal Writers' Project manuscripts. Most of these writings are reprinted in Part II. As explained in the introduction to Part II, these texts have been organized to give an orderly, readable overview of Hispano history and village life in the region. They are woven together with brief, interspersed editorial remarks. Occasional further editorial matter is bracketed within the reprinted material. Otherwise, all manuscripts appear substantially as Brown submitted them.

Brown's manuscripts have undergone minor editing to correct obvious grammatical and orthographic errors and for internal consistency. All Spanish words and phrases have been italicized and their definitions and translations enclosed in parentheses and quotation marks, a procedure which Brown generally followed in his work. However, only about a third of his manuscripts show handwritten diacritical marks on the Spanish words and texts, so the editors have placed such marks on all Spanish words and names except place names, which do not appear with accents in contemporary anglicized usage. On the whole, the Spanish texts and Brown's English translations have not been altered because they are indicative both of local usage and Brown's bilingual competence.

The appendix and bibliography place Brown's work in the larger context of the Federal Writers' Project and of contemporaneous sociocultural and literary work on Hispano folklife in New Mexico. The 1930s and early 1940s were a productive period in New Mexico studies, and Lorin W. Brown's contributions are among the most notable.

Above all, this is Lorenzo's book. We both hereby salute him foremost as friend and mentor. We also gratefully acknowledge the help of his children—Richard, Anna, and Francie—in the preparation of this volume. For her part, Marta would like to thank the men who helped her contact and meet Lorenzo—Mr. Henry Hughes, the late Mr. Ted LeViness, and Bob Kadlec, and to recognize Chuck and Nan Perdue, good friends who blazed the trail on these Writers' Project matters. Chuck would like to acknowledge the generosity of Cordova's current residents for sharing their understanding of the community's history with him, especially the sagacious and genuine human being, the late Don Federico Córdova, and to thank his wife, Helen E. Diodati, for help in drawing together loose ends in Part I. Gilberto Benito Córdova's 1970–72 work really opened the New Mexico Federal Writers' Project files and stimulated both Lorenzo's efforts and our own. Each of us has always received every courtesy and gained immeasurably from the competence and knowledge of historian Dr. Myra Ellen Jenkins and her staff, James H. Purdy and J. Richard Salazar, at the New Mexico State Records Center and Archives; Stephany Eger, librarian in the History Division, Museum of New Mexico; and Carl J. Mora, managing editor of the University of New Mexico Press. Finally, all three of us—Marta, Chuck, and Lorenzo—would like to pay tribute to the inspiration of a talented and spirited pioneer in the study of Hispano folklife in New Mexico, the late E. Boyd.

December 1977   Charles L. Briggs
Chicago and Santa Fe   Marta Weigle

PART I:

Lorin W. Brown in Taos and Cordova:

A Biographical and Ethnohistorical Sketch

From November 1936 until December 1941, Lorin W. Brown wrote almost two hundred manuscripts for the Federal Writers' Project in New Mexico. These included field reports, interpretive and impressionistic sketches, translations, and transcriptions of numerous folksongs, folktales, proverbs, riddles, and other genres. Although few workers on the New Mexico Federal Writers' Project received personal recognition at the time, Brown's contributions were soon noted both by regional investigators and literati. Charles D. Carroll early appreciated Brown's approach, describing him as "gifted with an innate, sensitive understanding of the Spanish-American . . . the best translator of their scene for the New Mexico Writers' Project."[1] Brown's edited manuscripts appeared in *The Santa Fean: a National Monthly,* on Haniel Long's "New Mexico Writers" page of the *New Mexico Sentinel,* and in the New Mexico FWP's magazine, *Over the Turquoise Trail.*

In addition to their value as exemplary contributions to a fascinating literary era in New Mexico, Brown's essays also deserve recognition for their uniqueness. There were three principal sources of inspiration contributing to their creation. Cordova, an Hispano community in New Mexico's Rio Arriba County, provided a primary stage for the drama. Its more than two-and-one-quarter centuries of history and local idiosyncracies were enhanced by an impressive landscape. The New Mexico Federal Writers' Project provided the opportunity for the writing of the papers; a number of talented individuals were given the time and freedom to record New Mexico's heritage. Finally, there was the drama that only comes into being through the work of a capable author. Lorin Brown's explorative spirit was forged from the experience of three cultures—Hispano, Pueblo, and Anglo—and annealed by the diversity and richness of the life he led.

Brown's life is largely inseparable from the drama of northern New Mexican society. His birth in a turn-of-the-century mining camp might as easily have cast him in the role of a Zane Grey protagonist as a poet of Hispano culture. Growing up in the Taos, New Mexico, home of his maternal grandparents, the Martínezes, the young Lorenzo established a relationship of great intimacy with the land and its inhabitants. Needless to say, this familiarity

3

played a large part in determining the nature of his later involvement in Cordova. By the same token, his schooling back in the Midwest with his father's relatives prepared him to become a spokesman in two languages for two cultures. It was this bilingual, bicultural capability and sensitivity, combined with a deep love of Hispano northern New Mexico, that informed and sustained his life and writing during the troubled years before the Second World War.

Lorenzo the Taoseño

Lorin William Brown, Jr., was born in Elizabethtown (E'town), New Mexico, on November 22, 1900. E'town is presently a deserted mining camp on New Mexico Route 38, five miles northeast of Eagle's Nest in Colfax County.[2] Brown's account of the events surrounding his birth indicates that his life was marked for adventure right from the start:

> The evening of my birth the cowboys from the outlying ranches rode into town, firing six-shooters and shouting their lungs out. Downtown the miners stepped out in front of whatever establishment they happened to have frequented, answering their playmates with a like fusillade. It was a customary prelude to the evening's carouse in the various dens which offered entertainment in that wild town. For years I cherished the belief that they were celebrating my advent into this vale of tears.[3]

Lorin W. Brown, Sr., must have been one of the most versatile entrepreneurs in the town. The elder Brown was born in Morning Sun, Iowa, and later moved to New Mexico in search of relief from the lung ailment which eventually took his life. Having arrived with his own printing press, he was active in the local newspaper business. Between November 1899 and August 1900, he and M. R. Baker served as editors and publishers of the *Mining Bulletin,* an English-language weekly. He was likewise responsible for the publication of a similar gazette, the *New Mexico Miner,* from June 1897 to September 1898.[4] Brown's previous editorial career included publication of Red River's *Mining Bulletin* and two Spanish (*Heraldo de Taos* and *Heraldo Taoseño*) and four English (*Herald,*

Taosonian, Valley Herald, and *Rio Hondo Miner*) newspapers in Taos.[5]

It seems hard to believe that this pursuit left the ailing Brown with much free time. Nevertheless, he served as acting postmaster in Elizabethtown and engaged in mining, mainly by grubstaking others. He also taught school in Red River and is known to have been "well liked by his pupils."[6] He was a portrait and field photographer as well; prints from his hand-camera negatives can today be found in the Museum of New Mexico, Santa Fe.[7]

The younger Brown's recollections of E'town show that this mining camp had much in common with other such communities of the day. It was a wild place where violence was frequent. Brown recently described some of the horrors of his native community in these terms:

> My mother told me so many stories of E'town and I heard tales of E'town from my Uncle Pedro Vigil of Talpa and others—how Charles Kennedy had been hung in the streets of E'town and how his decapitated head had served as football for days by the children of the camp. *Cháles Canadá,* according to grandmother's version, was found guilty of murdering wayfarers en route to E'town, robbing them and burying their bodies near his miserable cabin. It was even said that he served the flesh of his victims to passersby who stopped over at his cabin for rest and refreshment. His cabin was located at the foot of Flechado Hill, over which the road led to Taos. The hill was so named because of the many arrows or *flechas* which transfixed the trees of its crest after some bloody encounter with marauding Indians.

Although Lorin Brown, Sr., did not succumb to the morose dangers of E'town, neither did he profit substantially from its mineral wealth, his only "killing" having been made in the Arroyo Hondo area at an earlier date.

The Browns' stay in Elizabethtown ended abruptly after Lorin Brown, Sr., died on December 29, 1901, during a trip to his sister's home in Ute Creek, New Mexico.[8] His widow, Cassandra Martínez de Brown, moved to Taos, home of her father and mother, Vicente Ferrer Martínez and Juanita Montoya de Martínez. Young Lorin lived with his grandparents throughout most of his childhood and adolescence, and it is the influence of his maternal kin which proved to be the most important in terms of his literary vision of Hispano society.

His grandparents were fascinating figures in their own right. Vicente Martínez was a student of the rebel Hispano priest Antonio José Martínez of Taos. Father Martínez espoused a number of liberal causes, and he exposed his pupils to the works of Virgil and Victor Hugo. Subjects of study included astronomy, botany, and Greek mythology. Vicente Martínez's thinking was strongly influenced by this instruction, as evidenced by the names he chose for his children: Cassandra, Rolando, and Horacio Hugo. Brown recorded the following description of "Padre Martínez and the First College in New Mexico" as one of his later FWP contributions:

> The writer's grandfather attended Father Martínez's college which the Father had established in 1826 in Taos, New Mexico. I remember him telling me that the school was for the youth of both sexes, although I do not remember that he ever mentioned any girl students. Lack of equipment necessitated that problems be worked out on the whitewashed walls of the classrooms, charcoal out of the fireplace being used in lieu of chalk. When the walls became too murky the priestly schoolmaster would have some of his Indian servants give them another white coat and they were ready again for the dispensing of knowledge.
>
> The college was a self-contained institution run in a very efficient manner. Father Martínez maintained a large household of servants, students from afar who received their board and lodging free of charge and many indigent hangers-on who lived off of the Father's bounty. (89)

The young Lorin later shared in this academic tradition as well, because he "read omnivorously in my grandfather's library."

Needless to say, the topics of discussion in Father Martínez's school were hardly common fare, and the rebel priest and his followers paid the price for bearing the liberal standard. Vicente Martínez and his fellow classmates were excommunicated along with Father Martínez in 1857, thus setting them apart from the Catholic community in Taos. Many proved ready converts for Protestant evangelists. Vicente chose a different course and early espoused the cause of socialism. Together with a defrocked priest, he and other pupils formed the nucleus of a group with similar political ideas. Brown reports that "in that day and age they were looked upon as dangerous men and labeled anarchists and nihilists. When my father came along evincing similar political beliefs, the bond between the two men became stronger than just that of family ties."[9]

Lorin's grandmother was no less intimately involved in the Hispano community of Taos. Known as a *curandera* ("folk healer") and a *partera* ("midwife"), Juanita Montoya de Martínez ("Mana Juanita") was summoned to treat every type of ailment. Her versatility was demonstrated by her treatment of everything from severed limbs to third-degree burns. Claiming Taos Pueblo as well as Hispano ancestry, she visited the Pueblo frequently, staying overnight many times. According to Brown, "this was proof that she had blood ties with the Puebloans, for only an admitted Indian was welcomed overnight in the Pueblo." Lorin went along on many of these visits, and he remembers them vividly. Indeed, it was "Mana Juanita" who took the time to instruct the boy in Hispano beliefs and practices, and Brown, up until his death, still utilized a number of remedies she taught him.

Cassandra, Lorin's mother, was no less forceful a personality than her parents. She converted from Catholicism to Protestantism at the age of twelve, and she appears also to have made up her mind while still young about the importance of education. Much of her adult life was spent teaching in the rural villages of northern New Mexico. Between 1905 and 1925, Cassandra Brown taught in Arroyo Seco, Arroyo Hondo, Valdez, Talpa, Ranchitos, El Prado, upper and lower Cañon de Taos, and Cordova. In addition to frequent visits to these locations, Brown spent two school terms as his mother's pupil, and a good deal of the depth of his knowledge of Hispano village life derives from this variety of experience.

Nevertheless, the young Lorin generally remained in Taos with his grandparents while his mother waged distant battles on behalf of literacy. Brown recently recounted the intriguing details of how he came to reside with the Martínezes:

> It was the custom in those days for the *coyote* or *coyotito* to be turned over to the grandparents to be raised, presumably to be a comfort to them in their old age and a useful one for the running of errands and minor chores. The terms *coyote* or

coyotito were generally applied to the youngest of a family. In our case Vicente would have been the likely candidate, but he was quite young and much attached to his mother. I was outgoing and had already established a strong rapport with my grandmother, so, to my joy, I was the chosen one. Neither grandparent having any English, I learned Spanish from scratch. My mother never used anything but English with us, so I became bilingual early in life. I read everything I could lay my hands on, so that helped.

Brown has traveled far in the intervening years, but he still considers himself a Taoseño at heart. The splendor and freedom of his childhood days in the Taos Valley are the foundation of his love for northern New Mexico and the reason he could never quit the area for good. The importance of this part of Brown's life to his later participation in the Federal Writers' Project is shown in his recent description of several Taos exploits:

> The foods grandmother cooked were from the fields and gardens of Taos, each crop in its season. In winter we enjoyed beans, chile, dried fruits, *tasajo, chaquehue,* and *atole,* the inevitable evening bowl, laced with red chile or hot goat's milk. I absorbed all my knowledge of customs, traditions, *cuentos,* etc., with that evening bowl.
>
> And what a life that was—untrammeled, free as the wind, with all the streams and hills to roam, orchards to purloin. I wish every boy could have that kind of upbringing. There were no wars or hint of war, only occasional pictures of Kaiser Wilhelm reviewing his goose-stepping army. But that was far away across vast oceans.
>
> Horses were the mainstay of everyday life in the community. My peers and I knew every horse in the vicinity, from the saddle horses, to the harnessed ones (comprising the usual farm beasts), to those used by the freighters. It was no wonder that in our play we emulated horses. Cupping small milk cans in our hands, we lived on all fours for three or four years. We were the bucking bronc, the race horse, and the fancy gaited saddle horse. The object of our greatest admiration was the stallion which was penned behind a high board wall just above our play area. We would catch glimpses of his head and forefeet as he reared and snorted defiance toward any possible

rival when the wind brought him assurance that a mare was on her way. Such power and such defiant might thrilled us so that for days afterward we all were stallions, pawing the earth and shrilling defiant blasts to the world at large.

It was about this time that spending money, or lack of it, became a subject of great importance. In spite of our familiarity with the streams around Taos we had overlooked a fruitful source of revenue. Some of them teemed with muskrats. We had deemed them only occasional targets for our slingshots or thrown stones. Four of us acquired a dozen Victor traps and thereafter every Friday found us setting our traps on the stream south of Taos. Saturday morning we went out to gather our harvest. The afternoon was spent in skinning our catch, fleshing the pelts, and stretching them on willow stretchers to dry. Shipments were made to a fur and pelt house in Denver. The first payment put change in our pockets. We excited the envy of a group of four older boys, who summarily informed us that they were "muscling in on us" and told us to stay out of our trapping grounds. At the time of this ultimatum they showed us one dozen brand new house traps and offered to buy ours. We refused to sell and bided our time. How we outwitted this group is another story. We used brains instead of brawn, which we lacked, but outsmart them we did, and shortly after we were back in undisputed possession of our trapping grounds.

These early experiences in and around Taos are clearly reflected in Brown's succeeding essays (e.g., in manuscripts 25, 32, 82, 91, 113). Some memories have been incorporated directly, while the more intangible aspects of his youth served to increase his perception and understanding of the folklife materials he collected more than three decades later.

Lorin did not, however, share this stage with his grandmother and grandfather alone. He had two sisters, Amy and Floy, and three brothers, Bascom, Roy, and Vincent. Vincent was the baby of the family, while Lorin was next in line. Brown's childhood, like that of his siblings, was split between Taos and Sterling, Kansas. Lorin Sr. had a maiden sister who taught art at Sterling College. Lorin Jr. was primarily educated at the Presbyterian Mission School in Taos, but he attended kindergarten, seventh grade, and the last two years of high school in Sterling. Characteristically, the flamboyance of his high school years in Kansas was enhanced by the small newspaper stand that he and Vincent operated near the railroad station. In addition to newspapers, they sold contraband cigarettes and a slightly risqué magazine, *Uncle Billy's Whizbang*. This provided the boys with a living, but it also led to numerous run-ins with the members of the W.C.T.U.

A contemporaneous event was of great importance to Brown's later involvement in Cordova. Bascom, the oldest son, had been given a post as a ranger for the U.S. Forest Service near Llano Quemado, a small community just south of Truchas, which was settled by Cordovans. Cassandra followed in 1917, and she taught in the village school. Traveling through New Mexico during that year, Brown jumped on a buckboard headed for Truchas and joined his mother. Surprising Bascom at the ranger station, Lorin hired on as a trail rider and lookout for the summer. Shortly thereafter, however, Bascom packed up and joined the Army. Lorin manned the ranger station for the remainder of the season, becoming quite possibly the youngest ranger in Forest Service history. Afterwards, he headed back to complete his last year in high school in Kansas. His mother stayed that year in the Quemado school; she later moved down to Cordova and taught school there until the 1920s.

After finishing high school, Brown spent one year at Sterling College in the Students' Army Training Corps. He was released following the end of World War I. The next four or five years were spent roaming around various parts of Kansas and New Mexico. The wheat harvest in the former state kept him busy during several seasons, and he even worked an entire year on one grain and cattle ranch in northwestern Kansas. Various jobs in the circulation departments of the *Albuquerque Tribune*, the *Albuquerque Journal*, and associated newspapers prompted him to traverse much of New Mexico between Albuquerque and the Mexican border.

Cordova, New Mexico

While Brown was visiting Cordova around 1922, Cassandra convinced her son to fill the local teaching post which she was then vacating. He recalls that "this was my introduction to home life in Cordova, a village I appreciated more and more as I continued living there." Brown's residence in the community was of substantial duration. He made Cordova his home between 1922 and 1933, later staying there for varying periods between 1936 and 1941, while working for the Federal Writers' Project.

Cordova provides Brown's major thematic focus in his Federal Writers' Project manuscripts. The village is situated in a small valley enclosed by the foothills which connect the Sangre de Cristo Mountains with the Rio Grande Valley to the west. Cordova's sixty-nine hundred feet of elevation and semiarid climate allow the surrounding slopes to be dotted with piñon and juniper trees. The mountains just above boast more lush vegetation and tall conifers.

Thirty-five miles of paved roadway presently link Cordova with Santa Fe to the southwest, and fourteen miles of paved highway lead west into Española. One approaches the village from the mesa or plain to the north and west; the Pueblo ruins just over a mile in that direction provide the Quemado ("Burned") Valley with its name.[10] Cordova initially borrowed the title as well, and the village was known as the Pueblo Quemado or simply Quemado until the establishment of a post office in 1900.[11]

The facts surrounding the initial settlement of Cordova have not come to light. It was definitely founded as a frontier community by residents from less remote towns. Although it was established between 1725 and 1743,[12] Cordova, along with other villages in the area, was abandoned in 1748 following devastating attacks by nomadic Indians. The following year, Governor Joaquín Codallos y Rabál was petitioned by eleven citizens temporarily living in Chimayo who asked him to permit them to cultivate lands in Cordova while leaving their wives and children in the former community. The governor granted their request, and he further decreed that guards were to be placed on the high peaks to protect them.[13] Evidence of land conveyance in the succeeding years indicates that this attempt at settlement was successful.

The arduous existence of Cordova's first residents is well characterized by Brown. Produce was raised on small garden plots, requiring the use of irrigation. However, droughts and hail storms rendered farming extremely difficult. Goats and sheep were grazed on the hills around Cordova, and they supplied many of the villagers' needs in the form of goat milk and cheese, wool, and meat. Natural predators were a constant threat, however. In addition to these hardships, relations with nomadic Indians were not always friendly, and laboriously secured provisions and animals were frequently lost in raids. Bloodshed was likewise not uncommon.

The dictates of maintaining both an adequate defensive posture and placating the Spanish government necessitated a close-knit community both physically and socially. The settlement originally consisted of a single enclosed *plaza*, or town square, whose two sole entrances were barricaded with strong wooden gates. Walls were thick, and primitive weapons were kept close at hand. Oral history such as that presented by Brown describes this period as one of continual reliance on community-wide cooperation.

Providing for the religious needs of the village appears to have been no easier than accommodating physical necessities. The nearest resident priest was at the parish church in Santa Cruz. Cordova, along with Cundiyo, Truchas, and other nearby settlements, was classified as a mission, and clerical visits were at times as much as a year apart.[14] Brown's informants noted that priests were housed in the leading family's home during their visits to Cordova.

Once sufficient resources could be assembled for the purpose, Cordovans began building a chapel. Heavy timbers were hauled from the mountains by oxen, and a large quantity of *adobe* ("mud") bricks molded and dried. Although the date of the San Antonio de Padua Chapel's completion is not known, it is believed to have been finished by 1821 and licensed by 1832.[15] The structure, carefully described by Brown (67), still stands in the center of the plaza—a monument to the faith and perseverance of the many generations of Cordovans who have inhabited the valley.

The role of local laymen in preserving the faith hardly ended with the building of the chapel. One of the most important tasks that confronted the residents in furnishing the chapel was the provision of holy representations of Christ, the Virgin Mary, and the saints, generally referred to as *santos*. The exquisite main altar-screen was a product of local talent. José Rafael Aragón, who painted it sometime between 1834 and 1838, was one of the most popular and prolific of the nineteenth-century folk image-makers of New Mexico.[16] Oral history maintains that many of the remaining images were produced by Cordova artists as well. Brown well describes the responsibility of a number of local individuals and religious organizations in both the care of the images and their use in processions.

This brief history of Cordova reflects the life of the community and its inhabitants through the first half of the nineteenth century and, to a lesser extent, during the next fifty years as well. Between that time and the present, however, a series of major economic transformations have revolutionized the economic status of Cordova and surrounding communities. Some of the most significant modifications are related to changes in the relationship between Cordova and the dominant society. Even the briefest of visits to contemporary Cordova yields evidence of profound cultural alterations. Although it would be impossible to treat here the depth and complexity of these processes, a brief update of Brown's picture of Cordova better places his essays in their social and historical context.

One of the first and perhaps the most important set of events marking the turn of the century was related to a serious undermining of Cordova's subsistence base. Economic life in the community was never one of plenty; unmechanized agriculture and husbandry in a semiarid land often dictated a Spartan existence. This traditional subsistence system was pushed to the brink of disaster by two concomitant processes of encroachment on the community land base. First, population expansion led to further subdivision of the villagers' already small holdings of irrigable land. Secondly, lands surrounding Cordova on the south and east were transferred from the public domain and designated as national forest, thereby seriously reducing the community's reliance on livestock production. New grazing regulations were instituted following the consolidation of the Jemez and Pecos National Forests into the Santa Fe National Forest in 1915, and there was a limited number of permits for sheep and cattle. Goats were then excluded from these areas.[17] These developments, along with a gradual shift from a barter to a cash economy, confronted Cordovans with a growing need for cash income.

Villagers engaged in migratory wage labor to cope with this problem. Railroad building, mining, and other nonagricultural enterprises in New Mexico; harvesting sugar beets, onions, potatoes and other crops in Colorado; and the sheep camps of Colorado, Utah, Wyoming, and Montana all provided opportunities for outside work.[18] Prior to the Depression, an estimated seven to ten thousand workers from the villages of the Middle Rio Grande Valley, the land drained by the Rio Grande between Elephant Butte and the New Mexico–Colorado border, left each year to engage in such migratory labor.[19]

Brown accurately described the effect that this practice had on the village of Cordova.[20] Quite a number of men were out of the community six months of the year, generally in the spring and summer. He also documents the resulting augmentation in quantity and variety of material goods in the community. Unfortunately, such gains were based on a growing dependence on outside sources, and the relative affluence thus achieved was short-lived.

After the Depression engulfed the area, income from migratory wage labor was reduced by as much as 80 percent.[21] The subsequent crisis was acute, and widespread starvation was prevented only by the implementation of numerous federal projects. Estimated relief income for Hispanos in the Middle Rio Grande Valley in 1936 was $1,143,051.[22]

A more permanent resolution for this poverty was provided by the influx of population and capital into New Mexico during and after the Second World War. Much of this growth was associated with the federal installations in Albuquerque and Los Alamos. The latter facility and the service industries which grew up in its shadow provided a new source of cash income for the residents of the area—daily wage labor. According to one estimate,[23] over half of Cordova's work force is now engaged at Los Alamos, and the remainder is employed mainly in Española and Santa Fe.

The participation of Cordovans in the national economy was furthered by improved accessibility to the community. Before 1946, the road to Cordova was little more than a trail, and daily travel to Santa Fe or Los Alamos was impossible. In that year, however, the road that traverses the plain above Cordova (State Route 76) was graded and maintained with gravel. In 1953, it was paved.[24]

The appearance of the Quemado Valley has changed drastically since World War II. The subdivision and fencing of the valley into farm plots still results in a patchwork quilt pattern, and the four ditches continue to connect the fields in veinlike fashion. However, the early Cordovans clustered together in their "hive," the central plaza, leaving the precious fields for cultivation. Once nomadic Indian attacks were no longer a problem, income from wage labor could be devoted to further building. First, a family broke off to found the Plaza de los Trujillos about one-half mile up the valley. Two more plazas were later founded on the north side of the valley.

A change of far greater profundity has also occurred in the residential structure of Cordova. With defense no longer a problem and dependence on agriculture less critical, villagers began to build homes on formerly cultivated lands. In the late 1930s, there were only two houses south of the Rito Quemado; the valley is now dotted with individual homesteads, termed *ranchos,* from one end to the other.[25] Persons who have moved onto these *ranchos* vividly describe the greater isolation due to the transition.

Increased cash incomes have also enabled Cordovans to provide themselves with a community water system, electricity, and telephones. The local manufacture of most necessities, which greatly concerned Brown, has likewise largely given way to the purchase of mass-produced goods. While mud and timber construction is hardly obsolete, the use of cement block and the purchase of trailers is common. With the growth of retail dealers in Española, the influx of Sears and Montgomery Ward mail-order catalogues, and mass media advertising, Cordovan tastes in automobiles, home furnishings, and dress increasingly reflect the standards of American culture. Indeed, the articles most commonly produced in the community, wood carvings, are sold to tourists and not to Cordovans.

The pace of change is graphically expressed in the evolution of the school buildings. The "Old School" in which Brown taught was, as he describes in "The Deep Village" (52), replaced by the "New School," which lies just west of the main plaza. This structure proved inadequate in the early 1970s, and the recently constructed Mountain View Elementary School now overlooks the Quemado Valley from its perch on the plain northeast of the village. The many one-room schools which served turn-of-the-century Cordova, Truchas, and the Llano Quemado have been consolidated in this modern building.

Lorenzo the Cordovan

With the end of World War I and the completion of his studies, Lorin Brown once again found himself in his native state. In 1922 he obtained a teaching position in the Cordova "Old School," a job that brought him back into the mainstream of Hispano village society and provided him with an unforgettable experience in rural pedagogy. The only other teacher was Federico Córdova, who in 1977 was eighty-three years old and still resided in the village.

The two men were responsible for one hundred pupils between them. Incoming students were monolingual Spanish speakers, but all instruction was in English, as were the "Little Elfin" readers. Not surprisingly, Brown reports having used quite a number of props and a good deal of sign language. Even sitting two to a desk, the students were packed so tightly into the tiny room that they overflowed onto the window sills. Furthermore, with only a partition between the two classrooms, it was difficult to hold down the noise. Facilities were likewise limited; drinking water for the entire school was provided by one bucket with a single dipper, and water had to be hauled from the river.

Brown claims that the compensation was not bad; the mid-September to early April school term netted sixty dollars for each teaching month, and it left the rest of the year free for fishing and hunting. Parents would also frequently send the first fruits of their yield to the teachers, as educators were highly respected members of the community. Cassandra received an abundance of this sort of gratitude; not only was she a favorite teacher, but she was related to a substantial portion of the villagers through her marriage to Margarito López in 1928.

Brown taught school in Cordova until 1931, at which time he was succeeded by his younger brother Vincent. True to his entrepreneurial predilections, Lorin was involved in a number of other pursuits while in the village. Having brought in a 1922 Buick around 1924, he earned a few dollars by chauffeuring Cordovans to town, to dances in neighboring communities, and even to the regional "witch doctor." In the front room of the family house, Brown ran a tiny general store with yard goods, candy, and assorted small items. Mail was also sorted in the shop, and, as a Fourth Class Postmaster, Brown received 75 percent of the value of the cancellations. After quitting as schoolteacher, he even became the area's deputy game warden, adding licenses to the items available in his store. True to form, Brown acquired the job through sheer inventiveness: "I don't know how [I got the job], I just got a notion one day and called up the game warden in Santa Fe and said, 'We don't have an outlet for anybody to sell licenses here.' "

In spite of Cassandra and her son's intense involvement in village life, they did not sever their contacts with the world beyond the community. A number of their "Santa Fe friends" graced the Brown family with periodic visits, and these frequently coincided with Holy Week ceremonies in Cordova. Among such visitors were many artists and writers who had arrived in New Mexico with "great enthusiasm for the discovery of fresh material."[26] The landscape and ritual of Hispano villages proved particularly appealing to this crowd, and the Browns' location in Cordova provided an unusually propitious vantage point for observing the spectacle. The exchange was hardly one-sided, however, because the interests and perceptions of the guests impressed themselves strongly upon young Lorin. This influence is quite apparent in the picture of village life which later emerged in his contributions to the New Mexico Federal Writers' Project.

Among the Browns' regular Holy Week guests were Mary Austin, Frank Applegate, members of the "Cinco Pintores" (an association of artists Jozef Bakos, Walter Mruk, Fremont Ellis, Will Shuster, and Willard Nash), Aileen Nusbaum (one-time director of the Writers' Project), and others. Brown recently recorded his recollections of these visits:

> For the most part, my guests were annual visitors—writers, artists and friends from families with whom we were intimately acquainted in Santa Fe. In season, many were also my guests on pre-arranged fishing and hunting trips. We were a close-knit group, thoroughly enjoying the flow of conversation, which was as varied as the group itself.[27]

The parties would gather at the Brown house behind the chapel on Holy Thursday, and much of the evening was spent roasting apples and piñon nuts over an open fire while engaged in convivial conversation.

Such festivities were not, however, the primary object of the reunion. By the 1920s, the performance of public acts of penance by members of the Pious Fraternity of Our Father Jesus Nazarite was practically common knowledge among Anglo-Americans in the region. Annual treks to the Hispano villages during Holy Week, the temporal focus of Brotherhood rituals, had unfortunately become something of a tourist attraction. Therefore, at the first sounds of an approaching procession of Brothers the group sought a suitable vantage point from which to view Brotherhood activities. Some of the guests would also stay through the Tenebrae services on Good Friday evening.[28]

The interests of the Browns' visitors were not exhausted by the *Hermanos*. Brown, his mother, and his stepfather made a point of introducing their Santa Fe friends to Margarito's relatives and to notable Cordova personalities.[29] A number of these introductions resulted in lasting friendships, renewed each year during Holy Week. Brown served as go-between and translator on such visits. This contact was of more than passing importance to Guadalupe Martínez, who became a regular tour guide, and to José Dolores López. López, a carpenter, had taken up the chip-carving of utilitarian furniture in 1917. Most of his early work was given to relatives and neighbors. Brown introduced López to Frank Applegate, and Applegate persuaded the carver to market his work at the Santa Fe Annual Fiesta. Applegate also influenced the direction of López's work, for it was he who suggested the carving of religious images.[30]

The Applegate-Austin crowd likewise influenced Brown's perception of Cordova, and thus the later emergence of "Tía Lupe" (Guadalupe Martínez) and José Dolores López as leading characters in his writing is easily comprehended. Brown astutely perceived that the curiosity of educated Anglos was thoroughly aroused by these villagers as well as by the "Penitentes" (a term frequently used by outsiders to refer to the Brothers). In fact, excursions proved so popular that they remained an annual event even after the Browns moved to Santa Fe in 1933. Brown continued to open the Cordova house almost annually during the final days of Holy Week. It is therefore hardly surprising that the fruits of Holy Week conversations with Frank Applegate, Mary Austin, and other "Santa Fe friends" were fresh in Brown's mind when he returned to Cordova in conjunction with the New Mexico Writers' Project.

After moving to Santa Fe, the Browns purchased a residence on lower Agua Fria Street. As was the case with so many other New Mexicans, the Depression found Brown involved with a number of federal work projects. When the General Land Office decided to resurvey a number of Spanish land grants, Brown was on the crew "because I had a pickup." He also worked under the Public Works Administration and the National Recovery Act. One of his stints enabled him to put his knowledge of the region's language and terrain to good use: he was charged with covering Santa Fe County in search of all physically disabled or handicapped persons. During this time he also made the acquaintance of Santiago Mata and other members of embryonic labor movements such as La Liga Obrera de Habla Español ("League of Spanish-Speaking Workers").[31]

Having done a thorough job with the survey, Brown was hired by Brice H. Sewell, State Supervisor of Vocational Trade and Industrial Education, in charge of developing a number of community vocational schools. Artisans were employed as instructors, and students were trained in production and marketing techniques.[32] During his year and a half with the program, Brown was instrumental in founding and staffing vocational schools in three small communities close to Santa Fe—Cerrillos, Agua Fria, and Cienega. He employed teachers—nearly all of them Hispanos—skilled in carpentry, weaving, leatherwork, iron work, pottery, and woodworking. Brown's involvement ended two days after the defeat of his avowed senatorial candidate in the 1936 election because project officials were displeased by his vocal political partisanship.

Lorin W. Brown and the Federal Writers' Project, 1936-41

Lorin Brown joined the staff of the New Mexico Federal Writers' Project in November 1936, shortly after being fired from his vocational training job. Brice Sewell proved a loyal friend and recommended him to Ina Sizer Cassidy, then State Director of the Federal Writers' Project in New Mexico. When he arrived for an interview, Brown's old acquaintance, wealthy newspaper publisher Cyrus McCormick, was consulting Mrs. Cassidy on other matters. According to Brown, McCormick told the director that if she were to hire him, "I would heartily endorse him because I know of his knowledge of the villages, people, the language and his other capabilities." Brown attributes his being "hired on the spot" to this unexpected endorsement. Thus began a mutually beneficial though sometimes strained association which continued until 1941.

Perhaps a third of Brown's extant manuscripts are not dated, so it is presently impossible to document his Federal Writer's Project career with precision. At various times, he remained in Santa Fe translating Spanish archival documents, folk plays, and miscellaneous Project manuscripts and copying pertinent articles from library books and journals. These tasks exasperated him, and he endeavored to spend as much time in the field as possible. Cordova was his headquarters, but he also spent appreciable periods north in the Taos area and southeast of Santa Fe around Leyba.

Brown's earliest dated manuscript (117; March 22, 1937) is a short sketch about his favorite Cordova informant, Tía Lupe. This is followed by a number of Cordova manuscripts with April and May dates and a couple of personal reminiscences about Taos. He had obviously established himself as a field worker some four months after beginning the FWP job.

Aileen Nusbaum, Cassidy's assistant, was responsible for Brown's welcome field assignment. Recalling her own Holy Week visits to Cordova with Brown and their friends, "she told Cassidy [Brown would] be the one to interpret the village scene." Brown vividly recollects his feelings and modus operandi during the early days of his field work:

> I could conceive of no endeavor which could have pleased me more. I was back amongst old friends in a village I loved for its people and its setting and its general pleasant environment. I spent my days renewing old acquaintances, particularly the elders whose conversations I enjoyed because they smacked of old times, old customs, and traditions. Thus I would spend my afternoons and evenings talking here and there first with one and then another until it was time for them to retire. I would then take myself to my room, light the kerosene lamp, put the old #5 Remington into action, and start typing the salient features of that evening's conversation. I would type until about two or three in the morning, at which time I would hit the hay, sleep late, and saunter forth next day after a brunch to resume my pleasant conversations around the village. I mailed all my manuscripts in to the head office, rarely going in except on occasions when I went back to Santa Fe to visit my family and replenish my groceries.

At one point his salary for this enjoyable work, mailed to him in Cordova, was $108 per month.

It was not hard for the novice field worker either to contact old friends or to recall earlier experiences in both Taos and Rio Arriba Counties. Cordovans whom Brown had earlier failed to meet while he was working as teacher, postmaster, storekeeper, and chauffeur eventually became acquainted with him at dances, weddings, christenings, wakes, and the like. Many informants were friends of his mother, and most members of the sizable López family still consider him a cousin, recalling, of course, his mother's marriage to Margarito López. According to Brown, none of these neighbors knew what he was doing, thinking him to be "just *escriviando*" ("writing").

Lorin Brown lived in Cordova around the time of the Depression, and the community's incorporation into the modern capitalistic economic structure was far less complete than it was to become in the postwar era. Nevertheless, it is clear that many changes were nascent if not overt at the time. Therefore, while it may at first seem paradoxical to say that Brown discovered pre-1900s Cordova when he was there during the 1920s and 1930s, it is quite true that Brown sought to capture the first hundred and fifty years of village history in his writings. For this reason, he chose the oldest inhabitants of the village as his primary informants. Much of the information he recorded was drawn from such individuals' childhood memories and from their parents' and grandparents' stories. It is thus hardly surprising that Brown's essays deal with such topics as the abandonment of the Alto Huachin, the casting of the chapel's bell, trading expeditions to Mexico or the Comanche territory, and the like. Herein lies part of the uniqueness of Brown's contributions to the Writer's Project; his selection of materials anticipated many of the concerns of contemporary anthropologists, folklorists, and ethnohistorians.

When he periodically returned to town, Brown tried to avoid direct contact with the Santa Fe office for fear he would be fired or put to work on translation-transcription projects. By his own recollection:

> On one of these trips I was hooked into translating archives in the Museum of New Mexico. These archives were for the most part those which had not been translated ever, and were an interesting source of materials about early days in New Mexico under Spanish and Mexican rule, and brought forth many items of great interest . . . their relations particularly

with the Indians. One ritual of the Indians which seemed to
rile the authorities was the fertility rites which were held in
Tesuque, Santo Domingo, and other nearby pueblos and
which to the Spanish seemed merely an obscene and riotous
orgy. Little did they delve into the religious significance
which the Indians attached to the ritual, in that the Indians
believed that this was a very necessary rite to spread the seed
both amongst themselves and indirectly increase the fertility
of the land and the crops which would follow it. So many
bandos and decrees were issued to try to stamp out this rite,
seemingly to no avail and to the increasing chagrin of the
powers in charge. However, this sedentary occupation palled
on me soon, and I tried to find a way to talk myself out of this
boring type assignment.

Brown managed to escape the onerous library task by embarking
on another field project which fortuitously presented itself.

Early one evening, Brown chanced to encounter two friends—*El
Nuevo Mejicano* editor Tony Martínez and Francisco S. Leyba of
Leyba, San Miguel County—on the streets of Santa Fe. Martínez
showed Brown a memorial *corrido* Leyba had composed for the
paper. His interest piqued, Brown arranged to accompany Leyba
to his ranch for the weekend. On the way, they picked up Leyba's
brother Nicolás, himself a composer and poet. There followed some
three weeks' sojourn "first at one ranch and then the other,
enjoying the hospitality of both brothers, the ranch life, horseback
riding, and helping with ranch chores. The evenings were spent
listening to *corridos*, extempore verses, and songs and in delightful
conversation about old times and events." Brown considered many
of these pieces "valuable" enough for eventual submission to the
Writers' Project (e.g., 51, 71, 77, 78, 82, 119). The brothers' singing
abilities particularly entranced him, and he later regretted not
having a means of recording their considerable skills.

When he returned to Santa Fe, Brown was assigned to help
Eunice Hauskins, "a violinist attached to the Writers' Project." He
remembers this assignment, probably in late 1937, as follows:

We were, or rather she was to transcribe the songs of *Los
Pastores*. I was able to get a gentleman from Agua Fria who
knew all the songs of *Los Pastores*, and evening after evening
we would meet with him while he would intone the different

songs and Eunice would try or did put them down, transcribe them in notes until she had transcribed all the songs. . . . She did an excellent job and this assignment took at least two weeks.

In 1938, Brown made a series of brief studies comparing this Agua Fria version of *Los Pastores* (90) with the Galisteo, San Rafael, Santa Fe, and Taos versions (43–47).

Brown prevailed upon Mrs. Cassidy to let him return to Cordova, and, sometime in mid-1938, he began to extend his field activities northward through Truchas and Ojo Sarco into the Taos area. He recalls visiting "Los Cordovas near Taos, which was originally settled by people from Cordova," and several manuscripts from Talpa bear September and October 1938 dates (e.g., 34, 38, 60, 95, 98). One of Brown's informants there was his uncle, Pedro Vigil, who was married to his mother's sister, Jesusita. January 1939 seems to mark the end of his most prolific period, judging from the dated field-derived manuscripts.

In 1939, control of the Federal Writers' Project reverted to the state, and it became the Work Projects Administration Writers' Program. This year also saw the resignation of Ina Sizer Cassidy as State Director of the New Mexico Federal Writers' Project. Both these changes, plus the general Project pressure to finish the New Mexico Guide and his own marriage, doubtless influenced Brown's later output. Most of this was library-based rather than field oriented—translations, transcriptions, occasional reminiscences and original research, and copies of journal articles and book excerpts. Records show he submitted several articles for the "History of Grazing" project on March 13, 17, and 18, 1941, and these are probably among his last submissions. On the whole, it was uninspiring work he was glad to be free of when the Office of Postal Censorship job opened late in 1941.

There is an urgency to Brown's recollections of his first two years with the Federal Writers' Project. The constant threat of "403s"—termination forms—looms. In a letter of March 1976, Brown recalls that "at the time I was sending them [the manuscripts] in from Cordova, Truchas and other places I was only interested in meeting a deadline and keeping my job, and those were rough times and jobs were hard to get." Indeed, the Project had been reduced from sixty to forty-two workers in 1937, and that number never again increased.

Brown's difficulties with Ina Sizer Cassidy very probably contributed to his insecurity about the Federal Writers' Project. He recalls receiving no directives, guidelines, or specific instructions.
Furthermore, according to his March 1976 letter, "I never received
any word of approval; Ina just demanded a constant flow of
material." Despite his desire to remain inconspicuous, Brown felt
compelled to take issue with Cassidy on certain matters. The
incident he remembers most vividly occurred in the translation of a
popular song with the words *"vente chinita conmigo":*

> I translated this phrase as "come away with me my little
> curlyhaired one." Mrs. Cassidy objected to this translation,
> saying that couldn't be possible, that the words really meant
> "come away with me my little Chinese lass." Despite my
> efforts to prove her wrong, being the person she was (she was
> a dominant personality, very hard to swerve from her course
> of action), I could not make my point and so the translation
> had to go through as she had decided it must be.

Confrontations like this and rejections like the one described below
made Brown wary of the Santa Fe office:

> I'd been asked to repeat the conversations of a group of men
> around the campfire or bonfire [which] I had described as
> being one of the highlights of a *velorio*, wherein the men
> would build a bonfire outside in the patio and hunker down
> round the fire carrying on conversations and narratives on
> different subjects like horse trading, planting of crops, hunting
> and highlights in the life of some individual who was
> outstanding because of his feats, whether humorous or prodi-
> gious in strength or so on. I was asked to prepare a typical
> conversation around these bonfires and submit it for some
> special request made by a Washington official perhaps,
> anyway, the higher-ups of the Writers' Project. This I did,
> putting down the conversation just about verbatim, just in the
> Spanish as it is spoken up in the villages. I used the archaic
> and historic nuances of the language as it was spoken up
> there. For instance, I used the word *ansina* for *así, croque* for
> *creo que, p'alla* for *para allá, alao* for *alado, parao* for *parado,*
> and so on. These distortions, if you will, were common and
> part of the language up there. My manuscript was submitted

and sent to higher authorities for evaluation and was returned with the notation that it was at best very poor pedestrian Spanish and as such could not possibly be entertained as a worthwhile contribution. In my benighted understanding I had thought that that was what the Writers' Project was striving for—authentic reproduction of particularly the languages of people, and it was a blow to see this interpreted in such a manner. It is possible that whoever reviewed this, perhaps a graduate of Spanish from some university where academic Spanish was taught, did not realize the fact that in New Mexico the Spanish of three hundred years before has been preserved. . . . This rejection of my efforts made me strive for a permission to hie myself back to the villages and keep a low profile. . . .

This is a serious charge against the Project, and it should be borne in mind by all who consult the New Mexico Spanish-language materials.

Brown remembers Aileen Nusbaum, Cassidy's assistant to whom the materials were first submitted, as a sympathetic figure. Cassidy and most of her advisers were not. Since Mrs. Cassidy did not know Spanish, she relied on several who did for the evaluation of Spanish-language manuscripts and their translations. Brown resented his submissions sometimes being pre-empted by one of these advisers. He felt he had been "subtly used" and frequently recalled "what Brice Sewell had said to me when he recommended me for the job: 'Lorin, they are going to pick your brains.'" Despite this administrative unpleasantness, Brown apparently enjoyed generally good relationships with his fellow workers. According to him:

> For the most part all of the personnel of the Writers' Project were hard drinkers, not only at Christmas parties but throughout the year. We had many who succumbed time and again to the alcoholic fumes and were incapacitated for two and three days at a time. I was one of those who, having become addicted to Four Roses, many times did not show up on Monday morning when assigned to the office. I would call in saying I had a bad cold and could not show up, and Helen Shuster, bless her soul, would invariably show up at my house with a half pint of Four Roses, the hair of the dog that bit me, and several good magazines to read while I recuperated.

Mrs. Shuster was a typist with the Federal Writers' Project.

Besides Helen Shuster, Brown especially remembers Jack Thorp, John Looney, Lou Sage Batchen, whom he twice visited in Las Placitas, Jacob Scher, and E. Boyd. According to his letter of March 1976:

> The only ones who did voice approval were E. Boyd and Jack Scher. I took Jack on several field trips and he became most thoroughly sold on New Mexico. He would show me sketches he had written after one of these trips, then tear them up, saying "Lorin, you have to have soaked up this sunshine for years and eaten beans and chili with the natives to be able to interpret this scene."

Vardis Fisher was also called in when the New Mexico Guide volume was nearing completion, but he was not very approachable.

John Looney, who wrote several biographies of Santa Fe figures, mostly businessmen, was the subject of much rumor about his previous life and present ill health. According to Brown:

> I never have been able to ascertain the truth of all the stories told about him, but it was said that at one time he was a very influential and prosperous newspaper publisher in Illinois. It was said his newspaper enterprises were centered in Cicero, Illinois. He became an evangelist and fought the Capone outfit, at the time becoming so much of a thorn in Al's side that they took vindictive action against him in many ways. At one time he had a stronghold in Rio Arriba County to which he retired periodically to seek rest and relaxation and further his campaign against his enemies. It was said that he would drive from Chicago in an overnight forced trip by automobile with guards because he was always being threatened, and renew himself in the stronghold. It was surrounded by a fence with guards at all entrances. After a short period he would return again to Illinois to pick up his campaign against the forces he was fighting. At one time there was an accident which he always believed was rigged, [and this] cost him the life of his son. This was taken as an act of retaliation by his enemies and a threat to him to cease and desist his campaign of publicity against the underworld. At any rate his legal proceedings against the murderers of his son were lost in the

courts, undoubtedly due to the influence of Capone with the judiciary. So that John Looney took matters in his own hands and went out and slew one or two of the principals in his son's death. In his trial he lost and was imprisoned for a term of years. He emerged from the penitentiary with this tubercular condition and came back to New Mexico seeking the beneficent influence of the sunshine of the state. Somehow he got on the Writers' Project.

Brown recalls the frugality of Looney's lifestyle at the time he knew "this very sick and decrepit old gentleman":

> In an effort to recoup some financial standing Mr. Looney lived mostly on day-old donuts and milk, saving his money until he was able to buy a one and a half ton truck. This he took with him on weekends up to a coal ledge he had knowledge of in the Rio Arriba country. He would dig and get out coal enough to fill his truck and bring it into Santa Fe to sell . . . and next week he'd repeat this performance. He was hoping to promote it to an extent where he could make a profitable paying operation.

Brown accompanied Looney on one such two or three-day trip, and remembers him as "a very well educated man, conversing very little," but with "will and determination." Brown was fascinated with Looney's Illinois history, but he had no further knowledge of the man either before or after the Federal Writers' Project.

Of the Hispano workers, Aurora Lucero-White was the least congenial as far as Brown was concerned. He barely remembers Rosario O. Hinojos and recalls having met Reyes N. Martínez of Arroyo Hondo only once by chance at the Santa Fe office. Eulogio F. Ulibarrí, who did some translating and submitted a few manuscripts, "didn't have very good English." According to Brown, Ulibarrí used "some pull from Rio Arriba" to get onto the Project staff, and he remembers that Ulibarrí "never relinquished his big hat and boots like the Tierra Amarilla fellows [who] all dressed that way."

Members of the New Mexico Federal Art Project worked closely with the Writers' Project. Brown recalls that "all of the artists" seemed "ever present at the office." He particularly remembers Willard Nash's rueful reference to "Los Cinco Pintores" (Bakos,

Mruk, Ellis, Shuster, and Nash) as *"Los Cinco Pendejos"* for having
to take refuge in the Art Project. E. Boyd was another artist "who
was always in demand around the office to illustrate different side
projects." According to Brown, Boyd was friendly with Mrs.
Cassidy and occasionally acted as one of the director's "consul-
tants." He himself began a lasting friendship with Boyd, noting that
"due to her illimitable knowledge of Spanish folklore and the arts
and crafts of both the natives and Indians alike . . . [she] was
highly valued [and] because of her sense of humor, witty, sometimes caustic, nevertheless agreeably received."

Brown's later involvement with the Federal Writers' Project was
tempered by a most significant event—his marriage to Frances
Juanita Gilson on August 31, 1939. Like Brown, Gilson was a
product of both Hispano and Anglo ancestry. Their greatest
similarity emerged, however, in the bold and independent nature
of their personalities. Not surprisingly, their married life was
marked by numerous moves.

Frances Brown never experienced the same intimacy with the
land and people of New Mexico that her husband enjoyed. Her
grandfather, a dragoon with the United States forces in the
Southwest, became enamoured both with New Mexico and with an
Englishwoman he met in Santa Fe. While his fondness for the state
gave way to his roots in St. Louis, his love for the girl was more
substantial, and they married in Santa Fe. Their two sons were
raised in Missouri, but Gilson's enthusiasm for New Mexico
infected them, and they traveled to Tesuque, New Mexico. True to
their father's example, they married two sisters from that village.
Frances's mother and father left for St. Louis when she was four,
and she grew to adulthood without ever returning to her native
state.

At the age of twenty-two, Frances set out to reclaim her Hispano
roots. It so happened that the Roybals of Tesuque, her maternal
relations, were good friends of the Browns. On a visit to the
Roybals, Brown was asked to replenish the household's diminishing
supply of bootleg. Frances accompanied him, and this proved to be
the first leg of her whirlwind tour of New Mexico. Their marriage
was enacted in a civil ceremony which, true to the style of both,
took place during the Santa Fe Annual Fiesta. The newlyweds
lived first with the Roybals in Tesuque, then with the Browns on
Agua Fria Street, and finally in their own house on Palace Avenue

in Santa Fe. Brown immediately became a proud father by adopting his wife's two young children by a previous union—Richard, aged three, and Anna, two years old. Brown reports that it was "just like pouring a quantity of water from one glass to another."

The frequency and duration of Brown's stays in Cordova had begun to decrease toward the middle of 1939, and they further diminished following his marriage. During Charles E. Minton's tenure as director of the New Mexico Writers' Program, Brown was permanently reassigned to the main office in Santa Fe. However, he did take Frances up to meet his Cordova friends and relations on one occasion. Her courage and curiosity outweighed her halting Spanish, unused since infancy, and the experience was a positive one for all parties. According to Brown: "She loved it, loved all this countryside." Their week in the community was much like Brown's earlier Federal Writers' Project-inspired visits. This couple circulated from house to house, with Brown introducing his wife and, as he puts it, "becoming embroiled in conversation." The bombing of Pearl Harbor marked the end both of Brown's employment by the Writers' Program and of the couple's residence in New Mexico.

Lorin the Traveler

Having passed the Civil Service Examination shortly after reassignment to the Santa Fe Writers' Program office, Brown was asked to report to the Office of Postal Censorship just after war was declared. Following a brief stay in El Paso, Texas, the Browns were transferred to Nogales, a border town in Arizona. The family lived there for the duration of the war, and Nogales was remembered by the Browns as the birthplace of their daughter Frances.

The three decades following Brown's employment by the Federal Writers' Project found him engaged in various jobs in numerous locations—California, Idaho, Washington, Alaska, Mexico, and, of course, New Mexico. His life continued to be as colorful as it had been in childhood and early adulthood, but it no longer found literary expression. Wife Frances supplemented the family's income with regular submissions of original crossword puzzles, however, and she drafted a number of short stories and a novel.

Lorin Brown's Writers' Project manuscript copies also suffered from the years of oblivion which beset the New Mexico Federal Writers' Project materials as a whole. In 1962 a fire razed the family's mountain cabin near Sandpoint, Idaho. Until that time, Brown had treasured carbons of all his contributions, hoping someday to rework them. The fire forced him to rely upon the scattered and incomplete copies which were deposited in New Mexico. The tragedy appears irreversible; efforts to date have not succeeded in recovering a complete set of Brown's papers.

The depth of Lorin Brown's New Mexico experience was subtly influential in determining his lifestyle. For example, his knowledge of rural pedagogy and his understanding of Hispano culture once prompted a call from the New Mexico state superintendent of schools. Several troublemakers in Lamy, New Mexico, had exhausted a number of young female schoolteachers early in the 1948–49 school year, and Brown spent the remainder as their master. An immediate "council of war" revealed the true source of the problem—a lack of recreational facilities. This situation was quickly remedied, and the students shed their roles as incorrigible ruffians and displayed considerable creativity, especially in the impromptu theater they organized on Friday afternoons.

Lorin and Frances Brown's New Mexican heritage also contributed to their fondness for certain locations. Both enjoyed Mexico, and San Luis Soyatlán, their residence for several years, continued to be a paradise lost for Brown. They also shared a love of the outdoors. Many of their happiest moments were spent on the lakes and rivers of Idaho and Alaska. Frances suffered many years from ill health, however, and the rigors of the Alaskan winter cost her her life. Both came down with the Asiatic flu while working as Salvation Army volunteers in Anchorage. In Brown's words, their arrival at the hospital was "the last time I saw her, in the emergency room. Really rough. And I said, 'Well, I want to see my wife.' 'No, you can't get up, you can't.' And they wouldn't take the intravenous off me. They had me under oxygen . . . for days and days."

Frances Gilson Brown died on December 26, 1969, and her husband's description of her final disposition is most revealing of his wife's and his own approach to death and to life:

> So she enjoyed, oh she loved to fish; we went fishing all the time. And, all the time we were [at the lake in Alaska] she

really went for it. So I thought that was the best thing to do with her ashes, spread them on that lake where she liked to fish. She never did want to be buried. Well, we made a pact: if I went first she'd cremate me and vice versa. . . . I've got my will, it's with Henry Hughes, that if I die within the radius of fifty or sixty miles of Cordova, I want to be brought up here, doesn't make any difference where, just under a cedar up there, or a juniper. But if I die elsewhere, I want to be cremated. . . .[33]

True to her mother's wishes, Anna spread Frances's ashes on the surface of the lake near Anchorage. Released from the hospital in January, Brown soon returned to New Mexico.

By this time, the Brown clan had lost much of its foothold in the state. Brother Bascom had settled in California following graduation from engineering school. Roy had died much earlier, the victim of poisonous gas during World War I. Brother Vincent had died as well, but sister Amy was still in Albuquerque. Brown stayed with her for a while, and he began to sink new roots into the soil of his homeland. Perhaps he had foreseen that his wife's demise would usher in a return to an old pursuit and the emergence of a new identity.

The Writer Returns

A series of events which began in 1970 encouraged Brown to reclaim another element of his past—his brief career as a writer in the 1930s. Daughter Frances was attending Stanford University in Palo Alto, California, and he joined her and his grandson there. Both father and daughter worked part-time in a kindergarten, she as teacher and he as "Mr. Fixit."

During a trip to Santa Fe, Brown met Marta Weigle through the efforts of two mutual friends. Weigle had originally contacted Brown by mail while conducting archival research for her dissertation on the Pious Fraternity of Our Father Jesus Nazarite. Her interest in Brown's expertise on the subject and in his related contributions to the Federal Writers' Project rekindled his own interest in the topic and increased his confidence in his own work.

A trip to the Taos area with writer and friend W. Thetford (Ted)

LeViness gave Brown an opportunity to reflect upon his experiences there and in Cordova and to gain a new perspective on the materials. Upon returning to California, he sat down for the first time in over thirty years to elucidate the northern New Mexico materials. The resultant manuscript provided an overview of his involvement in Hispano villages. About a year later, Robert F. Kadlec of Ancient City Press and Marta Weigle arranged for the new manuscript's publication along with two Federal Writers' Project manuscripts on the Brothers—"Lent in Córdova" (75) and "The Wake" (122). Explanatory notes and a glossary were provided by Weigle, and the work appeared in 1972 under the title *Echoes of the Flute* and with the pseudonym Lorenzo de Córdova. Thus, nearly four decades after he began writing on Hispano northern New Mexico, Brown finally received recognition for his efforts.

Encouraged by these results, Brown moved to New Mexico in 1973. He stayed in Santa Fe at first, but the city's altitude was incompatible with his heart condition. Albuquerque proved more hospitable, and he maintained an apartment there until 1977. At first he was reluctant to attempt further resuscitation of his Federal Writers' Project manuscripts because "it seems like such old hat to me, such old stuff. And it's been kicked around so much." Nevertheless, Weigle, Briggs, and E. Boyd convinced him that the recent surge of both popular and academic interest in southwestern Hispano culture made his early writings of substantial contemporary relevance.

Beginning in 1973, Brown began to gather copies of his papers from the New Mexico State Records Center and Archives, the History Library of the Museum of New Mexico, and elsewhere, and to research related material. His efforts to write up additional information on the Hispano communities of New Mexico were hampered by ill health, but his attitude remained one of perseverance. As Brown would say, *"como vida haiga, tiempo sobra"* ("while there's life, there's time").

Brown's determination had begun to bear fruit. He continued the researches reported in *Echoes of the Flute*—renewing old acquaintances, visiting former haunts, and tracking down some of the loose ends of his Federal Writers' Project materials. This work had its personal rewards as well, for Brown came to define himself as a writer and to have renewed faith in his literary talent. His labors led him back to the land of his childhood—Taos, and at the time of his death he was engaged in writing a book called "Tales of Taos." This volume (see 127, 128) was to counterbalance the emphasis accorded his adopted Cordova in the Writers' Project manuscripts which follow.

Brown's Collection

The most moving aspect of the following essays is perhaps the serendipity of their execution. The community, the man, and the opportunity for their union in prose met, joined, and then separated along divergent paths. Cordova's ties with Latin America were not entirely severed when Brown entered the community, and New Mexico's Hispano villages continue to contrast sharply with the Anglo mainstream of American society. Thus, the body of traditional knowledge which underlies the people's manner of relating to each other and their surroundings, the main subject of the following sketches, is scarcely common fare for television serials.

Lorin Brown's uniqueness was forged from an alloy of Father Martínez's renegade school, *curandero* tradition, and staunch Kansas Protestantism. The independence and vigor with which he pursued life was augmented by close friendships with members of the Santa Fe colony of artists and writers. Brown's individuality was matched if not surpassed by that of his wife Frances, and he enjoyed the support of loving and determined children.

Finally, Brown's five-year employment with the Federal Writers' Project in New Mexico constituted an unusually fine opportunity for the exercise of previously concealed talent. The free rein which he was allowed with regard to the selection of materials and the use of his time greatly contributed to the originality of the manuscripts. It is unfortunate, however, that New Mexico has taken more than thirty years to rediscover the value of his work and the importance of his knowledge.

Scholarly appraisal and use of these manuscripts must be based on a sound understanding of their nature. Especially in the case of Brown's ethnohistorical and ethnographic sketches, the reader must keep in mind the intent of the description. Barring a few, Brown's sources are oral rather than archival. He generally attempts to characterize Cordova's past as it was visualized by the Cordovans of the 1930s. To utilize this material as an objective historical account, as one author has,[34] constitutes a gross misinterpretation of the data as well as a failure to appreciate the basis of its subtlety and richness.

The mosaic produced by the convergence of writer, community, and opportunity is rather a set of poetic portraits of Hispano northern New Mexico. Cordova is represented in most of Brown's frames, which highlight village personalities, places, history, lore, and language. His vision of Cordova is a deeply personal one, and the aspects of village life which he holds dearest are more meaningfully captured in the rugged spirit of the first settlers than in recent decades of wage labor at Los Alamos. The nature of Brown's relationship to Cordova is perhaps best summarized by his first impression of the village: "Cordova was a paradise; there were no cars, no radios, no TV. It was just a very simple life, and I enjoyed it immensely."

PART II:

Village Life and Lore from Hispano
Northern New Mexico:
Lorin W. Brown's
Federal Writers' Project Manuscripts

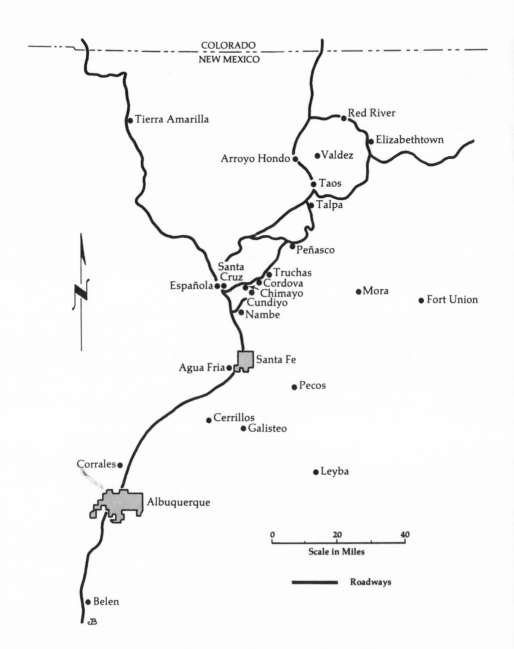

Principal Locations Mentioned in the Text

Introduction

The following sketches, stories, and texts represent the bulk of Lorin W. Brown's original contributions to the Federal Writers' Project in New Mexico. Except for the omission of titles and minor editing, the manuscripts are reprinted largely as found in the Santa Fe Federal Writers' Project files. Occasionally, longer or more complex pieces have been divided and presented at two or more appropriate junctures. Numbers in parentheses at the end of each selection refer to the "basic corpus" listing in the Bibliography, which gives the title, date, and a brief description of the original typescript.

Altogether, these manuscripts cover an astonishing range of Hispano New Mexican ethnohistory, folklore, and folklife. They have been woven into a narrative superstructure to enhance their aesthetic qualities and to animate village life and lore. Italicized editorial remarks between the Brown texts are therefore *not* scholarly notes but rather an ad hoc narrative suggested directly by the texts and only indirectly by historical, ethnographic, and folkloristic concerns. Texts and translations of hymns, songs, tales, proverbs, and riddles—all collected and most translated by Brown alone—are also interwoven to frame, to highlight, and to mark transitions.

The first selections after the morning hymn are arranged historically. Texts dealing with the Spanish and Mexican periods of Indian raids, buffalo hunts, and the early history of Cordova precede reminiscences of Taos, which postdate the American occupation, and Civil War legends. An "economics" section follows, with texts about trade, treasure, the *ricos*, and the cooperation necessary for survival in the poor villages. Play and pastimes are often the fruit of such cooperation, and selections on *bailes*, fiestas, games, riddles, and so forth, lead into storytelling by Tía Lupe and others. Folktales, tall tales, and legends of all kinds are included. The saint's legend of Santa Inés del Campo, patroness of the outdoors, provides the transition into the long piece about the lonely life of shepherd Basílico Garduño. Since this elaborate account ends with the promise of *Los Pastores* being performed around Christmas, a section of texts covering the annual cycle of village observances—the Christmas season, Lent and Holy Week, and various saint's days—follows. Despite inevitable changes, this cycle remained dear to the Cordovans of Brown's acquaintance, particularly the *ancianos*. This presentation thus closes with a rich perspective on old age, the Church, death, mourning, and life lived fully in the knowlege of death and the hope of life eternal.

Al Angel de Guarda

Angel de mi guarda	I beg you, Guardian Angel
Noble compañía,	Noble comrade of mine,
Vélame de noche	Keep vigil over me by night
Y guárdame en el día.	My footsteps guard by day.

Chorus:

Cantemos el alba	To the newborn day
Ya viene el día	Let's sing our morning hymn,
Daremos gracias;	And all give thanks;
Ave María.	Hail Mary!

Estas sí son flores,	These indeed are flowers
Estas sí que son;	Of a truth they are,
Gracias a María	Thanks to Holy Mary
Glorias al Señor	Hallelujah to Our Lord.

Que todos los santos	From all the saints on high
Del cielo nos valgan;	Protection we implore,
Oh Jesús divino	Our souls, Oh Lord divine
Cuida nuestras almas.	Guard fore'er from evil.

En suma pobreza	In lowly humility
Ya parió María	Christ to Mary was born,
Al Verbo encarnado	The Word in human form
Para amparo y guía.	Our Shield and Guide is He.

La mula se espanta	The mule afrighted was
Con el resplandor	By the splendor near the manger,
Y el buey con el baho	While the ox drew near the Babe
Calentó al Señor.	And tried to keep Him warm.

Ya nació María	He was born, Oh Mary
Para el consuelo	To be the Great Consoler
De los pecadores	To sinners here on earth
Y luz del cielo.	And to be the light of heaven.

Tan bella grandeza	The ugly dragon, Lucifer
No quiso ver	Essayed to close his eyes,
La ciega fiera	He did not wish to see
De Lucifer.	Such surpassing grace and beauty.
María divina	Divine and Holy Mary
Por ser tan pura	By reason of her chastity
Fué celebrada	And her surpassing beauty
Por su hermosura.	Shall e'er exalted be.
Viva Jesús	Long live Jesus,
Viva María	Long live Mary,
Cantemos todos	Shall be our song
En este día.	On this happy, happy day.
Bendito seas	Blessed be Thou
Sol refulgente;	Oh Sun so bright,
Bendito seas	Blessed be Thou
Sol de Oriente.	Oh Sun of the East.
Bendita sea	Blessed forever be,
Su claridad	That light we see
Bendita sea	Blessed also be
Quién nos la da.	He who grants it to us.
Quién la alaba canta	He who raises his voice
Muy de mañana	In this morning hymn
Las indulgencias	Indulgences of heaven
Del cielo gana.	Shall be granted him.

Fin

Al Angel de Guarda is a morning hymn sung in honor of the Guardian Angel, invoking his protection throughout the new day and the following night. (6)

From its first colonization in 1598, New Mexico was considered a dangerous frontier outpost of New Spain. Hispanic colonists clustered in tiny fortified plazas near Indian pueblos and in the Rio Grande Valley. By the mid-1700s, groups of determined settlers accepted land grants to establish buffer communities in the mountains and on the perimeter of the colony's core. Beleaguered by an inhospitable environment and beseiged by nomadic Indians, these staunch villagers nevertheless managed to entrench themselves and to perpetuate a proud heritage.

Más vale doblarse que quebrarse.
("It is better to bow than to be broken.")
Dónde hay gana hay maña.
("Where there is a will there is a way.") (100)

The Hispanos Lorin Brown knew in the 1930s preserved memories of their hardy pioneer forebears.

On a dark and stormy night or a day when the blizzard sweeps across the country on a cold norther one will hear some of the older residents of New Mexico say: "Este es día de herejes" ("This is a day for the heretics"). This saying alludes to the time when the Indians chose just such inclement weather to launch a surprise attack or raid on the Spanish settlements, hoping to catch the men of the villages napping inside by the fireplace. (55)

Some communities still staged "Los Comanches," a folk drama commemorating a skirmish between a band of Comanche warriors and a troop of Spanish soldiers. The version described below was performed by Hispano residents on the San Ildefonso Grant.

Los Comanches as put on in El Rancho under the direction of Sr. Martín Roybal is a play full of action, interesting and diverting. This play of all the many plays produced by troupes of players among the early Spanish settlers is one of the few which does not treat of a moral or a religious theme. It treats of an encounter between a band of Comanche Indians under the command of their chief, Cuerno Verde ("Green Horn"), and a troop of Spaniards commanded by their captain Don Carlos Fernández. These two with Barriga Dulce, the comedian of the piece, are the principal characters of the play.

As staged in El Rancho, December 28, 1938, the two forces, mounted on the pick of the saddle horses of the valley, meet on the sandy bottom of an arroyo close by the village church. The sloping banks of the arroyo make ideal vantage points from which the spectators can enjoy and follow the action of the play.

Previous to the enactment of the play, mass is said in the church, for this day is also the feast day of the patron saint of the village, San Antonio de Padua. While the devout villagers, with not a few Indians from the nearby pueblo of San Ildefonso, are listening to the service of the mass and the sermon which follows, the jingling of sleigh bells is heard through the open church door. Many knowing smiles are exchanged by those who are aware of the scene taking place outside of the church, for the actors who take the part of Comanches do not attend mass but are quite busy in the pursuit of a custom in which tradition grants them full liberty and protection. In their fringed buckskin garb, beaded vests, and plumed bonnets, they are busily engaged in pilfering articles of various kinds from the automobiles, buggies, and wagons which are parked here and there near the church. Individuals are not exempt, and every now and then a victim is surrounded by three or four of the Comanches or perhaps by all the band; they perform a brief dance of exultation around him, for he is now their captive and must pay a ransom in order to be set at liberty. The usual ransom is delivered to the captors in the nearby *cantina* and is usually a quart of wine.

In like manner the owners of the different articles pilfered from car, wagon, or buggy must redeem them when mass is over. This is the only source of revenue for the players who take part in the play. The most welcome form of payment is a quart of wine, but the victim may pay off with money, and many a quarter, dime, and nickel are collected and turned over to *el director* to be divided later.

After mass all the villagers join the procession, which forms at the church door, and exultantly accompany San Antonio de Padua as he is carried around the church on a gaily decorated pedestal, borne by four women and shaded by a canopy. The procession is very colorful, with the bright dresses of some of the younger women toned down by the long-fringed black shawls of the older women, the bright shawls and silken finery of the Indian women, the banners of the different religious orders, and the long robes of the priest and the altar boys as they lead the rest. The Comanches and the Spaniards of the play on their varicolored curveting horses, waving plumed headdresses, silken ribbons and tinkling sleigh bells, which the Comanches wear, lend their jingle to the music of the violin and guitar, the ringing of the church bell, and the *alabados* sung by the Brotherhood of the Penitentes, as in a group they followed the procession around the church.

Immediately after the procession has circled the church and the image of St. Anthony has been carried inside, the crowd streams down the hill on which the church stands to assemble on the banks of the arroyo mentioned beforehand.

The actors on their ponies have already reached the arroyo and are stationed about twenty yards from each other, the Indians at one end and the Spaniards at the other. Midway between the two groups stands a wagon on the seat of which are seated the musicians, a violinist and a guitarist. Seated in the wagon box behind the musicians are two boys who play a small part in the play. The wagon is supposed to represent the camp of the Spaniards.

The play begins as the musicians play the Santa Anna March, following which Cuerno Verde spurs his horse towards the Spaniards. Stopping a short way from them, he delivers a lengthy harangue from the back of his ever circling horse, in which he boasts of his prowess and the bravery of his warriors. Riding back to his men to the tune of the Santa Anna March and the beat of the *tombe*, he awaits the Spanish Captain, who in like manner rides up close to the Indian line and recounts his deeds of valor, lauds the power of the Spanish arms, and warns the Indians of the fate which they will meet if they should be so rash as to fight against him and his men.

After other speeches of like nature and challenges to single combat from both sides, the Indians make a charge and, surrounding the camp of the Spaniards (the wagon), take the two boys captive. Here, Barriga Dulce, the comedian of the play, a boastful character who hides under the wagon when the Indians attack, comes forward and cuts a ludicrous figure, as in his oversized helmet and with his enormous horse pistol he starts out to trail the Indians. He very bravely follows their trail, shouting threats and promises of vengeance to the empty air, but as soon as the Indians are sighted dancing around their two captives, he turns and flees for camp, stumbling and falling in his haste and terror. The Spanish soldiers, who have been following Barriga Dulce, recapture the two boys after a fierce skirmish with the Indians and return to camp.

The Indians return to their original station and between challenging speeches they have several fierce fights, heralded by the playing of the Santa Anna March and the beating of the *tombe*. Through all this Barriga Dulce keeps up his amusing acting, taunting the Indians when they are too far away to retaliate and shamelessly fleeing when they are close, first the arrant braggart, then the utter coward, but ever convulsing the spectators with his humorous remarks and actions. He never learns his lines, ad-libbing and distorting the lines which the director feeds to him from the side lines into impromptu jokes and remarks, of a rather shady character at times but always greatly amusing to the crowd.

In the final encounter, the Indians are vanquished and, fleeing from the Spaniards, are overtaken one by one as they race their horses up the arroyo and over the hills. The Indians are brought in afoot and unarmed. Here Barriga Dulce shows his true nature as he prods the defenseless captives with his enormous horse pistol, reviling and taunting them, and taking all the credit for their capture. (39)

One old Cordova resident recalled his own experiences as a comanchero *on the plains east of the Rockies.*

"Sí Señor, if my daughter had not put iodine in my eye in place of the medicine given me by the doctor I would be out with my sons helping them plow."

These were the first remarks from Sr. Vicente Romero of Cordova after we had exchanged salutations and I had commented on his good health. After a lapse of several years I had found my old friend partially blinded due to his daughter's unfortunate mistake.

"And for the grace of God who has given me my good health and the company of my wife I give thanks. Fifty-seven years we have gone through this life together. I was married quite old, when I had thirty years. I have lived a very active life and it is hard for me to be sitting here by the fireplace so useless." Around him were eight grandchildren, just a fraction of the twenty-six he has, not counting great grandchildren.

"Not always have I been so helpless. If I do say so myself I have never been afraid to work or to risk my life to acquire the necessities of life for my family. And when I was young we were surrounded by so many savage nations that any trip away from the village had to be made in force. Four times I have been on trading trips to the Comanches and three times to the plains on buffalo hunts. We used bows and arrows and the lance as weapons when hunting at first. Later we were able to trade for guns at Santa Fe. There were many deer then and the rivers were full of fish. But everything comes to an end in this world.

"The first two trips to the Comanches I went with my uncle Guadalupe Márquez, who was the *comandante* or leader. I learned enough of the language and customs so that the last two trips I went as *comandante*. Our first trip took us about three months. We took salt, blankets, and strips of iron for arrowheads. We also took big packs of a very hard bread, which our wives baked especially for trading to the Indians. Another article of trade was dried apples and plums.

"We went by way of Peñasco and Mora. When we came close to Fort Union we would wait until night to slip by the fort. The Americans did not want us to go into the Comanche country because it might cause trouble. After we had gotten by the fort without being seen we would have to hunt for the Indians. These savages were always traveling, hunting, or following the buffalo herds, so that we never knew where we would find them. We went here and there over the plains looking for signs of the Indians. When we finally found the trail of a large group in which there were signs of women and children, we knew we were close. Following this trail until the sign was quite fresh, our *comandante* ordered us to make camp. Locating the closest water supply we started to unpack. While we were doing this our *comandante* made a smoke signal on a high point near camp.

" 'Now boys, in the morning we should have the Indians here and we can start to trade,' he said. 'Be very careful how you act with the Indians.'

"We did not sleep very much that night. In the morning we were surrounded by a large group. They made camp next to us, the women doing all the work. The children and the dogs made lots of noise. At first the children were afraid of us but after a few days became very friendly, always begging for something. The Comanches are very fine looking Indians, light complexioned and well built. There are many savage nations on those plains. On one trip we traded with a group of Kiowas. It is a good thing the government guards these savages because if they ever fought us all together they might kill us all off now that they can get good rifles.

"After a sort of feast with the Indians we started in to trade. This would take a long time because there would be much talk over each trade. Sometimes an Indian and one of us would fix up a horse race. They liked to bet and that way we won many articles from them.

"We did not stay in the same camp but traveled from spot to spot with our customers, following the buffalo trading as we went. I enjoyed this life very much. It was very new to me; we were always watchful and on our guard for some act of treachery on the part of the Indians. But they had need of the goods we had to trade so they treated a trading party with a certain regard and usually avoided any act which might cause trouble. We were more careful than they were perhaps, always thinking of our families and the goods we were to take home with us.

"The younger men in our *escuadra* would run foot races with the Indians and amuse ourselves in other ways, such as breaking horses and contests with the bow and arrow. We had wrestling matches in some of which I took part. I very often raced a *grullo* (dark gray, with a black stripe down his back and on each shoulder), which was my favorite hunting horse, with first one and then another of their horses. I won six out of about nine races and not being held back by thoughts of a wife and children at home bet many blankets and other articles and so added considerably to my store of goods, because my *grullo* was pretty fast.

"Another young fellow, Anacleto Mascareñas, two years older than myself (remember I had only eighteen years), almost brought calamity on our little *escuadra* ('troop' or 'gang'). For some time several of our group had had conversation with a young girl of the tribe who had been taken captive from some place in Texas, San Antonio del Arbol she called the place. Where that place is I don't know. She had tried to persuade us to take her away from her captors, promising us that her father would pay us in gold and cattle, should we return her to her home. Her story was that the Comanches had seized her as she was taking some clothes to some servant women washing at a stream near the house. As she was passing a clump of wild plum bushes, three of these painted savages had jumped out, took hold of her, and one of them closed her mouth with his hand to keep her from crying out or screaming. They led her to where they had left their horses. One of them took her on his horse and rode off, followed by the other two. A short distance from her father's ranch they were joined by others in charge of stolen stock, also belonging to her father. She was shown the mutilated bodies of two of her father's herders and by sign shown what to expect if she did not go quietly. One of the men who had carried her off had made her his wife. *¡Pobrecita!* She had to work very hard like the rest of the Indian women. Her pleas were very pitiful and some of us younger fellows felt like risking a rescue.

"In every important decision our *comandante*'s word was final because we had entrusted ourselves to his care and given him full authority. Some of us took up the girl's case with him for his decision. We could almost guess what his decision would be. There were two of us who did not care so much about the gold or reward from her father, but had dreams of taking this really *muy bonita* captive as a bride and enjoying the surprise she would cause when our folks saw her after the salvo to San Antonio. It was the custom for any group returning to Cordova from a hunt or trading trip to discharge their firearms at the crest of the ridge circling our home village. This salvo was in honor of our patron saint of the village and was a means of announcing our arrival. Those were very joyous times and I will never forget the first time I belonged to one of these returning parties. But let me finish telling you about this girl. I was one of the two who wanted to take the girl back with us, but our *comandante* said, 'No, it can't be done. Any effort to free her or take her away might destroy our whole party, as far away as we are from home and as few as we are for the number of Indians against us. Even if we were so lucky as to get her away with little or no loss none of us could ever return to trade with these Indians.' But Mascareñas insisted and threatened to carry her away against the *comandante*'s orders. He secretly made preparations to do so. When the *comandante* found this out he ordered Mascareñas seized and bound until he gave up his plan and promised to obey our leader's orders in everything. This seemed very cruel, but it was very necessary for the good of our whole party. So the *pobrecita* stayed there with the Indians, perhaps for life. *Asi le tocó* ('That was her fate'). Those were very hard times.

"I remember now something that happened on my last trading trip with the Comanches. Among our party was José Antonio Vigil and his son. This man was later known as El Capitán Vigil. He was afraid of no Indian or twenty of them even. I could tell of many deeds of valor of his against the savages, but now I will tell you of what happened on my last trip. I was in charge as *comandante* and our whole group was composed of men from Cordova or El Valle. This man Vigil had a very fast and enduring sorrel horse which was known as El Alazán. The Indians coveted this animal and Vigil received many offers for his horse. One Indian even offered him two captive women amongst other things. This was a good offer, for these captive slaves were very much in demand among the *ricos* and prospective bridegrooms and brought a very good price. But Vigil refused all trades because he could not bear to part with this very excellent animal.

"Early one morning Vigil and his son left camp after antelope without my permission. He was very far from camp when he and his boy were overtaken by an Indian known as Capitán Corona. This Capitán Corona was so called because of the peculiar way his hair grew. At one time in some fight his enemies had started to scalp him while unconscious, thinking him dead. The operation revived him before his scalp had completely parted company with his skull. Being a renowned fighter he had scattered his would-be scalpers. However his scalp did not fit back snug to his skull like it had been before. It had grown back in a bunch on the top of his head making a crown-like growth. And that was the reason for his name, *corona* meaning crown. At any rate he was a very tricky Indian and a fighter with a reputation, being a chief amongst the Comanches. This day he hailed Vigil and his son and catching up with them rode along between them. Being as eager as any of the others for Vigil's horse he started talking trade as they rode along. José Antonio being always on his guard pretended to agree to trade so as to keep Corona in good humor. The tricky savage decided to get the horse for nothing because without warning he knocked the boy off his horse with a club which he carried in his left hand. At the same time he reached over with his right hand and pulled Vigil off his horse. All this was done very suddenly. However he was not quick enough for Vigil, who at the instant drew his knife. Catching Corona in the pit of the throat he ripped him open, completely disemboweling him.

"His first thought was of the trouble he might cause the rest of his companions. Putting the body on the Indian pony they covered any marks of the fight and buried the body quite a way from the scene of the fight. His horse was taken to the edge of a cliff where he also was killed and his body pushed over the edge. Riding back to camp late that night I was awakened and told what had happened. Vigil after telling of the fight said, 'I have brought this trouble on us myself. My boy and I will leave tonight. The Indians missing us will think that Corona has taken us captive. If you folks make no fuss the Indians will believe as I have told you. As soon as you finish trading you had better leave because they might accidentally find the body. I leave all my goods in your care to take to my family in case I do not get home. But I will not stay and make trouble for the rest of you. This is the only way. *Adios, amigos.'* '*Vayan con Dios,'* I answered.

"There was no doubt that everything was for the best this way. Luckily it rained very heavily that night, covering their tracks and the Indian's. They finally must have believed as Vigil thought they would when Corona failed to show up also. This was another time when one or two individuals suffered in order to preserve the safety of the many. I am glad to say that Vigil and his boy arrived safely home after many narrow escapes from the Indians and from hunger.

"José Antonio lived to found Cundiyo, settling it along with his sons and their families. His descendants and the descendants of his eight sons were the reason that in Cundiyo today the only family name you hear is Vigil. Here in the defense of Cundiyo from Indian raiding parties José Antonio received the name of El Capitán Vigil. The Indians learned to leave him alone after he had killed several of them, and Cundiyo was fairly safe from their raids.

"One time I remember Capitán Vigil was taken to Santa Fe to show how he fought against the Indians. With his body wrapped around with a rawhide rope and with his shield he kept off the arrows which were shot at him. I think it was the captain of the American soldiers at Santa Fe who took him there for this exhibition. I do know that he came home with a team of mules and, as he said, with $800 American money. He was a very valiant man, very famous for his valiant deeds.

"After finishing with our trading we made preparations to leave the Comanche country. The Indians escorted us for three days out of their country. They did this with all trading parties when the trading was over. After again slipping by Fort Union we were very happy to be on our way home. We were still in some danger from Apaches or Navajos who liked to come through that part of the country to raid the Pueblos and even on horse-stealing trips among the Comanches. The Comanches were very great enemies of the Navajos. One Comanche told me that the Navajos were all magicians or practiced witchcraft. To prove this he said that whenever they were about to overtake a bunch of horse-thieving

Navajos the latter would turn themselves and the stolen stock into soapweed and the Comanches would have to return emptyhanded. That is why they had no use for the Navajo.

"The closer we got to our homes the more we pushed our poor horses with their loads. And, thanks to God, we finally reached Truchas and now we were practically home. Soon we were firing our firearms in the salvo to San Antonio. We could see the people on the roof-tops counting us as we rode down into the village to see who was missing. My poor mother cried with joy to see me back safe. Blessed be God; those were the times. This was my first trip to the Comanches and I was to make many more, but I always remember this one especially." (41)

Another less fortunate cibolero from Galisteo was commemorated in a melancholy ballad.

This ballad treats of an accident which overtook a young buffalo hunter of Galisteo, New Mexico, on the Great Staked Plains in the year 1873. With his hunting lance held on high, Manuel Maes was riding at a dead run towards the galloping herd of buffalo. Suddenly his horse stumbles, having stepped in a prairie dog hole, throwing his rider over his head. What might have been only a nasty spill turns into a plains tragedy, for Manuel's lance has fallen in such a way as to receive and transfix his body as it fell.

The ballad is written as if spoken by Manuel as he lay dying after his accident. First Manuel speaks of a premonition he had had of his death. He had heard a bell toll and had had a distinct vision of himself dying in his mother's arms. Yet next day, a Sunday, he goes out to the hunt and his premonition comes true as the ballad tells us.

Through several verses Manuel takes farewell of his mother and father and his several brothers and sisters. He even bids a fond goodbye to a mountain peak which he tells us he could see from the door of his humble *jacal* in faraway Galisteo. He also regrets he has not been able to try out a new mount which he had brought along for the hunting.

He is left in a lonely grave near the Colorado River. In the last verse of the ballad, its composer, giving his name, Cecilio Roybal, asks that a prayer be said for the repose of the soul of the unfortunate Manuel Maes. (81)

An old cibolero and ranchero recalled his youthful experiences with Indians and Hispanos west of the Rio Grande.

Don Juan José Gonzáles was seated on the ground with his back to the wall soaking up the warm sunshine. Eighty-four years old, the warm sun's rays were gratefully received after a winter indoors.

"How are you Don Juan?"

"Very well, *mi amiguito.*" He no doubt recognized my voice because his eyesight had almost failed him completely. "Stay and talk with me." Usually alone because his son was a very busy fellow, Don Juan was always anxious to have somebody to listen to his reminiscences. Having nothing better to do, I sat down beside him.

"How good the sunshine is. My old bones can stand lots of it. But I thank God he has let me live so long and granted me such good health. I have only been really sick once in my life and then it was due to a *maldita bruja* ('accursed witch')."

"Really," I said. "I have heard many tales about witches but never quite believed them."

"No, this is the truth because I remember well. You know father was very well fixed. His home ranch was on this side of the Rio Grande near Corrales. I was the *coyote* or youngest son and my father was very good to me. I was the *consentido* ('indulged son'), and he kept me home just to carry his orders to his hired help around the ranch and to accompany him to town. My other brothers were out in the sheep camps and on the other ranches we had, one ranch as far away as Cuba.

"Now listen and I will tell you how I was bewitched and cured by a *médico* or witch doctor. I had gone to Albuquerque returning about the time that everybody was sleeping in the heat of the day. I left our coach on the west bank of the river, then I fired a shot from my revolver to attract our ferry-man so that he would row over after me. He had been sleeping in the shade of the cottonwood, but my one shot was sufficient to wake him. Upon landing on the other side I was quite thirsty and thought to stop at María's house and get a drink of water. María was a Navajo Indian slave who had been given in marriage by my father to one of our sheepherders. They lived in a two-room house close to the river. Here I stopped and María coming out of her house I said, 'María, for God's sake give me a drink of water. I am very thirsty.'

"María was usually of a bad visage or sullen. Some thought it was because she wanted to go back to her people and also because she didn't like her husband. Maybe she was mad at my father for making her marry Antonio. Father married her off to get her away from our house, where she only went for two days to wash clothes every week.

"That day she was more *gente* or cordial than I had ever known her to be. 'Sit down, Juanito, and rest. I have some very nice apricots, very sweet. Let me bring you some.' I like all kinds of fruit and thought I would wait for her and she was soon back with them. I ate two or three and taking some with me left, thanking María and wondering what had changed her.

"Hurrying as fast as I could I reached the portal [of our house] and started crying out for help. My voice was very weak and when my mother and some of the women arrived I had fallen into a faint. I did not know about being carried inside and my mother was very much frightened not knowing what could have happened to me.

"Later I became delirious and in my delirium raved about María and apricots. My mother sent a girl to María's to see what she knew about this sudden sickness. The girl returned with the news that María was gone. *Sí, Señor,* she had bewitched me with those apricots and had run away perhaps to the reservation. My mother sent some men to try to find her and bring her back. '*Maldita bruja,*' she said, 'she is the cause of this. All Indians are *brujos* and that "long face" wants to pay us back for some wrong she thinks we have done her.'

"Calling for Pedro, one of our helpers, he was ordered to saddle two mules and go immediately and bring Secundino Padilla, a famous witch doctor who lived on the road to San Ysidro. As you know when you have been bewitched only a witch doctor can cure you. This Secundino was one of the best in the vicinity. So Pedro set out with the two mules, one for Secundino to ride on the way back.

"That evening I was very sick, I would become transfixed, my jaws would become tightly clenched for long intervals. I was treated with many applications of herbs, but with not much faith on my poor mother's part, because she did not know the right cures for my case. And the horrible visions or apparitions I could see, some with horns, others with eyes like the flames of hell. I was very much tormented by the devils called up by that evil woman, and it's a miracle I did not die in that state.

"Early in the morning Pedro returned but without the witch

doctor. '*Por el amor de Dios*, didn't you find Don Secundino? Now my son will surely die bewitched,' said my poor mother. Pedro had not found the witch doctor home, only his wife, who gave Pedro something to eat. While he was eating, she told him Secundino already knew of Juanito's sickness, how she didn't say, but only that Secundino had immediately left to gather some herbs or medicines which he knew were necessary. Before leaving to gather these, Secundino had told his wife, 'Don Buena Ventura Gonzáles's son has been harmed by one of their Indian women and there will be a man after me. Give him something to eat, then send him home immediately telling him I will be with Juanito as soon as he.'

"Pedro had no sooner finished telling my mother about his trip and was starting to refresh himself with some wine when Secundino stepped up on the portal. How he arrived nobody knew; there was no horse or mule to be seen. These folks must have some alliance with Satan or else how can they do the wonderful things they do?

"Yet Secundino used his arts to cure me. I do not know just what he did; neither did any of my folks. He asked to be left alone in the room with me, first asking for some pots and hot water. About two hours afterwards my mother was called in. I had regained my senses but was still very weak. My mother said there was a very strong smell of sulphur in the room. How he cured me we did not know. It is not wise to try to find out too much about those things. It is enough to take advantage of their knowledge of those hidden things for well-being, because acts of the devil have to be fought by those who have an understanding with him.

"After drinking some wine and eating some food Secundino left the house. We did not see him again around there. He had gone home, no doubt the way he came. Next day my father sent Pedro with a wagon loaded with flour, fruit, and wine to Secundino's home near San Ysidro. He was given a buckskin purse with many coins in it for Secundino also. You may be sure my father sent word with Pedro to my brother to drive some fat sheep down to the witch doctor's home also.

"In a few days I was as well as ever, riding my favorite horse around our ranch, very glad to be well."

"And how about María?" I asked. "Did she ever return?"

"No! We never saw her again, although for many days I never let loose of my revolver, hoping to see her. I had it loaded with bullets marked with a cross, the only kind of bullets that will kill a witch, though some say silver ones are as good. *¿Quién sabe?*

"One of the men my mother sent to try to find María after she disappeared was Tiburcio Chávez, son of Abelino Chávez, a neighbor of ours from across the river. This young man had been a captive among the Navajos. He had seven or eight years more than I. He had been captured when only about ten years old, while herding cows in the foothills close to his home. His boy cousin about the same age was taken captive at the same time. The men of the village organized and pursued the Indians but were unable to even see them. Maybe ten or twelve years later a troop of soldiers stopped to camp on the river. They had with them a band of Navajos which they were guarding or conducting as prisoners to Bosque Redondo.

"Everybody went to see the soldiers and their prisoners—men, women, and children. We were all curious to see these savages who had caused us so much trouble and had killed so many of our people. One *vecina* of ours, an old lady, was very much astonished when a tall Indian reached out and took hold of her shawl. She screamed, attracting the attention of the captain of the American soldiers. *El Capitán* jerked the Indian's arm loose, while all the time the Indian was speaking very excitedly in his language. Two words in Spanish could be understood. They were: *'Mi mamá,'* or my mother. This old lady was very mad that a dirty Indian should call her mother, but *El Capitán* became interested and called an interpreter. You will not believe me but this tall Indian was one of those two boys who had been taken captive so many years before. He recognized his mother but had no more Spanish than those two words, *'mi mamá.'* What strange things happen in this world, no?

"After this woman, the wife of Abelino Chávez our neighbor, was convinced that this was her son she just shook hands with him. She was still afraid of him and could not greet him affectionately as she should have. She said she could not until he had washed and changed his clothes. It was very funny but when he brought his wife out to meet his mother, our *vecina* was almost ready to let him go on with the rest of the savages to the reservation.

"Finally she asked both her son and daughter-in-law home for a meal, first getting consent from the captain. The Indian wife ate so much, maybe she was very hungry, that she died that evening. The young man stayed with his folks, where he soon learned enough Spanish to be able to make himself understood. He was a very good hunter and trailer. Anybody losing stock was sure to come for Tiburcio. He nearly always returned with the lost animals. Later on he married and raised quite a family. I am not sure whether he is still living because some time ago a daughter of his took him to her home near Socorro.

"He was a great fellow to take on a buffalo hunt, using a spear like the Indians did, and nobody could beat him when it came to riding a horse. But everything comes to an end in this world and my *compañeros* on the buffalo hunts are nearly all gone.

"Sea por Dios," the old man sighed, and I left there, thinking to come back some time and ask him to recount his experiences on the buffalo hunts of long ago. (123)

The Spanish colonists pushed beyond established settlements in search of new land to be brought under cultivation and, hopefully, defended from hostile nomadic tribes. Above Santa Cruz de la Cañada and Chimayo lay the Quemado Valley, site of contemporary Cordova. The first settlers soon discovered that the place had not always been uninhabited, however; a Pueblo Indian village had existed on the mesa above and been abandoned before their time.

About twenty million years ago, lava flows and changes in earth structure caused the Rio Grande to become a series of lakes from which the water flowed and was drained off as the river changed its course. [Brown here cites E. R. Harrington, "Rocks of the Ages," *New Mexico Magazine*, February 1941, p. 16.] These exposed lake beds are best seen around Española, which is in the neighborhood of Cordova. Fantastic forms, telling the story of eroded sedimentary deposits, are seen singly and in groups, mostly of a tawny color but with some red showing in the Chimayo Valley to the east.

The road to Cordova turns off US 64, which is the highway from Santa Fe to Taos, skirts the village of Santa Cruz, and runs alongside the Rio Santa Cruz over a fairly level but winding road into Chimayo. From here the road climbs on the shoulders of hills that rim the valley until it attains the eminence where the ruins of the Indian village of Pueblo Quemado lie concealed under mounds of dirt. Just beyond, far below and down to the right, are glimpses of cultivated fields, but no evidence of habitation. Up ahead, the road continues the rise to the distant village of Truchas, which lies at the foot of the highest mountains in New Mexico. To the left, where the valley floor has become a canyon, foothills march north and east. Except for an occasional jack rabbit, no sign of life appears among these piñon-dotted hills. The vast bowl of the sky sweeps up from behind the Truchas Peaks in a blue glory and stretches for miles and miles to the Jemez and Nacimiento Ranges to the west. (52)

About one mile after one leaves the Plaza del Cerro [Chimayo], one reaches Rio Chiquito, a small village to the right of the road whose inhabitants are engaged in the peaceful pursuits of weaving and chile raising. Here the grade of the road becomes definitely much steeper and it is necessary to use second or low gear. The first breathing spell is reached when you have topped a high hill from which you can see the village of Truchas outlined against the eastern horizon, some five miles away and mostly up.

This spot may be identified by the many mounds on each side of the road which form a rough circle enclosing a small plain some six acres in extent. No vegetation except cactus and a fuzzy growth of Russian thistle, which never seems to grow beyond the incipient stage, is to be seen on these hills or mounds. This height or the site of these mounds is about three-fourths of a mile from the spot where one leaves the ridge road to Truchas on the left and descends into the valley in which Cordova is located. This site may be identified also by a cross which stands on a mound on the eastern edge of the circle. This cross was made and erected there by the late Don José Dolores López, well-known wood carver of Cordova, remembered by many for his hospitality, graciousness, and keen sense of humor.

This is the Alto Huachin, the site of an Indian Pueblo of long ago inhabited by Tano Indians. Its location lent itself admirably to freedom from surprise attack, guarded as it is on the north and west by steep slopes and on the south by the steep rocky gorge of the Rio Quemado. These ruins should be of interest to the archeologist since they have never been excavated except for the tentative test holes dug by amateur seekers of curios. However, if you are headed for Cordova, drawn there by the unique attractions of this typically New Mexican adobe village, you will be interested in the connection between these ruins and the history of the settlement of Cordova.

Alto Huachin, or Huachin Height, was so named after the last chief or governor of the ill-fated Pueblo. These Tanos dwelt here, continually harassed by the Navajos, Apaches, and other predatory tribes, as they tended their scant crops in the valley below or hunted small game in the rocky outcroppings of the surrounding hills. To the north and west of Alto Huachin and across a sandy arroyo there is a high butte which to this day is called *La Sentinela,* or The Sentinel. This was a lookout point on which a watchful sentinel was posted to signal the approach of any band of enemies which he might sight.

How many attacks the Pueblo survived we do not know, but we can imagine that they were many and unrelentingly fierce. We do know that sometime previous to the year 1751 the enemies of the Pueblo on the Alto Huachin finally prevailed, killing most of the inhabitants, after which they set fire to the buildings; for at this time the site of the erstwhile Pueblo was known to the settlers of Santa Cruz de la Cañada by the name *El Pueblo Quemado,* or The Burned Pueblo. This fact is established by a document dated as above, in which document a group of settlers of Santa Cruz petition the viceroy for permission to resettle the lands of El Pueblo Quemado. The word resettle argues that they had previously settled on these lands, and whether they had been driven out or had abandoned them for other reasons is not touched on in the petition.

However, the settlement which sprang up in the valley of the Quemado River was henceforth known as El Pueblo Quemado and was not known as Cordova until a United States post office was established there in 1925. The name Quemado was not permitted by the United States Postal Department because there existed another town of that name in the southern part of the state, so that the name Cordova was selected, honoring the most prominent and progressive family of the village.

A few of the surviving Tanos from Alto Huachin took refuge in a small valley about two or three miles above, where they lived a miserable and fugitive existence. Here they finally died out, and the pitifully small ruins of the last stand of a one-time flourishing community may be seen today. This valley is still known as La Cañada de los Tanos. (24)

It was more than natural that Cordova's first Spanish residents quickly set about constructing a defensible plaza or town square; the governor backed up their efforts with the force of law. When Brown first entered the community, Cordova's fortified appearance continued to remind visitors of the precariousness of the settlement's infancy, and he described its enduring contribution to the vistas surrounding the road into the village in the 1930s.

Where the ridge road [State Highway 76] gives to the right, a steep, twisting descent, hazardous in rain or snow and thrilling at all times, looks out and down onto more fields; an *acequia* ("irrigation ditch") is crossed, and the narrow way straightens out briefly before climbing up past corrals and a small, new, flat-roofed school building. Without warning, the traveler is in Cordova.

On the left, houses line the rocky, narrow road that becomes the village street, while on the right the ground slopes down to more corrals and the village grist mill. Midway in the settlement, space between a small store building and an adobe house forms a short, wide path, and a few hard bounces take the visitor off the road, around the store, and into the plaza, onto which look the little church and the old school house, now a dwelling. From the plaza, heart of this hillside hamlet, one looks up to the Penitente *calvarios*. These are visited by members of the local *morada* during Lent when, to the accompaniment of the medieval *pito* and the thud of yucca whips swishing against blood-soaked naked backs, the barefoot Brothers make their tortured way to their own calvaries, accompanied by companions chanting the appropriate prayers.

In the spring, the irrigation ditches dash busily along to the fields, and the blossoms of the fruit trees are miracles of pink and white against the brown adobe. In the autumn, pumpkins, corn, and squash make mounds of color on the rooftops, *ristras* of scarlet chile hang down the walls of the houses, and the miller is busy grinding corn and chile pods for the housewives. In the summer, the men and boys are busy in the fields, which lie away from the closely huddled houses, while the women and girls are busy indoors. In the winter, when the trees are bare, the houses seem to move even closer together, squat a little lower, and draw in more closely the deep stillness of the village. The work horses are left out to graze, but the goats are driven out from the corral each morning, grazed, then penned up for the night. Everyone knows, especially the grandmothers, what everyone is doing or has done, how each one meets the times. While there are many blood ties, there are other ties too, and there are few secrets.

Cordova has changed very little in its physical appearance from

the time when it was known as El Pueblo Quemado. Both of the
original *Puertas de la Plaza*, the upper and lower, afford entrance
into the central, open square dominated by the buttressed adobe
church. These entrances are no longer barricaded with the stout
wooden doors or gates, which formerly were closed at night after
the stock had been driven inside the square for protection against
the raiding Indians. The square has had no houses built within its
original confines because it is communal property and no title
could be obtained by an individual. If it had not been for this
obstacle, many of the villagers who have built homes on rocky
exposed points south of the river would have preferred this
location; but the demands of farming preclude building on any
piece of land that could possibly be used for cultivation, hence the
use of home sites unfit for anything else.

The houses of the village still keep guard on the central square,
but they have had doors and windows placed in their outside walls,
which in pioneer times had been left solid, except for loopholes.
(52)

*The arduous nature of subsistence in the struggling new community
necessitated the men's departure for numerous trading expeditions
and other enterprises. Nevertheless, the women who remained at
home faced no less formidable tasks in the struggle for survival.
Among their duties was the preparation and storage of food for the
extended family.*

The early inhabitants of Cordova did not have far to seek for
material for making dishes, cups, and cooking utensils. Close to the
village there are substantial deposits of a micaceous clay that is
good for pottery. Certain women made pottery as a means of
acquiring those necessities of life that they lacked because they had
no land on which to raise these necessary foods.

The process of making these bowls, pots, and other articles is
relatively simple. Care must be taken to select lumps of the purest
clay, with a minimum of foreign matter. Careful washing and
kneading of the clay leaves it in a smooth condition easily handled.
For the most part, no attempt was made to decorate these pots:
everything was utilitarian; decorations were superfluous. The clay
was formed into long rolls about the consistency of dough and the
thickness of a lead pencil. These rolls were built layer by layer into

the shape desired. Careful scraping and modeling by hand left both inside and outside surfaces fairly smooth. The pots and other articles were left to set but not allowed to dry. A fire was built of pine bark and left to burn down to embers. The moist pottery was placed thereon and more bark was fed to the fire in just sufficient quantities to allow the pots to bake slowly. This was a slow process, a primitive one, yet the results were eminently satisfactory. After the pots were baked, they were smeared inside and out with pitch and again placed on the coals until the pitch had been thoroughly burned into them. This process waterproofed the pots and they were ready to be traded to the village housewife.

In those days, barter was the only method of commerce feasible. Money was of no use to a widow who made pots for a living; if she were in need of an *almud* of corn meal, there was no store where she could buy it. So a system of barter evolved to solve this problem. A pot or any other article would be traded by its maker for as much corn meal, flour, and beans as the pot would hold. This was a fair solution and one practiced for many years. The larger the pots were, the more meal they would hold, and everyone was satisfied with this arrangement.

The Apaches knew of these deposits of clay. Every summer large numbers would camp near the source of supply. Here the squaws would make and fire pots, while the braves hunted and fished in the nearby hills and rivers. The people of the villages dreaded the summer invasions . . . of these nomad Indians. Stock was kept close to the village, instead of allowing it to run loose in the hills, for the Apaches dearly loved fat beef and mutton. These Indians also fashioned baskets from the slender willows that grew along the river. These they would trade to the villagers for food, clothing, or grain.

The pottery trade was followed by widows and women who had no land from which to expect to stock their larder. Because their neighbors needed pots and jars as well as the flat griddles called *comales*, on which tortillas were baked, this craft supplied a need in the community and gave a livelihood to women who otherwise would have suffered privation and who would have had to accept charity.

Troja is the name given by the early Spanish settlers to bins or openings in the wall in which grain was stored for safekeeping. As used locally, the word *troja* is a corruption of *troje*, which means granary. The bin type of *troja* was made by building an adobe wall three or four feet out from the main wall of the kitchen or of the *dispensa* ("storeroom"), this wall being made about three feet high and usually running the length of the room. The space thus enclosed was divided by adobe partitions to make separate compartments for different kinds of grains. *Trojas* in the kitchen held the flour, meal, prepared grains, and other foods handy for the housewife. The *trojas* in the *dispensa* as a rule were larger and held the carefully selected seed grain for the next season's planting as well as other grains used in feeding the stock and the chickens.

Another type of *troja* was dug out of the wall or was a hollow place in the wall with a hole at the top into which the grain was poured and a hole below through which the grain would pour out, impelled by its own weight. These hidden *trojas* were used as secret caches in which seed, grain, parched corn, and meal were stored. By plugging the two holes with mud and then plastering them over and whitewashing them to conform with the rest of the wall, they were hard to detect. These hidden stores were prepared by the early settlers as emergency stores in case an Indian raid should force them to flee their homes. On their return they would be fairly certain of food and seed with which to begin life again. This type of *troja* is found in an old house at Cordova. Its shape was something like that of a hopper, wide at the top and narrowing funnel-like at the bottom, the whole smoothly plastered to facilitate easy movement of the grain. (88)

Not all pots were used for food; some held crude cosmetics.

Even amidst the perils of Indian raids and the arduous uncertainties of pioneer life, the women of the adventurous Spanish settlers gave thought to their appearance. One of the first articles of trade which was welcomed by maid and matron alike was the product of some inventive mind who, using the materials found at hand, laid the foundations for the wealth of later merchant families. This article of trade was nothing more or less than the first homemade face powder. The wily trader who invented it had no trouble disposing of the little pots containing it.

The powder was made of deer antlers which had first been reduced to an ash. This ash was then ground to a fine powder on the *metate* or grinding stones found in every home. Still it was not fine enough for the purpose to which it was then to be put but had to be dissolved in water. The resultant settlings were collected and placed in little earthen pots, ready for the buyer. These little pots, of a uniform size, commanded a set price and were one article of trade over which there was not much haggling.

In the making of the pots, the trader utilized material from the self-same hills from which came his raw material for the face powder, for they were made of the micaceous clay that abounded there. They were gleaming little pots, the mica in the clay imparting a shine to their round sides. These pots were soon to be seen sitting in the chimney corner or in some cases hidden behind the carved doors of the *almarios* and their contents surreptitiously applied because there were some who frowned on the use of face powder.

Should some maiden apply too much of the powder to her face, she would be sure to hear *"A esta se le volcó la olla"* ("This one had the pot boil over on her"). The witty ones referred to the cloud of ashes which would erupt when the boiling pot on the open hearth would boil over, sending ashes all over the person of the housewife. The embarrassed girl would retire to rub off some of the too-evident whitening powder. (109)

The men were responsible for woodworking to equip home and ranch.

Three common articles of useful homemade furniture found in every home of the early Spanish settlers were *trasteros, almarios,* and *goteras.* The similarity of the needs which they filled allows them to be logically grouped in one classification.

The *trastero* or cupboard as a rule was the most outstanding of this group. In it, next to the wedding chest, the early craftsman exercised his most loving skill and ingenuity, for in most cases these articles of furniture were made by the bridegroom for his prospective bride.

These *trasteros* were more or less of the height and depth of the cupboards we all are acquainted with today, but there the similarity ends. In the *trastero* no glass or glue was used. No nails were employed in its construction. In fact, the only iron-work on them was the hand-wrought hasps and hinges with which the doors were hung and secured. One pair of doors was the rule in most *trasteros,* though some had two pairs, one opening onto the shelves where dishes and foods were kept, the other or lower pair opening onto the shelves for pots and kettles.

The feature common to all *trasteros* was that all of the sides were constructed so as to allow air to circulate freely throughout their interior. This utilitarian end was artistically and ingeniously achieved by the use of carved spindles or slats cleverly fitted into the framework of the doors and sides in a carefully planned design. Joints were dove-tailed or tongue-and-grooved, held more firmly still by wooden pegs at points of juncture.

The head-board at the top of this piece of furniture was usually fashioned in a flowing, symmetrical shape nicely suited to the rest of its dimensions. On this head-board the artisan carved some design, the most common being the squash blossom, the sunflower, or the rosette design. The legs or corner pieces, which usually extended four or five inches below the lower shelf, were decorated with a continuation of the design carved on the head-board. The whole effect was never that of something overdone or elaborate, rather of something most pleasing in its simplicity and harmony of design.

Armarios, or *almarios* as they were commonly known, filled a need similar to the *trastero* and were a natural outgrowth of the ease with which adobe walls may be dug out to accommodate them. For *almarios* were nothing more or less than a hole dug in the wall of the home of the required size. This then was fitted with shelves and whitewashed. As in the *trasteros,* the unique feature of the *almarios* was the doors with which they were fitted—doors made of carved spindles or slats of different designs fitted into slots in the framework. However, rarely were hinges used to hang these doors; rather they were of the type known as *zambnigo* or *zambuso.* That is, the doors turned on elongations of their own framework fitted into snug holes in the crosspieces of the supporting frame. Here also the only metal used was in the hand-forged latch or lock. This article of furniture, if we may call it so since it was not movable, was used as a storage place for valuables and for finer articles of clothing such as laces, scarves, shawls, and so forth.

Goteras were long narrow shelves made by fitting a horizontal length of board, some three to five feet long, into two perpendicular end pieces, and included a railing of three or four inches in height. The four pieces were firmly knit and held together with tongue-and-groove joints, reinforced by the ever helpful wooden pegs. They were suspended on the wall by leather thongs or held up by two iron spikes driven firmly into the wall. The end pieces as well as the railing were neatly carved. With its load of vari-labeled bottles and glasses, which was the accepted cargo for this type of shelf, the *gotera* fulfilled its duty in the dispensing of liquid cheer. (68)

> Quién adelante no mira atrás se queda.
> ("He who does not look ahead will be left behind.")
>
> Tanto va el cántaro a l'agua que allí queda.
> ("The pitcher that goes oft to the well is soon broken.")
>
> Vale más una chica sombra que una grande resolana.
> ("Better the smallest bit of roof overhead than all of the
>   open spaces.") (100)

The United States Army of the West occupied New Mexico in 1846. The military governed until 1850, when Congress passed the Organic Act of the Territory of New Mexico. Native Hispanos reacted to the newcomers with curiosity, suspicion, and some hostility.

> El que a hierro mata, a hierro muere.
> ("Who lives by the sword dies by the sword.") (100)

Brown was also familiar with the Spanish frontier settlement of Taos. In the early twentieth century, there were still Taoseños who recalled the American takeover. Their reminiscences stirred the young Lorin Brown, and he recorded his own memories of the stories for the Federal Writers' Project.

One of the interesting ranch homes of old Taos was the home of Don David and Doña Marcelina Martínez of Taos. This rambling, many-roomed dwelling four miles west of the Taos Plaza is remembered by the writer as the scene of many hours spent in play and exploration of its many corners. Possibilities for amusement for myself and the grandson of *Mana* Marcelina were many. There was the ditch in which we waded, made water-wheels, and tried to catch the elusive waders, that quick darting insect which can skim

over the surface of the water with so much agility. The orchard, the
corrals—all were used in turn as the scene of our activities.

When tired of play we would turn to the conversation of our
grandmothers for diversion. These two, cronies and contemporaries, never tired it seemed of talking over old times and events,
many of which centered about this same farmhouse. Shortly after
the American occupation, troops had been quartered here, the
location of the farm making it a natural outpost for the defense of
Taos from the raids of Apaches and Navajos. The former Indians
were the most feared for their sudden savage attacks. Although the
Navajos were equally ferocious, they seldom ventured that far
north.

We would listen with interest as they would tell of the curiosity
with which the population of Taos would flock to the vicinity to
examine and comment on the different activities of the cavalry
troops. Sundays would always find a good portion of the townspeople there, gaily dressed and in family groups, bringing their
lunch with them so they could spend the day. They watched the
soldiers drilling, grooming their mounts, and at target practice.

Relations between the people of Taos and the soldiers were very
friendly because there was a realization on the part of the former
that these new conquerors were serving as a guard against their
much feared enemies *los herejes,* or the heretics as the Indians were
usually called. Then it was that many friendships were begun
which resulted in the marriage of some of these soldiers with
Spanish families, making for mutual appreciation.

The arrangement of the different parts of the old farmhouse
made it a natural fort. The walls of the living quarters on the south
and east were continued on the west by a high adobe wall
continued on the north. An adobe wall pierced by a strong wooden
gate closed the gap between the northern end and the front of the
house on the east. All doors to living quarters were fashioned of
thick hand-hewn lumber, and the windows were guarded by thick
shutters fitted with loopholes. The north walls of the stables and
dispensas, or granaries, were blank except for conveniently placed
loopholes. The enclosed corral served admirably as safe quarters for
the troop's mounts.

In the northeastern corner of the large kitchen was a fireplace of
huge proportions. I have seen only one other of its size and
construction. Open on two sides, made entirely of adobe, it was

large enough for myself, a ten-year-old boy, to enter without stooping and, standing erect under its bell-shaped roof, to gaze up to the sky through a chimney large enough for the entrance of an exceedingly fat St. Nicholas. Here meals for a whole company were put on to boil in large iron pots and to roast on the long iron spits which we had found and used for spears.

The part of the narrative for which we always waited impatiently was the account of the disastrous rout which the Indians inflicted on these troops on one occasion. I have no recollection of any other battle being recounted; perhaps there were, but the horror with which this one filled our young minds effectively erased memories of any other account. It seems that shortly after the posting of the troops at the farmhouse, they were ordered out in pursuit of a group of raiding savages. These Apaches, ignorant of the presence of the troops or in defiance of them, had raided some ranches nearby and had escaped with stock and captives, leaving behind not a few dead settlers. Their trail was easily followed as they were all for making haste in their getaway.

Now these troops, new to the West and to fighting Indians, spurred their horses into a furious charge when the trail signs showed they were close to the Indians. This charge led them into a small, thickly wooded valley surrounded by outcroppings of rocks. Here the wily Indians had dismounted and hidden after sending their stock and saddle ponies ahead under guard of certain of their party. As the troops rushed in, their horses were stampeded by a horde of painted savages uttering their demoniacal war whoop and fluttering blankets to further frighten the troop's horses. Many of the troopers were thrown or impaled on the junipers or scrub piñon which were so thick there. Completely demoralized, the scattered soldiers were made easy victims by the Apaches, who easily dispatched the fallen or lanced the plunging horses as they came by them and finished the rider before his dying horse had fairly fallen to the ground.

Not all of the troops were killed, some having been saved by the very headlong rush of their frightened horses. Reassembling, the survivors returned cautiously to the scene of their defeat. The Indians were gone, satisfied with their surprise attack. They left behind them the mutilated remains of nearly half the troop and took with them some of the cavalry horses as an added insult to the crestfallen survivors.

As ready with their sympathy and help as they were with their admiration and interest, the women of Taos hastened to minister to the wounded and prepare shrouds for the dead. My grandmother, although only twelve years old, had accompanied her grandmother, María Teresa, wife of Pablo Montoya, leader of the ill-fated Taos Rebellion. (So it was that she could recount from her own recollection the events above set forth.) This ready solicitude strengthened the bond of sympathy between the civilian population and the new government. It was further demonstrated by the crowds which followed coffin-laden military wagons to the graveyard, where one grave received all of the victims of that fatal ambuscade.

Another house which served as an outpost was the home of the Jeantettes, located on a high point on the southwest edge of the town. Here a small group of soldiers had their quarters. Here also a large hall was the scene of many *bailes* which the officers gave and to which the townspeople were invited. Some artistic officer had decorated one wall of this hall with the figure of an American eagle with outspread wings. This figure was left there for many years after the soldiers had disappeared.

It is no wonder that after hearing these tales my friend and I would be moved to get on the slow plow horses and try to make them break into the semblance of a cavalry charge, firing at imaginary Indians with imitation muskets. Tangible evidence of the troopers remained in the distorted lumps of lead which we dug out of the thick adobe walls of the stables, which had served as a back-stop for their target practice. These we hammered into sinkers for our fishing lines. (25)

Still another grand old Taos home occasioned further lively memories.

Some say that he came from Truchas and others that he came from Spain. This guess was because of his peculiar speech; it bore a resemblance to that which they were accustomed to hear from the Spanish priests and other isolated Spaniards in their midst.

In later years, I found a family in Truchas of the same surname as Juan S——, all of whom spoke in the same abrupt, rather brusque manner. They were known locally as *Los Gachupines* (Spaniards) and by most were ridiculed as being purposely affected in their speech. At any rate I established that Juan S—— was their *pariente* (kinsman), and proud they were to acknowledge him as such, for he was known far and wide as the merchant prince of the Taos Valley, owner of vast and productive lands and countless sheep and cattle.

His initial arrival on the Taos scene could not have been more propitiously timed for himself and for the aficionados of the sport in progress at the time. The stranger seemed to arrive at the same conclusion after a preliminary survey of the activity which engaged the men and boys of the village. Entrusting his *mochila* ("bedroll"), comprised of two sheepskins and a large heavy blanket, to his dog, he took off in the direction of the communal spring. He reappeared in a surprisingly short time with his arms full of limbs and roots of the piñon tree. To have come back so soon, he must have purloined them from someone's woodpile. Diving into a flour sack attached to his *mochila*, he abstracted from its depths some lumps of *piloncillo* ("raw brown sugar"). Handing these to an alert-looking boy, who with others had clustered around him with the consuming curiosity of his tribe, the stranger asked the boy to run an errand for him.

"Bring me some nails, *dos puños, nuevos o viejos* ('two handsful, new or old')." The lad darted off and soon was back with the right quantity of nails clutched in his grimy hands.

From a sheath pendant from his belt the stranger withdrew a razor-sharp hunting knife, and from the flour sack he produced a smaller knife in its own protective sheath. Adding a small file from the same source, he carefully laid all of these tools side by side on a flat stone he had drawn up to his working area. For he had made this particular corner of the plaza his shop, and soon the onlookers were treated to a finished product of his skill and dexterity with knife and file.

From a piñon stick of the desired thickness he proceeded to cut and carve out a piece roughly 2½ inches long. One end he carved into a convex, smoothly rounded form, leaving a round tip in the center. This he whittled through to separate it entirely and leave it free of the parent stick. The other end was tapered carefully from the lower rim of the convex top to a well-defined point. At the tip of the point it was cut free also.

"*¡Es un trompo!*" cried out one of the boys.

Recognition could not deny that a top had evolved from that inert piece of wood. Not finished, true, but this the artisan proceeded to remedy. With his smaller knife he neatly rounded the sides and carved the knob at the top so that it centered exactly, trimming it to hold the loop of the winding cord securely yet to operate to release smoothly when released from the player's hand.

The final touches were done under the rapt scrutiny of a score of eyes drawn to the spot by the boy's cry of *"Es un trompo"* ("it's a top"). With his file the topmaker rounded the pointed end of one of the hand-wrought nails, then drove it into the top to the desired depth. Cutting it off at the right length, he then filed this end to a point. The top was finished except for a little smoothing of its sides and top with a rubbing stone.

Taking a top string from his pocket, Juan S—— wound the top tightly, then flung it forcibly to the ground with the practiced throw of an expert. Whipping the cord back and away, he gave the top the needed impetus to set it spinning. Critically he watched it as it rotated. It deviated slightly from the perpendicular. Arresting its motion, the top was taken up and carefully inspected. It was then subjected to infinitely minute filing and paring. Once again it was wound and cast to spin, this time giving off a quite audible hum. So truly was it shaped that at the peak of its spin it appeared to be entirely motionless—only a faint blur encircled its spinning form.

"¡Se durmió! ('It has gone to sleep')" came the admiring cry from several onlookers. A tribute to the skill of this topmaker, for only a well-balanced top will achieve that state of seeming immobility.

"¿Cuánto quiere por el trompo? ('How much for the top?')" was the spontaneous query directed at Juan S—— by several would-be buyers.

"Lo echo en rifa ('I will raffle it off')." A shrewd move by the topmaker. In this way he would not have to select one buyer to the exclusion of the rest. Let chance decide. Being compulsive gamblers, this suited the crowd. Collecting five cents from fourteen of them, he left it to them to decide ownership.

La babita they all agreed would settle the issue. With a straw broom a space was carefully swept clean on the floor of the street. Stooping over, one spat a large gob of spittle (*"la babita"*) in approximately the center of the newly swept area, leaving a wet spot roughly the size of a fifty-cent piece. Since it was top season, it was agreed that ownership of the prize should rest with the most adept at shooting at the mark with a well-aimed top.

Sequence was determined by each one calling out whether a quarter tossed in the air would alight *cara o águila* ("heads or tails"), or face or eagle, the mark of the quarters of that day. As each contestant correctly guessed the side showing, he became number one or number two, and so on. If he missed he took his place at the end of the line to await another turn.

When the trial order had been determined, the winner took his stance, wound his top, and made his throw. The rules further provided that after each throw the top must be picked up and held spinning in the contestant's open palm. Failing to successfully accomplish this threw the hapless one out of the running. There was much bantering and hurrahing as each player made ready. This was done in an effort to rattle him, as well as engendered by the excitement of the contest itself. Also there were many side bets offered and taken.

The closest mark was carefully preserved, all others neatly erased. When one lucky throw pierced the exact center of the *babita*, there was much altercation when the target was renewed to its original circumference and degree of wetness. This elicited much advice and close scrutiny from the remaining aspirants as fresh spittle was applied to the satisfaction of all.

When a winner finally emerged and held his trophy admiringly in his hand, Juan S—— remarked for all to hear, "To the second best thrower I will make a top as good as that one for one *tostón* (fifty-cent piece)." He had been carving away at his second top all the while the contest had been going and had it practically finished when he made his offer. Now that they had an assured source of supply, the men took up the serious pursuit of gambling, pitting their skill with the tops against each other in various forms of the sport.

The favored form was one which promised a quicker turnover for the gamblers. A *babita* was enclosed in a circle drawn with a sharp stick approximately five feet in diameter. Spike throws at the *babita* fixed the order in which each player took his turn. Each player deposited a top within the circle. The object of the game was to drive tops out of the enclosure. Tops driven out became the property of the successful player, who could continue as long as he drove a top out with each successive throw. Losers could redeem their tops at a predetermined price, usually a *tostón*.

The larger and heavier tops were chosen or reserved by the

players for this game. A heavy top with a sharp point could be so driven that it would split the target top in two. In this case the luckless loser was not only out a top but must pay a *tostón* to the sharpshooter. There was one rule which held that after each throw, successful or not, the top thrown must spin after the throw. If it failed to do so its owner must throw it into the ring to await its fate.

This game was called *El Corte,* perhaps derived from the practice of cutting individual animals from a herd or flock. Players became so adept at this game that many tops were split. All of this brought a thriving business to the shrewd woodcarver.

El Aguante consisted in simply pitting spinning tops against each other. At a given signal all participants spun their tops, endeavoring to transmit to them the ultimate in velocity with a practiced whip of the launching cord. Each one then had to pick up his top and hold it spinning in his outstretched palm. The last top to waver and fall won for its owner all of the other tops or a sum agreed upon beforehand. *El Aguante* roughly denotes an endurance test.

One top contest was an unusually boisterous one with lots of action and a fair chance for bruises or for being spiked by a thrown top. This fast game was called *La Arriada* ("The Drive"). This term was also applied to a round wooden ball whittled out of piñon wood. It was about the size of a golf ball and in due course became as pitted as one. Goals were established and teams of players chosen, usually the same number on each side. A purse was made up by each side, both sums being left with some onlooker as stake holder.

The wooden ball or *la arriada* was placed midway between the two goals. The leader of each team stood on either side of it. At a given signal each launched his top with a sideways motion, striving to strike the ball and send it toward his goal. Teammates stood poised with wound tops, ready to further the ball on its initial course or to turn it in the opposite direction. In this exciting drive the pace was fast and furious; the ball was driven hither and yon. Tops and their humming filled the air.

Shouts of encouragement and jeers for a bad throw came from the spectators, who greatly enjoyed this test of skill and team work. As usual, much betting went on. If not cash, *almuds* (dry measure, approximately two U.S. gallons) of corn, beans, piñons, corn flour, chickens, *cabritos* ("kids"), or whatever were wagered on the outcome. The women of the town were enthusiastic viewers and backed their men's efforts with wagers as those above. They were as vocal in their shouts of encouragement as were the small fry.

A heavy top with a blunt point was reserved for this game. The object was to drive the *arriada* forward and not to split it. These heavy tops became veritable missiles if the player threw one which had not been properly wound. It would fly off at a tangent with disastrous results if it encountered an unprotected face. Some tops which despite repeated shaving and trimming would not spin in an upright manner but which would skitter off in an erratic course were called *Iscariotes*. This name perpetuated Judas Iscariot's infamous reputation as one who was untrustworthy and false to his kind. Boys usually fell heir to these rejects.

Simpler forms of gambling with tops consisted of merely spiking at a *babita* or a *rayita* ("line"). Closest at either mark was the winner of whatever stakes were wagered—tops or coins. All this made for a thriving business for the enterprising topmaker; split tops had to be replaced as did tops lost as wagers.

Having found quarters for himself and his burro, Juan soon became an established resident and fixture in Taos. There were those who did not fully take him to their bosom, but the gambling fraternity accepted him wholeheartedly, the more so when it became known that he was readily available for small loans, with interest of course—*cinco centavos* on the *peso* per month. By fireplace light he prepared a stock of tops at night, so that his mornings were free for other pursuits.

He disappeared from Taos for a period of over a week, returning with a well-laden burro. The next morning the townspeople awoke to find that a small business establishment was on display on the corner of the plaza. Two sturdy *tarimas* ("wooden benches") held an assortment of small articles constantly in demand: needles and pins, tobacco and cigarette papers, small mirrors prized by the Indians of the pueblo—numerous items, all small, so that one burro load furnished quite a variety. Hard candies and marbles for his small clients brought him in a steady stream of nickels and dimes.

He soon bargained for and acquired the lot on which his *tarimas* had stood, a deep lot which soon held a two-room building. In one room he installed his store and displayed his stock on plank shelves behind a counter he made himself, strictly utilitarian with storage room beneath. The other room was a storeroom and living quarters combined. Behind all this he built a corral with stout wooden gates and enclosing adobe wall. Here was kept the stock taken in lieu of cash. From these were drawn animals selected for butchering to supply his meat market.

Everything was grist which came to the mill of this intelligent and canny trader. He acquired pasture land where he could hold his surplus stock. This soon led to flocks of sheep on the range and herds of cattle in the hills. His storehouses bulged with grain of all kinds, hides, and pelts. Periodically this would be transported by burro trains to the Rio Abajo country. Here this cargo would be traded for wine from Corrales, chile, fruits, and other products which grew abundantly in the milder climate of the lower Rio Grande.

Within five years an imposing two-story residence rose on the site where he had carved his first top. The lower floor was a complex of workshops, storerooms, and quarters for his numerous *criados* and *criadas* (Spanish domestic help, either adopted or attached to the family permanently). There were also many Indian slaves of different nations and other retainers, all busily employed in the various activities of the household and its outlying possessions. Here Navajo women wove blankets from the wool of his sheep. Hides were tanned and turned into buckskin for various uses.

A carpenter shop supervised by Don Juan himself was the training ground for Santiago, a Navajo slave who soon became adept in the art of carpentry. The same Santiago, later given his freedom, married a Taos woman and carried on his trade to become an honored and independent citizen in the community. He took his patron's surname and fathered sons who became prominent in the civic and political life of the state and their own village.

When it came to embellishing the upper quarters of his patron's house with the gingerbread in vogue in that era, Santiago put forth his best efforts. The outside staircase and panels, shutters, balustrades, and palings which acted as a protective barrier on that area which looked out over the plaza all had one dominant motif. Yes, you've guessed it. Either surmounting or pierced through, as in the shutters, was the figure of a top. Whether surrounded by whatever curlicues or figures fancied by the artisan or not, the top stood out in supreme prominence. In this manner did Don Juan pay tribute to the top which had spun him to success and fame.

Don Juan's family lived in aloof seclusion in the elaborately furnished rooms reserved to them. These were decorated lavishly with a mixture of both cultures—the best of the local artisans' craft, tin work enshrining figures of the saints, and *almarios* whose shelves were filled with bric-a-brac and mementos brought back from their travels by the peripatetic daughters of the household. Early they had evinced a love of travel and in due course had journeyed to San Francisco, Denver, and even to St. Louis. Waited upon by a bevy of *criadas*, they lived a life of leisure, venturing forth only to attend to their religious duties in the nearby church. They would appear in all their jewels and finery in the area just outside their front door. Here, guarded by a stout railing, they would overlook any activity in the plaza below. In the evenings, seats would be brought out so that they could enjoy the view of the mountains to the south and west with the purple sage spread out in between.

I was often in this home, going there in the wake of my grandmother's skirts. She was a *parienta* ("kinswoman") of Don Juan's wife and was particularly in demand by the daughters, who looked to her for advice and treatment for minor ailments. Grandmother had a well-deserved reputation as a *médica* learned in the practical application of the local herbs and household remedies. But most of all they appreciated her as a purveyor of gossip, relying on her to fill them in on the local news. Her pungent wit and accurate descriptive faculty sent her hearers into gales of appreciative laughter.

These young ladies in their silks and fine clothes exuded the perfume of other worlds. Convent-schooled and full of tales of their travels, they held me spellbound by their chatter and the fuss they made over grandmother. It often happened that I would be given a treat of candy with a suggestion that I might rather go downstairs and see what I could find of interest in the corral or the store. This I had learned meant that the conversation would take a turn not meant for the ears of an eleven-year-old. I would gratefully disappear since I had already grown restless. The horsehair-covered chair was a most uncomfortable seat; sharp ends of its covering penetrated my clothing as if to anchor me to its slippery surface. I gladly relinquished it for the interesting world of activity which awaited below.

A great event took place during these early years of my life. One of the first governors of the state, possibly the first, was invited to a big feast at the Taos Pueblo. Much preparation went into receiving this dignitary in proper fashion. The townspeople participated to some extent, but primarily the Indians of the Pueblo were the hosts. It was their show.

The *hornos* had been lighted and turned out sweet breads, *bizcochitos*, and the savory bread unequaled anywhere else. Pots of beans and chile simmered in delicious fragrance. Rice and raisin pudding and other goodies were prepared in abundance. Lambs and *cabritos* roasted over beds of coals. The day before the great event the braves of the Pueblo haunted the banks of the Rio Lucero. With horsehair loops they spent the day snaking trout out of its icy cold waters. Grilled trout was to be the pièce-de-résistance of the lavish spread under the cottonwoods of the Glorieta, and only the stealth and patience of the Indian could employ successfully this unusual method of adding such a treat to the festive board.

The feast was a glorious success, a tribute to the hospitality of the Pueblo. Although regulations forbade it, there must have been not a little Taos Lightning dispensed from surreptitious flasks, as well as some *vino* from the Rio Abajo. On his return to the village of Taos, the governor was to be received in the home of Don Juan. Here a bedroom had been prepared for him. Here it was thought he would wish to retire and refresh himself for the festivities scheduled for the evening.

We youngsters had been loaded with flowers and blooms of all kinds and told to await his entry into the Taos square. On his arrival we were to pelt him with the flowers or strew them in his path, I do not remember which. But when the governor finally arrived it was evident that he was in no condition to receive or appreciate the floral tributes awaiting him. During the feast on the banks of the river he must have partaken too freely of the circulating flasks, and the several nips had taken their toll.

Screening his condition from the crowd, several officious citizens hustled him up the staircase and into his bedroom. Here his senseless form was laid under a lacy coverlet with decorated pillows to match.

We flower bearers, still clasping our floral tributes, also made our way up the staircase, a shoving, curious, and intent troop. We watched through an open window as the recumbent form was left on the bed. With one accord we tossed the blooms and bouquets on the bed, completely covering it. We withdrew satisfied that we had not been altogether thwarted in our part of the day's ceremonies.

I often wonder what the governor thought when he came to. Did he think that somehow he had been transported to the Elysian Fields, or did his befogged mind merely wonder where in the hell he could procure a hair of the dog that bit him? (128)

Brown's grandmother, Juanita Montoya de Martínez, was a familiar figure in Taos County because of her abilities as a curandera *or* médica. *A fictionalized sketch recalls the days he spent accompanying her from house to house and placita to placita.*

Everybody in Taos knows Doña Juanita; she has become an institution through many years' practice of her profession. She is what is known as a *médica* or healer, versed in the knowledge of massage treatments, bone-setting, and familiar with the large assortment of native herbs and the efficacy of each in the treatment of different ailments. A great faith is attached by the native people to the benefits of massage treatments, and this is Doña Juanita's long suit, her unusually large frame and strong capable hands being admirably suited to this type of healing. So it is that at one time or another she has been in every home in Taos County, or its individual members have been in her home for treatment of minor ailments.

With her talent for healing, which is mixed with a slice of shrewd native psychology, she has a great gift of narrative, so that her visits to a home are looked forward to because of the fund of anecdotes and gossip which she always brings with her. On one of my visits to her during a series of treatments she was giving me for a sprained arm, she related an incident that occurred in Taos and which shows the persistence of old beliefs and superstitions today in the face of modern scientific knowledge. Or perhaps science chooses to ignore what it cannot explain, an argument I have heard from those who do believe. But to get back to Doña Juanita:

"Were you at the wake of Guillermo —— the other night?" was her first question leading up to the following account.

"No, Mana Juanita, I was not there," was my reply. "Why, what happened?"

"*Pobrecito*, what a sad death he had," she went on to say. "But I will tell you about this from the beginning.

"You know Guillermo was a hard-working man and happily married. He took good care of his family and enjoyed himself at the

bailes and the *cantinas* as a man does who has good work and no
great cares. But about a year ago he changed. He became sullen
and would get angry and disagreeable at nothing so that his poor
wife did not know what to do about it. He seemed to fear his best
friends and especially did he change toward his wife, even accusing
her of trying to kill him. His wife came to me about it, to see what I
could do for him. I said I would see if I could help but that she
would have to bring him with her. But he could not be persuaded
to come to see me and continued getting worse. When his poor
wife came to tell me of this I thought I had better tell her of
something I heard and which I felt might explain his illness.

" 'Now,' I said 'your husband became quite friendly again with
your cousin Gertrudes and started visiting her home some time
ago. Now you know that before you and Guillermo were married
Gertrudes was very friendly with him and she thought as everybody
else did that he would have his folks ask for her hand in marriage.
So that when he married you Gertrudes felt quite angry at both you
and Guillermo. She has never forgotten and well you know the
reputation she and her mother have. You know that they practice
brujería. And your Guillermo is so good-hearted that he can believe
nothing bad of anybody. He stayed away from Gertrudes's until
shortly before he took sick. When he did start going there it was the
chance they were looking for. Your husband is *embrujado* ("bewitched"), and you had better get him cured right away.'

"The poor girl started crying and said that she was afraid of
something like that but that she didn't think her cousin would treat
her or Guillermo like that. 'Well,' I told her, 'you might as well
believe it because a woman will do anything in a case like this, and
what is easier than to bewitch Guillermo in a cup of coffee or a
drink of wine or whiskey?' Then she begged again that I do
something for him but as you know I am not that kind of a *médica*.
I just use my poor knowledge and with God's help do my best for
my patients. But those others are in league with the Devil, *Ave
María Purísima*, and so can cure the evil done by *brujas*. May God
never permit that I should sell my soul to the Devil as some of these
others do. But I did advise her to take Guillermo to that *médico*
over near Española right away because no ordinary doctor could do
anything for him.

"At this time Guillermo was confined to his bed at home and was
very weak and his mind was affected. He was afraid of his wife and

his friends and insisted on his mother being there all the time, so you can see how those *malditas brujas* had turned him against his own wife. And now I will tell you of the strange part: all this time while Guillermo was at home in bed a large black dog hung around the house persistently trying to get in where he was. If driven away it returned immediately. And what an ugly dog, black with ugly green eyes! I know because I saw it more than once and, *Madre de Dios*, I have dreamed of its devilish green eyes many times since.

"After my talk with Guillermo's wife, Ignacita was convinced that he was *embrujado* and took him to the witch doctor. The witch doctor was certain he could cure him, especially after Guillermo confessed to having had some wine at Gertrudes's house. And in other ways he assured them that Guillermo was bewitched, how I don't know, but they have the Devil's own wisdom in such cases. On leaving again for Taos they were told to expect some medicine by mail and to be sure and follow the directions which would come with it, as that was the only way he could guarantee a cure.

"As they were leaving the doctor's yard, Ignacita swore she saw the same black dog slinking away. She says she crossed herself and swore that if it was possible she would have her brother kill it if it came to the house after their return to Taos.

"Guillermo seemed to be a little better and was kept in bed awaiting the arrival of the medicine promised by the doctor. But that black dog was there again the evening of their return. How could it have come so soon unless it was one of the devil's own, and the form which the *bruja* took when she was on her wicked errands? There was an attempt to kill it but it seemed to know and was not to be seen when anybody had a gun for that purpose.

"But the strange part I will tell you now and Patricio who works in the post office swears that it is true. While he was opening the mail pouches from the south a black dog came in the back door and picked up a package. He tried to catch it or scare it into dropping the package but with a great leap it went out the door again and disappeared. He did not know of course until later what the package was which had disappeared. *La pobrecita de la* Ignacita would go to the post office every time the mail came in, even after three days had passed since the medicine should have come in. All this time Guillermo grew worse and that devilish dog now would come and howl near the house from midnight until the first roosters crowed.

"Well, he finally died as you know, and no doubt that dog was the cause of his death. Oh yes, Gertrudes was the dog or the dog was Gertrudes, however you like. Guillermo's death rests on her soul, but *brujas* do not think of that because they are already sold to the devil."

"But, Mana Juanita," I said, "can't anything be done to punish such ones?"

"*Pero no,* how could our testimony sound in these American courts where they do not believe in such things? No, everything rests with Him. There is He who will punish." A significant up-pointing finger showed me whence Doña Juanita's trust expected justice to reside.

"But the most horrible part of this happened at the wake, which is why I asked if you had been there. We were all sitting around in the room where the body was. We had just finished praying the rosary and everybody was silent. You know how it is at that time. Nobody had started an *alabado,* and it was very quiet. And you will not believe me, but there were many there who will tell you the same thing. Ay! my body creeps every time I think of it. Suddenly a black shape came in through the back door which was open. It trotted over to the coffin and, raising its forepaws to the side of the coffin, looked in at the corpse. *¡Santo Dios!* I'll swear that it smiled, a wicked smile as I have never seen before and I hope never to see again.

"And none of us could move. We were as if paralyzed. Ignacita sitting nearby let out a shriek and cried, '*¡Santa María líbranos!*' and fainted, falling to the floor. At those words the beast disappeared, some say through the door but to me it seemed that it just disappeared like smoke in a breeze. But right after, just outside the door, we heard a long howl which finished freezing the blood in our veins. And that is what happened at the wake. Believe it if you wish, I know, I was there. May God keep us safe from such vengeance of these Devil's servants." (32)

His grandmother also recounted personal anecdotes like the following:

The magpie, a voluble and noisily entertaining bird found in New Mexico, is generally believed to be able to speak if first its tongue is split. In proof of this contention I relate the following incident with regard to a pet magpie:

My grandmother had found a young magpie while she and her family were out in the hills gathering piñons. She took it home with her and induced my grandfather to split its tongue. After the tongue had healed, she very patiently made a pet of the bird and taught it to say many phrases and to call her by her name, Juanita.

The bird was kept in the yard of their home on a small platform atop a post, securely tied by one foot with a long string. This precaution was necessary after it was known that the bright-eyed little rascal was an arrant thief with a special liking for bright and shining objects such as thimbles, spoons, and articles of jewelry. Once he made off with them, these were found with much difficulty in odd and out-of-the-way hiding places.

After his liberty was curtailed, the magpie would amuse himself by calling out to the passersby from his perch: ¿Cómo te va?" and "¿Pa' dónde vas?" and other short phrases of like nature. When some danger menaced or when he craved attention from my grandmother, of whom he was especially fond, he would call her by name: "¡Juanita! ¡Juanita!"

One San Gerónimo day [September 30], my grandmother had gone to the Taos Pueblo to watch the Indians dance. Suddenly, above the noise of the crowd and of the drums and the singing of the Indians, she heard her name called, seemingly from the sky above. As she looked up, she was greatly astonished to see her pet magpie flying overhead with a flock of six other magpies, trailing the long string with which he had been tied and calling "¡Juanita! ¡Juanita!" My grandmother called to him, "¡Urraca! ¡Urraca! ¡Ven! ¡Ven!" but her pet did not return to her. Yet he continued calling her name as he followed his kind, until he was lost from sight and hearing. (96)

Roving bands of hostile Indians had forced Hispanos in the Taos area to live in or near the Pueblo until almost 1800, and they long continued to frequent the ceremonies of their early benefactors. Brown also remembered another custom showing the reciprocity between Pueblo and plaza.

In the old church in the Pueblo of Taos there used to be a very large image of *Nuestra Señora de Dolores. Nuestra Señora de Dolores* was the patron saint of the village to the east of Taos, known as El Cañon de Taos, where the people possessed a small image of their patron saint, but nothing as large and as handsome as the one that the Indians had in their church.

For many years the people of the community observed the following custom: some time during the late summer or early fall they would send a delegation to the Taos Pueblo to ask for the loan of the Indians' image of *Nuestra Señora de Dolores.* The Indians having agreed and a day having been fixed, the delegation would return to their village with their report.

On the morning of the day agreed upon, all of the villagers of El Cañon de Taos who could possibly leave would set out for the Taos Pueblo in wagons, buggies, on horseback, and even afoot. In the lead would be a small group carrying their image of *Nuestra Señora de Dolores* to the accompaniment of hymns sung in her praise. This group would be relieved from time to time by others of the procession, all eager to render this service of devotion to their patron saint.

Upon reaching the church at the Pueblo, the larger image and object of this pilgrimage would be ceremoniously carried out of the church, and now with both images in the lead the procession would repair to a secluded corner of the large communal grazing grounds of the Pueblo, close to the river. Here under a leafy bower or shrine both images would be enshrined, beloved objects of adoration throughout the ensuing wake or vigil, which lasted all night. The crowd of devotees would alternate in singing *alabados* (religious hymns) and in praying during the entire wake.

At midnight a plentiful supper was served to all present. The food, prepared beforehand and brought thither in the wagons, as well as meat roasting over the fires surrounding the shrine, would be more than sufficient to feed the throng. Although the greater number of the crowd at the wake would attend with a purely religious motive, there were many, especially amongst the younger folks, who were attracted by the social side of this observance. Many Indians attended also.

Whether or not this custom is still observed, I cannot say. (87)

In due time, Hispanos entered the government and joined the armed forces of their new fatherland.

Por dondes fueres haz lo que vieres.
(When in Rome do as the Romans do. [Literally: "Wherever you go, do what you see."])

Más vale maña que fuerza.
("Wiles are better than force.") (100)

One Taos Civil War veteran recalled a strange encounter in a cave near Fort Union.

A veteran of the battle of Val Verde [1862], Don Miguel Archuleta is around ninety-six or ninety-seven years old, he is not sure. I arrived at his approximate age by taking his guess as to his age at the time in which some historical incident took place, for instance, the abovementioned battle. Erect, firm of step and in full mental vigor, he could attribute his vigorous old age only to the fact that he had enjoyed life to the fullest at all times, taking the bad with the same degree of cheerful acceptance with which he received and enjoyed the good.

After a drink of Burgundy, he stated that he had acquired a taste for wine while in Rio Abajo before and after the battle of Val Verde. "Before that time I drank *aguardiente,* of which there was plenty distilled in and around Taos where I was born. *Seguro es,* that it must have been good whiskey because it never seemed to have harmed me. Even now I like my whiskey at times, especially my *traguito* before breakfast."

Just then a red-haired young lady passed along the street. Don Miguel's eyes lit up and he smiled as he gazed after her retreating figure. Even after she passed out of sight he seemed to be lost in a reminiscent reverie. Offer of another drink broke in on this, and after sampling it, Don Miguel started in:

"You know, I never see a pretty redhead but I remember the enchanted woman of the cave near old Fort Union. I was a soldier and there were two very good friends of mine stationed there who were also from Taos. We were together at all times. Young we were then and all we gave a thought to were the good times we could have together when duty permitted and money was in our pockets. Blessed be God how long ago that was! Both of my *compañeros* are long since dead, and I trust God has already pardoned their sins and granted them eternal peace.

"Pablito Martínez was one of these *compañeros,* a very happy fellow who was afraid of nothing, not even the devil. He was very high-spirited and very proud too. I remember how my mother used to describe him. She would say: 'This Pablito is like the rooster, who always bows his head on going through a gate, thinking in his pride that his comb otherwise might brush the cross beam many feet above him.' Thus he was, but a great friend. The other, Manuel Esquibel, was very quiet but very loyal, and the three of us were together at many *bailes* where we made ourselves respected when the young men of the village tried to run us away.

"Now near Fort Union there is a cave of which we had heard tales. The people living near there had told us that it was enchanted, that a beautiful red-haired woman was to be seen at times at the mouth of the cave, usually in the morning and evening. Those who confessed to have seen her said that she was very beautiful and would appear with her red hair hanging down over her shoulders and beg them to disenchant her, that whoever would do so could have her for his wife. After making this plea she would disappear into the cave again, leaving them astonished at her beauty and wondering what kind of enchantment kept her prisoner.

"Three men had ventured into the cave at different times. Of these, only one had stayed in overnight, and not only overnight, but forever, as he never came out again. The disappearance of this poor fellow led the people to believe that *La Rubia* was a witch who took this form to entice her victims to some horrible death inside the cave.

"One evening Pablito came into the *cuartel* ['barracks'] very much excited. He had been out in the hills on some duty and swore he had seen *La Rubia* of the cave. 'I saw her, *por Dios que sí,*' he swore, and he was not one to swear in vain. *'Tan linda,* as no other woman.' He was going to go in that cave next day if he had to desert. And so on. He was like one who is mad, we hardly slept listening to him and trying to persuade him to wait until we could all go with him. We promised that next leave we would both go with him. Three would be better than one if there were dangers to be met. *Buen Dios*, we finally calmed him and he slept, but even in his sleep he tossed and muttered, no doubt dreaming of rescuing this *Rubia* and fighting *Dios sabe* what kind of monsters.

"So we waited until our next leave, which we asked should fall on the same day. Guns and food we took as well as many pitch

sticks as we could find and prepare. We even had the *padre* confess
us and bless our venture to prepare ourselves in every way. On the
way to the cave Pablito was full of talk about the *Rubia*. He was
sure we would disenchant her. How happy he would be with her as
a bride. And certainly his two friends would be happy also, *seguro*
we would rejoice in his happiness. Maybe she was a princess from
Spain or some other king's daughter and he would become rich
through marrying her. '*Y queridos compañeros*. I will not forget
you, you will share with me, riches, glory, everything.'

"*Pobre* Pablito, he was dreaming we knew. What could be found
in a hole in the ground in these sun-baked hills except that maybe it
was the home of some *bruja* who took the form of the *Rubia* to lure
men into the cave for her own wicked ends? But Pablito had seen
her. '*Con estos ojos la ví*, with these eyes I saw her,' over and over
again we heard him say. 'Beautiful she is and we are not men if we
do not go to her aid.' Maybe he was already a little bewitched, but
as good friends and *compañeros* we would all go together and fight
together as we had so many times at *bailes* or fiestas because of
other women. Perhaps not *Rubias*, but fight we did because the
village boys resented their preference for us. Or maybe it was only
because of our uniforms. *¿Quién sabe?*

"Nearing the cave, we pitched camp, examined our pistols and
powder, and prepared a meal, the last one before entering the
cave. We first hobbled our horses so that if anything happened to us
they would not starve and could in time get back to the fort. Now
the entrance to the cave is not very large and it is hidden by brush
and the overhang of the bluff in which it is located.

"Inside a short way it was necessary to light our torches in order
to see. At first it was very narrow and low, but in about ten *varas* it
opened up into a large room. We held our torches close to the floor
to see if we could make out any footprints.

"Suddenly Pablito jumped with a yell saying that he had seen a
footprint of *La Rubia* and ran on farther into the cave shouting:
'*¡Sal Rubia! ¡Sal cabeza colorada!* Come out Red! Come out
Redhead! We have come to disenchant you. *¡Salgan diablos o
demonios!* Come out devils or demons! We have come to fight you
and to free *La Rubia*.'" So quickly did he get away from us that we
did not stop to see the footprints but hurried after our impetuous
friend. We could see the glow from his torch ahead of us and hear

his shouts. We called to him to wait for us and ran after him. He must not have heard us, and the next thing we knew a turn in the cave hid his light from us, although we could still hear his voice.

"Soon we came to where three galleries branched off. Not knowing which one Pablito had taken, we stopped, puzzled as to which one to follow. The rocky floor showed no marks we could go by. We went up quite a ways in one on the chance it was the one Pablito had taken, but no sign could we find. We then returned to the point where the three galleries branched and decided to leave one of us there to stop Pablito if he should come back. Also we arranged on shots as signals to recall or guide us in returning to this meeting place.

"I cursed *La Rubia* and even Pablito as I followed down another part of the cave. Sometimes it would open into large rooms and then it would narrow again. At one time I could hear the noise of running water somewhere near me, whether underground or not I did not stop to investigate. At one place I found two skeletons huddled near the signs of a fire; nearby were some broken pieces of pottery so I judged they were the remains of Indians. At different places the walls of the cave were streaked with smoke, but in my hurry and anxiety I did not stop to look for other signs. Finally I decided to turn back, as I was getting hungry and tired and also I was not so sure of finding my way back to our meeting place since several small galleries and rooms ran off from this main passageway.

"With great joy and relief I finally reached a place where I could see the glow from a torch and knew I was near. With a shout I let my *compañero* know I was near. His answer was a very welcome sound to these ears. It was a disappointment not to find Pablito there, but we decided to wait a while before seeking him further.

"After lunch I lay down to sleep. It seemed as if I had barely closed my eyes when I was awakened by what sounded like a battle. Very much alarmed I jumped up. Then we heard a voice calling our names. It was Pablito, and it was the shots he had fired which the echoes made sound like a thousand shots fired all up and down the cave. Gladly we answered him and soon he was with us. He had not been able to find *La Rubia* or any sign of her or any other living thing. Like myself he had seen bones and signs of fires at different places. At one place he had taken the wrong turn, wandering around for quite a while before getting on the right track again. He had not reached the end of the cave either but had turned back to locate us. Very much disgusted at the result of our hunt, we decided we needed rest and lay down to sleep.

"It was so dark in the cave we could not tell whether it was night or day, and we had no idea of the length of time we had been in there. On awakening we decided to explore the third corridor and if we found nothing to return to the outside. This corridor or branch of the cave was similar to the others, opening up into large rooms and side passages, but we had no fear of getting lost because we marked the walls with soot from our torches as we went along. Upon reaching a place where the floor of the cave dropped away at our feet and our lights showed that this drop was very steep and deep, we decided to explore no further.

"As we turned to leave, Pablito called down into the pit—'*Rubia*, if you are down there you can stay there!'—and added other expressions which I will not repeat. Now we saw that our friend's good humor had returned, because before this he had been so quiet we did not dare joke with him about *La Rubia*. So joking and laughing we returned to our meeting place and after picking up different articles we had left there we made our way to the cave entrance.

"*Por Dios*, with what joy we welcomed the blessed sunlight! By the sun we could tell it was near the end of day, but what day it was we did not know. Since we could not find our horses we had to make our way back to the fort on foot, first hiding our saddles. Arriving at the fort we found out that we had been in the cave two nights and the greater part of three days.

"Pablito was called *El Rubio* for some time after that, but to his face only by his good friends. For anybody else to do so usually meant a fight. We had many a good laugh over his enchanted princess. Those were the times! I hope that in heaven the good God will permit me to rejoin my *compañeros* of those days.

"And that cave, *mi amiguito*, is there close to Fort Union. If I were younger I would go with you to help you locate it. Maybe *La Rubia* is still there under enchantment. What say you?" (104)

The American military eventually managed to control the nomadic Indians. As a result, annual trading caravans to Mexico became much less dangerous, although no less arduous.

A pan duro, diente agudo.
(Set a thief to catch a thief. [Literally: "Sharp teeth for a hard
loaf of bread"]) (100)

*Guadalupe Martínez, one of Brown's favorite Cordova informants,
remembered the glamour and treasure associated with these
nineteenth-century expeditions.*

"Which way and how far is Old Mexico from here?" asked Tía
Lupe.

I had stopped in to see her and found her seemingly absorbed in
profound reverie and at first indifferent to my entrance. This
opening remark gave me a clue as to where her mind had been
wandering. It was difficult for me to give her an idea as to the
distance between Old Mexico and Cordova, but I tried to explain
in terms of the number of days it would take to reach Mexico on
horseback.

"Oh, then it is beyond Rio Abajo?"

"Oh, *sí, señora,* much farther," was my answer to her next query.
Rio Abajo was the local designation for the lower stretches of the
Rio Grande including all settlements from Belen to Socorro.

"Yes, it must be because my foster-father, José María Martínez,
used to start out with his trading caravan from Chimayo for Mexico
and be gone for six months from the month of María (May) to the
month of the *Muertos* (November). He always tried to get back
before the month of *Noche Buena* (December). He liked to be here
for the feasting, and besides there was more time for trading then.
Everybody was enjoying themselves then; there were many *bailes*
and the Matachines amused the people every afternoon until the
New Year. Blessed be God, what wonderful times those were! The
people really enjoyed themselves then, though they endured more
dangers and hardships than now.

"I was quite small but I remember all this well. And all the
beautiful and curious things that my foster-father brought back. Ay!
what silks, shawls, and *rebozos* for the women! Also oranges and
lemons, dried pomegranates for medicinal use, anil and brazil for
the weavers. And many other curious things to trade. Oh yes,
piloncillo and *meleocha* (brown sugar and a kind of taffy) and the
wines for the feasts. All kinds of good things which we lacked here.

"My foster-father was very rich and we lived very well in a big house near the Potrero. With the gold he brought back from his trading trips he had bought many Indian slaves so that Doña Paubla his wife had only to give orders. And he needed all this help because there was always a big feast when he arrived from a trip and before he left. The house was always full of people trading with him and making arrangements for going with him on his next trip. Always much noise and excitement while he was home. I must have been very curious because I was around all the time and that is why I remember all this so well. Myself and the other children they raised were treated as their own would have been if they had had any.

"And the gifts they would give me from my grandfather who lived in Chihuahua! What handsome things for me alone! What do you think? A grandfather whom I never saw. I was told he was very rich, a merchant in Chihuahua with whom my father stayed while in Mexico."

"How did it happen that your grandfather was in Mexico and you here?" I asked.

"That is a long story," she answered, "but I am going to tell you so listen well:

"My grandmother died when my mother was a little child and soon afterwards my grandfather married a widow. This widow, Salomé Baca, had two sons who weren't much account and were of no help to my grandfather. But we will leave that. My grandfather was very unlucky in his second wife because he found out she was a *bruja* or witch. And I will tell you how this happened. These *brujas* are very sly people and are not always known as such. That any one should sell themselves to the devil like they do I can't understand, but there are people for everything in this world. And this Salomé was one all right. It seems that she would cast a spell on my grandfather on the nights when she wished to get to a witches' gathering or to go on some wicked errand for the devil, her master."

Here Tía Lupe made the sign of the cross and murmured an *Ave María Purísima*. Any evil spirits having been thus dispelled, she continued.

"These spells which Salomé would cast over my grandfather would keep him asleep until she returned from these trips. One morning he got up rather late and could not hear his wife getting breakfast. Thinking she had gone for water, he went on into the kitchen. Now he knew something was wrong because there had been no fire built.

"Looking around, what was his surprise but to see his wife lying by the fireplace apparently dead. On closer examination he found that she had a bad wound in one shoulder and had apparently fainted from loss of blood. Calling in two neighbor women to take care of his wife, he then went for his *padrino* or godfather.

"Returning they found the woman revived but could get no information from her. She seemed to be very angry and cursed them while they were questioning her. 'Let's see what we can find out for ourselves,' said the *padrino*. 'How did this woman get hurt?' 'I do not know,' answered my grandfather, 'but see here, there is blood inside the fireplace and in the chimney. Look! The ashes look like they have been brushed by some bird's wings. Let us go up on the roof and see what we can find.'

"You will not believe it but they found blood on the edges of the adobe chimney and near it some bloody wing feathers. These were owl feathers. There was no doubt then that this woman was a witch and was returning home in the shape of an owl. Somewhere she had been shot and was just able to get home before the first rooster crowed. You know witches can be out only until the first rooster crows, and no matter what shape they take for their deviltry they return to their own body at that time.

"Even after his wife confessed, my grandfather did not believe her promise to quit, the more so since she seemed to hate him for having found her out. So really he was afraid of her and what she might do to him.

"One day he came home to find the door locked and nobody home. Breaking the lock he went in and looked for his wife. But from the looks of the house he guessed she had gone for good. Very much relieved, he started to get himself a meal. Near the fireplace was an earthen pot covered over with a cloth. Dough was kept in this. Hoping to find dough ready for tortillas he lifted the cloth. He found dough, yes, but lying on top of the dough he found a large toad. He was very much frightened because he didn't know in what way his wife might try to bewitch him with the things left in the house.

"Leaving the house without touching anything more in it, he never returned. Finding my mother at his sister's house where Salomé had left her, he made preparations to go to Mexico.

Arranging for my mother's care, he left and never came back. Fear of this *maldita bruja* made him get as far away from her as possible.

"But as I say he always remembered us by sending presents, first to my mother and later to me. On my foster-father's last trip my grandfather gave him directions for finding a buried treasure over there between Cundiyo and Nambe, on or near the Cerro de la Patada. He described this place as being on the west slope of this *cerro* down near a little plain. As I remember, the best marks to be looked for were two peach trees between which the treasure had been buried. These fruit trees must have been planted there by a member of some caravan, as that vicinity was a favorite camping place and on the regular route through here and on to Truchas and Peñasco.

"It seems that this treasure had been buried by a party who had been attacked by Indians. Having killed most of the party, the Indians stole their pack and saddle animals. It must have been all the Indians wanted, or maybe the three survivors were too much for them. At any rate these three buried their goods there and made their escape.

"My grandfather was told this tale in Mexico and he passed it on to my foster-father. He made one effort to find it with no success and being old never went again. That treasure has never been found. At least nothing has been known of its recovery. Those fruit trees would be hard to find now. I suppose their trunks are completely rotted away. That's the way it goes. Years ago I tried to get my nephews to go and look for it, but they have always been lazy and disinterested, even if they are my nephews.

"This treasure was supposed to have been of gold and silver, coin and bars, a golden image for one of the churches, and other goods such as silks, shawls, *fajas* ['sashes'], besides all the equipment of the party.

"*Bendito sea Dios*, that which is not supposed to belong to one will not be. So many beautiful things from Mexico have I seen displayed in the *bailes* and fiestas by beautiful women. Of all that only the gold and silver ornaments remain, I guess. Even the pretty women that wore them are gone. That must be the way it is in that hole where that treasure is buried. All the pretty shawls, *fajas*, and silks have rotted away a long time ago no doubt. Only the gold will be there until found or until the world is no more."

With this bit of philosophy Tía Lupe wound up her tale, which

had me in imagination on the trail to Mexico beset by witches. On
hearing the part about the treasure I made a firm resolve not to be
bitten by the treasure-hunting bug again, but piñon season found
me on the sides of Cerro de la Patada searching more for the ghosts
of departed peach trees than for piñon. (61)

*Twentieth-century expeditions were no less eventful, according to
Cordova raconteur,* rezador, *and singer Higinio Tórrez.*

Don Higinio Tórrez had just returned from the salt lakes near
Willard. Through some arrangement with a friend from Chimayo
he had made this last trip in a little truck. Knowing that this was
Higinio's first ride in any kind of an automobile, I had gone to greet
him on his return and also to hear his account of his trip. It was
bound to be humorous, as were all his conversations.

The whole village loved this old gentleman because of his
entertaining qualities. His humble little home was always crowded
during the long winter evenings. Then Higinio was in his element
singing songs and spinning tales. Any incident which he chose to
relate, however commonplace, would be related in such a humorous way as to keep his audience doubled up with laughter.

Another function for which Higinio was much sought after was
that of *rezador* or leader of prayers at a wake or at the death-bed of
one for whom there was no time to call the priest. As a recompense
for his indispensability to the community Higinio was usually
elected Justice of the Peace. Occasional cases brought before him
should have brought him in some spending money from the fees
due the Justice of the Peace. But Higinio's good-hearted endeavors
were usually extended toward a settlement out of court. As an extra
inducement he usually would agree to forego any court costs so that
really the position of Justice of the Peace was only an honorary one
with rarely any monetary remuneration.

As an added source of income Higinio would bring in salt from
the salt lakes and *yeso* or plaster of Paris from near Cienega. These
commodities he would trade for grain, beans, or whole wheat flour,
measure for measure. These trading activities brought him in the
necessary food for himself and his diminutive wife. So on the whole
he lived well according to his simple wants and he enjoyed life
wholeheartedly.

This evening of his return I found that others of the village had preceded me, and his house was already full of his neighbors, their children, and his grandchildren.

"*Buenas tardes Don Higinio, ¿cómo le fué en su viaje?* ('How did you come out on your trip?')" was my greeting as I entered.

"*Bien, amiguito* ('Very well, my friend'). We flew all the way. Look you, we stopped to eat lunch the first day where I used to camp on my second night when I went in my wagon and team. What wonderful things these automobiles are. And that evening we arrived early at the lakes. And now you have me back here on the evening of the second day with a load of as white and pure salt as I have ever brought back.

"Now you all know it used to take me a week to make the trip with my little team staying the first night at Santa Fe and the second night I usually camped at San Cristobal near that old Indian village. You know that during the war I made a trip for salt and on the second day I camped as usual near San Cristobal. I noticed when I was making camp a group of men near the old church. They went by my camp as I was getting supper and I noticed they were covered with dust. Soon my little grandson Remigio came back from picketing the horses where they could graze.

" 'What could those men be doing digging near the old church, grandpa?' *'Quién sabe, hijo.* How many were there?' 'There were four and a fat *Americano* was watching them,' replied Remigio. 'Well, let's eat supper and then we will go see," I promised.

"It was still light as we neared the large hole back of the church ruins. We had nearly reached the edge of the hole when a big fat *Americano* stepped around the corner of the church. He had a rifle with him and asked us, 'What do you want? What are you doing here?' *'Nada, señor,'* I answered. 'Just wondering what those men were digging for. A well perhaps?'

" 'Yes, a well, and you had better leave. You have no business here. Where are you from?' was his angry reply.

" 'We are from Quemado and are camped over here on the stream. We are leaving in the morning.'

" 'Well, see that you leave in the morning and don't come snooping around here again.' With this reply he waved us away.

"We went back to camp wondering what they could be digging for, maybe one of those springs which the Indians stopped up when they left, or maybe digging up graves. Why couldn't they leave the poor dead Indians in peace?

"Next morning as we were preparing to harness our horses this fat *Americano* came up to our camp. He was smiling now and gave us a good morning very pleasantly. '*Amigo*, are you in a very big hurry to leave? If you are not I can give you maybe two days' work. Only one of my men came back this morning to help. The rest of the *tontos* are afraid of being bewitched. They don't like digging in this Indian pueblo. If you will help me I will pay you well and give you some corn for your horses.'

"Well my poor horses were thin and there was good grazing around the camp. The grama grass was this high, about up to my ankles, and I could use the money which I would earn. So taking the harness off the horses I agreed to work. I was curious to see what was going on.

"The *Americano* went with me to the old church and got me a shovel. I started digging with my *compañero*, a man from Galisteo. I can't remember his name.

"Near noon the *Señor Americano* measured the depth of the hole and shook his head and, cursing, started measuring from the corner of the church. 'You fellows eat your lunch and we will try another place afterward.' Sure enough, after lunch he had marked another spot a few feet from where we had dug before.

"All that day and the next day we worked hard and the fat *Americano* didn't help us any. He was too fat for work. Toward evening of the second day we struck some poles laid crosswise in the earth. Now the fat man was all excited. He almost fell in the hole trying to tell us how to dig. Following his instructions we dug around the cedar poles and lifting them up carefully uncovered a sort of pit walled and floored with the same kind of cedar poles. In it were several objects wrapped in buckskin and tied with thongs. As I was lifting the largest of these out, and it was very heavy, the buckskin wrappings came loose and it fell back in the hole leaving the buckskin in my hands. I stooped to pick it up, and you will not believe me but it was a golden image of San Cristóbal about so large."

Here Higinio extended his hands to indicate the size of the image. From this I judged the size to be about eighteen or twenty inches.

"Did you get to see any of the other articles, and do you think it was made of gold?" I asked.

"No, I didn't get to see any of the other articles, only as I could

feel them through the buckskin. The *Americano* seemed angry
because we had seen what we had and told us to put the other
things outside the hole near the edge. After he was sure we had
taken everything out he told us to climb out. 'This is all the work,
men. I will pay you now. You had better leave right away.' He gave
me ten dollars for my work, more than I had expected. How much
he gave the other man I don't know."

"What did the other objects feel like?" was my next question.

"Oh, some felt like big cups and plates, others just like heavy
bars. There were not many, and none weighed as much as the gold
image, if it was gold," was the old man's response. "On the way
past my camp I asked my *compañero* from Galisteo who the
Americano was. He called him *El Panqueque*, something like those
little tortillas I ate in a restaurant once."

It was not hard to figure out that the name hinted at as
"Pancake" must be Pankey. Perhaps I was right, although I have
heard nothing more to substantiate the old man's tale. If his
account is true this may explain Mr. Pankey's financial standing of
later years.

"Every time I pass that place I remember about that golden
image. I suppose the priests buried it there to hide it from the
Indians, ¿quién sabe? But how did this *Americano* know where to
dig for it? The tale is true that when God was passing out gifts to
the different races he granted *Los Americanos* the gift of riches
which they asked for. And us Mexicans we asked for enjoyment of
life in the form of wine, women, and song. That is why we find
ourselves so poor but always enjoying life." (65)

*Whenever possible, trade was brisk both within New Mexico and
between villages there and in southern Colorado.*

The trader in his covered wagon drove into the busy little village
early one morning, even before its inhabitants had departed on the
all-important task of gathering in their harvest. As he drove by the
first houses he heard the wondering exclamations pass from one
hastily opened door to the other: "I wonder what he has to sell."
"*Ojalá*, I hope he has brought watermelons or oranges." The trader
brought his horses to a stop in the center of the group of houses
which comprised the village. The team of diminutive horses
welcomed with evident relish this opportunity to rest, as they

relaxed in their harness with drooping heads and hips aslant, resting their weight on one hind leg.

Soon the word spread, after his first customer departed with her purchase, that this stranger had brought beans to sell for cash or barter for produce, onions, chile strings, cornmeal, fruit—anything which the trader could not raise on his unirrigated farm in the southern part of the state. A hailstorm had wrought havoc with the upland dry farms where the villagers usually harvested enough beans for their own consumption, so the coming of the trader gave them an opportunity of acquiring their winter's supply of that most essential of foods.

The wagon became the center of a bantering, laughing crowd, above which stood the shrewd and jolly trader trading joke for joke as he busily measured out beans and accepted produce or cash in return. The measure used by the trader was the old Spanish *almud*, a square wooden box holding approximately a peck. This measure is preferred by most of the people of the smaller communities in New Mexico because they do not understand and therefore are distrustful of scales, which measure by the little-known quantities of pounds and ounces.

There had been some comment with regard to the measure which the trader had brought with him. Some had voiced the thought that it looked smaller than the regulation *almud*. The trader had been able to quiet these first questioning remarks with a joke or by flattery if the outspoken one happened to be a woman.

A tall, grim individual stood on the edge of the crowd, watching the scene and listening to the various comments but making no comment himself. When the crowd around the wagon had dispersed with the exception of the ever-present mob of children, he drew near and said:

"Friend, sell me six *almuds* of beans. I will give three strings of chile in part payment and the rest in cash, but first let me see your *almud*."

The trader handed down the measure for inspection.

"Por Dios, friend, this is no *almud*, this a matchbox," was the comment after the measure had undergone a careful measurement of its dimensions.

"Oh, but yes, this is an honest measure. 'Tis the one I have always used," was the trader's defense. "Shall I measure out your six *almuds?"*

"Yes, if you'll use my *almud* which I shall bring from my house," said the would-be customer as he turned to leave.

"No! No! I would not think of bothering you. It would not be right, and besides, *mire!* Look!" said the trader as he held up his outspread hand.

The customer needed but one glance and yielded, knowing that in the quickminded trader he had met his match. Also, he could not help but admire the ingenuity of the man. For the outspread hand was an eloquent though silent symbol for a Spanish proverb which goes thus: *"No todos los dedos de la mano son igual"* ("Not all the fingers of the hand are of the same length.").

"Muy bien, amigo ('Very well, friend'), measure me out those beans." And with a handclasp of mutual appreciation the transaction was completed. (99)

Peddlers and traders provided excitement in the humdrum of village life. These adventurous men brought goods, news, and a fund of novel stories and anecdotes.

The trader had stopped for the night at his friend's home in Truchas, as was his custom on his frequent trading trips to that upland mountain village. After sitting up most of the night before the fireplace trading gossip and news with his loquacious host, Don Melitón Vigil, the trader went to his canvas-covered wagon for his bedroll. He took his bedroll into his host's front room, unrolled it, and lay down to sleep.

He had been asleep a short while when he was awakened by a most ungodly noise. It seemed to come from just outside the door. In his half-awakened state the trader did not at first identify the sound. After a while, his mind clearing, he knew the sound to be the hooting of an owl, but not just one owl; one owl could not make all that noise.

Opening the door, he looked out and saw two owls sitting on the crosspole of the gate which opened into his host's patio. There was a full moon and the huge birds seemed much larger as the moonlight etched their horned figures against the sky. It is very strange to see two owls together, and at best they are fearsome beasts, but that could not explain the trader's evident fear as, crossing himself, he hastily slammed the door.

Crossing the room, he bowed his head as he entered the low door which led into the room where his friend slept. He found his host awake; he too had heard the owls and was sitting up in his bed, rolling a cornhusk cigarette. The trader asked him if he had a gun, saying that he was going to shoot the owls and adding that they had been following him from village to village, and that now he was going to put a stop to it.

The old man pointed to the corner where his rifle stood and said: "If you think that those two owls are some evil ones who mean to harm you, you had better cut a cross in the bullets. Otherwise you will not touch them."

The trader complied with his host's suggestion by levering all of the cartridges out of the rifle and making a cross on two of them with his pocket knife. He loaded the gun with them as he crossed the outer room. Reaching the door, he threw it open and, raising the gun to his shoulder, fired two shots in rapid succession.

One of the owls fell to the ground with a dull thud but the other bird flew away with one leg trailing, showing that it had been wounded. The trader crossed the moon-drenched patio and gingerly picked the dead bird up by one leg, hurling it across the road and down the hillside.

On his next trip to Truchas the trader recounted the sequel to the killing of the owls. It seemed that he had had some difficulty with two Indians of the Tesuque Pueblo over a horse trade, and they had sworn to get even with him. Those two Indians had the reputation of being witches, and the trader was certain that they were the two owls which had followed him so persistently, seeking to harm him in some manner.

On his return home from the trading trip on which he had killed the owls, the trader was met with strange news concerning his Indian enemies. They had gone hunting at the time the trader had started out on his trip. One morning they rode back into the Pueblo, but one of them was slung across his pony. He had shot himself accidentally, or so said the survivor, who himself had a broken leg. His own horse had fallen with him on the way in was the story the surviving Indian told.

The trader, however, was certain that he and his friend Don Melitón alone knew the truth of how the Indians had met their fate. The Indian with the broken leg recovered. He must have ceased practicing witchcraft, for he never again bothered the trader after the death of his companion. (124)

*Even as late as the 1920s, a stranger's arrival was a singular event,
as this personal anecdote illustrates:*

The chattering and laughter of the women could be heard
coming from the east side of the house. This was a sign that they
were nearly through with their task for in the morning they had
started plastering the west side to avoid the sun, which could still
direct its rays with some force this late in September. Swinging
around the house in direct opposition to the sun's rays, they had
succeeded in keeping in some measure in the shadows cast by the
walls.

However, neither the heat nor the hard labor seemed to bother
these four women as they labored at a task which in this
community was acknowledged as one for women only. Men, if
tolerated at all, were allowed only to mix the dirt and straw into
mud of the required consistency. Even then, one of the women
would work and knead small batches at a time, carefully extracting
stones and other objects and leaving the mud a smooth paste. When
expertly applied by her coworkers, this left an outer covering fully
protecting the house from the elements for many seasons.

Nearing the end of their task seemed to add more zest and spirit
to their joking and gossiping. Passersby were cheerfully answered
as they joked with them in passing: *"¿Ya acaban las golondrinas
con su nido?"* ("Are the swallows nearly through with their nest?")
This allusion referred to the barn-swallow, which expertly fashions
its nest while clinging to a wall. Also there was a hint of the
constant twittering that the swallows indulge in while so employed.

Suddenly I heard an exclamation from one of the women in a
louder voice and with some measure of awe injected into it.
Thinking I had not heard aright, I rushed out of doors to see what
this could be—a practical joke or some real cause for alarm. The
women on the scaffolding had half turned at their companion's cry
and the one on the ground where she stood repeated the phrase
which I thought I had not heard correctly, this time with more
emphasis: *"¡Miren! ¡Miren! Ay viene Jesú Cristo a caballo, viene
bajando del alto."* ("Look! Look! There comes Jesus Christ on
horseback coming down from above.")

Following her pointing finger with our eyes, we could see the
reason for her surprised ejaculation. The slanting rays of the sinking
sun seemed to spotlight the figure of a man on horseback on the

steep hill-road which climbed toward Truchas. Yet what held us was the remarkable resemblance of this figure to the more familiar representations of the Christ. His features, full golden beard, and uncovered head were so very much like those of the Christ as depicted in the lithographs of the Saints and the Holy Family with which these people were familiar that it was no wonder that this astonished woman was deluded. The incongruity of a Christ on horseback and leading a pack-horse was not at the instant apparent, for the slanting rays of the setting sun bathed the stranger in such splendor as to make him a glorious figure.

The awe which the first speaker had injected into her exclamations had communicated itself to the others and held them speechless for a while, but only a short while, until the figure had advanced out of the direct rays of the sun. *"¡A tonta! Tu Cristo a caballo no es más que un Americano barbón."* ("You fool! Your Christ on horseback is only a bearded American.") And more! The poor woman was taunted and ridiculed by the others amid a burst of laughter. Thus they revenged themselves on her who through suggestion had fooled them for a moment of credulous amazement. But they all agreed that the *Americano* was *muy bonito* and really looked like *El Señor Jesu'Cristo.*

It so happened that this stranger on horseback was directed to my house when he stopped to inquire with regard to a night's lodging. This genial giant of a fellow with the full beard was hugely amused when I told him of the consternation he had aroused as he rode into the village. He liked New Mexico and had chosen to see some of its natural beauties from the back of a horse. Leaving Santa Fe some two months before with only his bedroll and simple equipment on a pack horse, he had swung around by Las Vegas, Mora, the hill towns near Peñasco, a side trip to Taos, and now he had arrived in Cordova which delighted him both as an artist and because of the memories it brought to him of his native Switzerland.

I enjoyed his company most of the next day, but this was brought to an abrupt close when he happened to ask the date. Upon being informed as to the correct date, he found that somewhere in his carefree ramblings he had lost two days and that he must be back in Santa Fe next day so as not to lose his return trip ticket back to Chicago.

So a hasty bargain was struck by which I became possessor of his horses and equipment in consideration for which I was to transport him to Santa Fe by hook or crook (this was before cars in Cordova or vicinity) in time to make use of his ticket. What cash was involved in the transaction was needed by him now that he had come back to the reality of trains, hair cuts, and Fred Harvey lunch rooms. Use of the Forest Service phone brought a car from Santa Fe which duly transported *El Cristo a Caballo* to Santa Fe beard and all, and that is the only name I have to remember him by.

Another reminder he left behind was one of his saddle-horses, called Cynic by him. This name was well bestowed; I have never known another horse with so many individual characteristics peculiarly his own. His traits, most of them sheer perverseness, made us regard him as almost human, and we remembered him long after we parted with him. His present owner, a very kindly one who indulges his idiosyncracies, is very fond of him. Perhaps, being a widower of long standing and set in his ways, he has a fellow feeling for Cynic and his humors.

The only horse in the village to boast of a given name, *El Cínico* is known to all but loaned to few would-be borrowers. As his owner rightly says: "*Caballo ajeno y espuelas propias hacen corto el camino.* ('A borrowed horse and your own spurs make for a short road.') But it's not so good for the horse." (73)

Few traders accumulated great wealth, but certain old village families combined careful management of local resources with shrewd trading to become patrones *in their communities. Cordova* patrón *Don Pedro Córdova was one such* rico.

When it was first settled, the little village in the valley of the Rio Quemado boasted a group of settlers alike in one respect at least: they were determined to conquer the land, reclaim it from the forest, and through their industry make a home for their children. The land that had already been cultivated by the Tano Indians of Pueblo Quemado was at first communal property. All the men who were able to work took part in its cultivation and the harvesting of the crops. Each family received its just proportion of the grains and other produce grown. The men who served the community as hunters received an equal share of the crops and shared with the others the game that fell to their flintlocks or bows and arrows.

As the danger from Indian attacks diminished, families branched out and fathers and sons picked suitable spots to clear for their own use. That which had been communal property was divided to the satisfaction of all. The day of cooperative effort and equal division passed; it now devolved on each family to fend for itself. The land cleared by their efforts was their own as was its yield.

In this group of settlers there were, of course, some with more foresight and initiative than others. Acquisition of property and land being the gauge by which a man's ability and standing were judged, it was to be expected that some would bend their efforts in that direction.

The outstanding qualities of Don Pedro Córdova made him a natural leader in his community, and his shrewd instinct for commerce and barter soon gave him possession by one means or another of most of the cultivated land in the valley. Before his death, nearly all of this land passed into his control, making him the *patrón* of the village to whom everyone looked for livelihood. Having virtually no land on which to raise any crops and little, if any, stock to depend on for a living, most of the men of the village had to work for Don Pedro in the fields or guard his flocks in the hills. Most of the women had to serve Don Pedro's household in some capacity or other. These families, virtually slaves, received for their labor not money but produce of the fields they helped till, meat from the flocks and herds under their care, and meal and flour which they helped grind on the metate.

Don Pedro, of necessity, maintained a large household; many of his servants lived entirely off his bounty. Besides the care of his fields and livestock, he engaged in overland trade with nearby and distant communities. He sent large herds of cattle and sheep over the mountain passes between Cordova and the valley of Taos, known as the granary of the province. His *mayordomo* in charge of these drives would trade the livestock for grain, a valuable commodity. This grain would be stored in the *trojas* built into the large *dispensas* of Don Pedro's home in Cordova. To him would come the farmers of the immediate vicinity for seed grain and grain for grinding into meal and flour. (80)

Don Pedro was the *rico* of the village. Owner of all of the tillable lands of the little valley in which Quemado was located and of the land grant to the east, he virtually controlled the destinies of the rest of the inhabitants. He was the *patrón* to whom all looked for their material welfare. His large establishment swarmed with all kinds of help, villagers as well as several Indian slaves. Although a seeming confusion, there was a well-ordered division of labor. In the kitchen Indian women were continually busy, some as *tortilleras* with no other task than to round out and bake tortillas. Others were kept busy bringing water from the river, grinding corn, and so forth; while yet others, the more reliable, were the actual cooks and had supervision of the lesser help. As for the men, some had charge of the planting and harvesting of crops, others of the herds of cattle and sheep and yet others were continually arriving or leaving on trading trips to Ranchos de Taos or Taos, driving herds of fat steers before them which they would trade for grain in that fertile valley.

A hard worker himself, Don Pedro saw to it that everybody else was kept busy. To those whom he paid wages he was very liberal, not confining himself strictly to the wages earned but giving them additional help as needed. Wages in those times were an *"almud* of cornmeal for a week's work and a fat mutton for two weeks' labor." It was enough for the simple needs of that time and could always be supplemented with game, which was plentiful. All in all, Don Pedro was considered a good *patrón*, and his people found a certain measure of security in the plenty which was his. (30)

Don Pedro Córdova contributed substantially to the construction of the village church, and, three years later, he sponsored the casting and christening of a beautiful church bell.

To this end, he secured the services of one Francisco Martínez from La Puebla, a little settlement in the lower Chimayo valley. This Francisco Martínez had followed in his father's footsteps as a maker or caster of bells. His father had brought knowledge of this art with him from Mexico. (30)

The bell that hangs in the adobe bell tower atop the old church was cast in the patio of one of the villagers and hung in the tower after a christening ceremony. For this ceremony, Don Pedro Córdova and his wife, Doña Ramona, served as *padrino* and *madrina* of the bell, giving it a name just as if it were some baby for whom they were sponsors. As the wealthiest couple of the little settlement, no one disputed them this honor, especially since Don

Pedro had contributed the greater part of the gold and silver that had gone into the melting pot. . . . True, others of the village had donated rings and ornaments of gold and silver to the melting pot to give the bell a sweeter, clearer tone, but Don Pedro had given thirty gold *escudos* and some silver coin, a large sum even in those days. However, in those days of barter, money was of little use.

Don Pedro lived in what might be called feudal state; the whole valley was his, and his inhabitants depended on him for their livelihood. Besides herdsmen, farmers, traders, and ox drivers for the trading caravans that Don Pedro sent out over the country and to Mexico, he had many Indian slaves, and these were assigned to tasks for which they were individually fitted. A long string of water carriers was kept busy bringing water from the river; these were for the most part old men, boys, and those simpleminded persons who could not cope with any task more complicated. The home of this man was a scene of bustling activity at all times, for with so many mouths to feed—his own household, the many domestics, hangers-on, and visitors—everyone must be about his appointed task. A *mayordomo* or overseer saw to it that everyone kept busy. This steward was an important individual and exercised authority around the house second only to Doña Ramona.

The varied interests outside the household were under the direction of another *mayordomo* who saw to it that Don Pedro's commands were carried out. There was no set wage paid to these workers, nor was it paid in coin or money. The head of a family received a set allotment of meal with a fat mutton at intervals. This was enough to satisfy the simple needs of those days, and Don Pedro could always be relied upon to supply the extra trimmings that a wedding or a christening demanded. All in all, the community was well enough pleased with the paternal overlordship of this wealthy man, accepting his bounty and enduring his domination with meek resignation, as if they were children in a large household.

In those days, what gold and coin came into Don Pedro's hands was of small use to him, so that when it occurred to him to donate a bell to the church, he found use for some of his hoard.

The caster of bells built his oven in Don Pedro's patio, and under the latter's watchful eyes stoked his oven so as to melt the different metals. A cast of clay had been prepared into which the molten metal was poured. A period of suspense ensued while the metal cooled. Perhaps the bell would be cracked or some bubble would render it useless and necessitate recasting.

Everyone rejoiced when the first casting was a success and immediately began to prepare for the christening of the bell and the ceremony and feasting which would be part of that event.

The visiting priest from Santa Cruz was always Don Pedro's guest whenever he came to say mass in the village and was entertained in Don Pedro's own private room. This room had the loftiest ceiling in the large establishment. It had but one door, which led to the outside. No one entered except at Don Pedro's express invitation or command. A small window in one wall opened into a small kitchen, in which only Don Pedro and his guests' meals were prepared. Dishes were passed through this opening to his personal body servant who saw to the arrangement of the table and waited on them. In this room Don Pedro entertained the priest in conversation throughout many courses, during which the choicest viands of those days were served with wines carefully brought in from Rio Abajo, as the lower Rio Grande Valley was known.

On the morning of the christening ceremony, the little village seethed with excitement. Visitors from nearby villages and outlying farms arrived in ever-increasing numbers—afoot, on horseback, and in creaking *carretas*—all eager to join in the festivities and anticipating the social interchange that a gathering of this kind was certain to produce. Bake ovens were emptied of loaves of enticingly fragrant bread, together with steaming pots of *panocha*, cakes, and baked meats. Don Pedro, as *padrino*, had ordered that a huge repast be prepared so everyone could eat and drink his fill. Whole beefs, sheep, and kids were roasted to satisfy the hunger of the assembling crowd.

The appearance of the sexton on the church roof and the sound he made as he banged on a copper pan, the improvised bell soon to be discarded, signified that mass would soon be said, giving them time to get ready before the last signal was sounded. Everybody who possibly could, crowded into the little church after the new bell had been carried in on a small platform, the whole gaily decorated with ribbons and wreaths of flowers. After mass, Don Pedro and his wife, resplendent in their finery, followed the bell as it was carried before the officiating priest.

The christening of the bell differed in no way from the christening of a baby. The *padrinos* made known the name they wished conferred on it: María Antonio. After the ceremony was concluded, the priest blessed the bell, and it was carried around the church yard in a joyous procession during which the singing of the crowd was punctuated with the sound of musket fire.

After the procession had circled the outside of the church, stout ropes of rawhide were called into play as the bell was hoisted to the church top. Brawny fellows heaved and tugged, glancing in disdain at those who proffered useless advice but no other aid, and, amidst shouts of the crowds, the clapperless bell was hung from the supporting timber that rested on top of the tower. Don Pedro proudly struck the bell to send its clear sweet tones ringing out over the valley, and the hills were still echoing the sound as the crowd knelt to receive the priest's blessing as he stood beside Don Pedro. (36)

Now the real festivities began. Groups gathered around the great fires where the different kinds of roast meat were to be had and helped themselves to the bread which was piled high in one corner of the long portal. Long tables held the rest of the feast, and everybody was welcome to help himself and eat his fill. In the crowd were some Apache Indians, notorious gluttons, who did not need a second bidding and who soon rendered themselves easy victims for a scalping knife if the laws of hospitality could have been suspended.

Horse racing, horse trading, and other amusements took up the afternoon. In the evening, the *baile* in the long hall was well attended by an ever-changing crowd, who danced awhile, ate awhile, and then went back to dance again. Fine straw spread on the earthen floor created a cloud of dust which the many candles tried to dissipate with little success. But no matter that it was not a brilliantly lighted ballroom with waxed floors—the polka, the *valse redondo,* the *cuna,* and the other dances of the period were danced with a lighthearted enjoyment. The extempore couplets sung by the guitar player in honor of the bell, Don Pedro, and his wife, and everybody else in turn were heartily applauded and cheerfully rewarded. Now and then there would be a sudden commotion—two jealous young men, hot words, then a thrust for outdoors, hands on knife hilt. There in the dark their differences would be settled in a manner satisfactory to both or of no more moment to one.

The feast and the merriment continued far into the next day.

Don Pedro with a few favored guests and relatives feasted apart, overlooking the tumult from his portal which commanded a view of most of the village. (30)

For many years this bell has sounded its tale of sorrow or rejoicing, calling the faithful of the valley to worship. Don Pedro's gold and silver imparted such a sweet and resonant tone to it, that often a shepherd far up in the hills hears and kneels to join his family in the village in prayer. Don Pedro and his wife sleep side by side just inside the door of the church, beneath the place where their clear-voiced godson hangs suspended and keeps their memory fresh.

Doña Carmelita Molina de Mondragón knows the very place pointed out to her by her grandmother as the spot on which the bell was cast. This spot was in what used to be the courtyard of Don Pedro's private dining room. She has a lump of heavy metal, resembling a piece of *malpaís* rock, which she asserts is a piece of slag, some of the overflow or waste from the metal which had gone into making of the bell. A cut into this chunk of metal with a file exposes a yellow, shiny interior with the same glow and sheen that shows on the side of the bell where the stone wielded by the bell ringers strikes a slow and measured toll or a staccato summons to mass. (36)

Inevitably, Don Pedro Córdova's wealth became legendary.

Tales were told of the vast quantity of gold and silver that reposed in some corner of his establishment; stories were common of his measuring the different kinds of coin in *almuds*, as one would wheat. These disclosures were said to have been made by a trusted servant while under the influence of wine: how he had helped Don Pedro measure each kind of coin, so many *almuds* of each, so many bars of silver. He could not remember the totals; he was just a poor, ignorant servant who did not know the number of days he lived, but Don Pedro kept tally. What was done with the gold after it had been counted and measured, he did not know, but "I know what I have seen."

This was, in substance, the information on which these tales of treasure were based. The basis for their truth was the knowledge everyone had that much coin and other forms of metal wealth came into Don Pedro's possession; it needed only his *mayordomo's* assertions of the different amounts they would bring back from Taos and Santa Fe to give color to what might have been explained as wild flights of imagination. Then, too, there was the tale that Don Pedro, having received notice of impending rebellion in the lower villages or some such disturbance of a political nature, something very hazy and not clearly understood by most of the villagers who knew nothing of the outside world, had had his treasure carried a short distance into La Cañada del Ojito, where he stayed alone with it. Those who carried it stated that it was contained in rawhide bags fashioned out of whole calf skins. Whether Don Pedro buried his treasure there and removed it later or whether it is still there has been a subject of conjecture and sporadic search for many years. For Don Pedro died and took his secret with him, dying from the effects of poison which he took accidentally.

Not many of the townspeople have undertaken to find this treasure because superstition has too strong a hold on them. Who wants to risk incurring the displeasure of the spirit that guards this treasure?

One young man who had experienced the delights of the city and who had received a fine education outside the village determined to come back and make an effort to locate this wealth, thus enabling him to return to the city and enjoy its advantages. Choosing for his companion a lad of the village who had been his lifelong chum and whose valor equaled his own, they ventured into Cañada del Ojito after dusk so that no one would see them. They carried with them equipment consisting of a shovel, a pick, and a lantern, along with several canvas bags in which to transport their treasure. It is said that they left all these indications of their hopes behind, close to a shallow hole that was the only visible sign of their night's expedition.

The truth of what happened finally leaked out, as such things will. It seems that they had been engaged in digging at a likely spot for a very short while—the small results of their efforts proved this—when a cold rush of air from beneath their feet extinguished their lantern. Strange noises assailed their ears—sounds of groaning and muttered imprecations. It seemed as if cold hands clutched at their throats. Wildly, desperately, they fled the place, scrambling up the intervening hillside between themselves and the village as if it were level ground. Terror stayed with them, not leaving them even after they had burst into the home of the confident lad who had scoffed at the old women's tales. Their staring eyes, disheveled hair, and sobbing were eloquent of their condition. They could not speak of anything for several minutes. Thus ended one attempt to find Don Pedro's treasure.

Men from outside the village, hearing about the treasure, brought magic needles and gadgets of different kinds guaranteed to locate any treasure, however well hidden, but all returned empty handed. One, who professed to be a seer, after some preliminary rites of a mysterious nature, told the man who lived in the room that used to be Don Pedro's own inviolate sanctuary that the treasure was hidden someplace within its walls. He assured the owner that the treasure would be found, but there were certain measures to be taken before the actual discovery. He obtained the owner's permission and promise of cooperation in every way.

To the seer's inquiry as to when mass would next be said in the village church, the owner replied that the following Thursday would be the day for the visiting priest to make his regular monthly visit. The owner was then told to be sure and go to mass, to confess himself, and to fast the rest of the day. The seer would do likewise, joining him in the church. All this the owner of the room did, and he was joined by the seer as promised. The seer had brought his little son, a child three years old, with him. It was necessary, the seer said, that an *inocente* should join them and that they should cleanse their hearts of all envy, spite, and wicked thoughts. To this end the rest of the day was spent in prayer within the room where the treasure was supposed to be hidden.

When night fell, the seer busied himself with mysterious, impressive preparations. He lighted seven candles, placing one in each corner of the room and three before a small altar which he placed in the center of the room. His little son was made to kneel in front of this altar with the owner of the room close behind, both with rosaries in their hands. Whether the seer knelt also, the owner could not say, but upon being exhorted to cleanse his heart against all evil or malicious thoughts and to follow the seer in the prayers that he would recite, the owner became absorbed in obeying the commands of this strange man. They prayed the rosary, after which the seer launched into a fervent incantation which the owner could not follow. He tried his best to keep his mind on his own prayers, inaudibly spoken, through which he heard the seer's voice raised in passionate exhortation. All this lasted about an hour, when the seer interrupted him in a tone of disappointment: "No, *amigo*, it is no use; your heart is not free of envious thoughts. Your thoughts were on the treasure, wondering how to keep me from getting my share. The spirits are angry and the light which should have indicated the treasure has been denied us. These rites are successful only when all who participate are free of evil thoughts. We shall try another day, perhaps."

When the seer took his departure next morning, the owner resolved never again to be mixed up in such doings. He was content to let the treasure rest where it lay. He did, however, give permission to another young man to sound the walls of the room. This one thought he had located a spot which might be the hiding place so eagerly sought. He started to dig into the wall close to the site of Don Pedro's fireplace, carefully at first, so as not to weaken the wall. Suddenly the little pry bar he was using sank into a cavity in the wall. Enlarging the hole through which the bar had plunged, he could glimpse a whitewashed wall cupboard. Further efforts disclosed the ends of two shelves, on one of which could be distinguished the rounded form of an earthen *olla*. Excitement seized both. Part of the treasure must be in that black pot! With no regard for damage done to the wall, both seized ax and pick and speedily opened a gaping hole, disclosing a small *almario* which had been plastered over.

Eagerly they snatched the earthen pot, scarcely visible through the dust raised by their strenuous, feverish efforts, from one of its shelves. To their great disappointment, the pot contained only a handful of thin, pitched-pine slivers which Don Pedro had used in lighting his corn husk cigarettes. Cursing Don Pedro and his motive for fooling them thus, they sadly set about repairing the damage they had done to the wall.

"Never again," said the owner of the room," will I make any attempt to find Don Pedro's treasure. The other time I fasted all day and my knees still ache from kneeling so long. Now I have weakend the wall of this room. I must put a *muerto* ('dead man,' a supporting beam) above this hole we have made. And with that, I will leave all dead men to rest in peace."

One of the villagers of Cordova relates that one night as he was returning from Truchas by way of the Cañada del Ojito, a bright light arrested his footsteps near the spot where Don Pedro's treasure was supposed to have been buried. Rooted to the spot, he was astonished to see the hillside open, and he gazed in amazement on the streets and houses of an enchanted city. For all its beauty, it seemed a city of the dead, for no one walked its streets, yet he could distinctly hear roosters crowing somewhere within its walls. He says he felt no fear, only awe and a great astonishment. Suddenly the light went out, the hill closed, and the city vanished. It took his eyes quite a while to become accustomed to the darkness. When he could see the path before his feet, a late terror seized him, and he fled the spot in fright.

With thumb over his doubled forefinger, he will swear that this is the truth, that it was no hallucination induced by drinking *mula*, that not a drop had touched his lips that night. That Don Pedro's treasure is buried there, he does not doubt, but for no money could he be induced to make any effort to recover it. "No good can come of meddling with things of the other world," is his firm belief. So the spirit of Don Pedro has been left to guard his treasure in peace. (80)

Many villagers knew of other elusive treasure.

"If my father had known gold when he saw it, he would have been a rich man, at least that is what he used to say after he came back from working in the placer mines in the Moreno Valley." Donaciano Romero accepted a cigarette and continued. "But when these *Americanos* were taking out gold from this hidden mine my father had many sheep, and there was no necessity for his leaving home until long after this had happened. So he had no knowledge about gold at the time.

"He summered his sheep in the Cañada de los Alamitos on the north slope of Jicarita Peak. My father told of seeing these men ride up this *cañón* towards the Jicarita. They always came out at sunrise and, returning, entered the dense forest at sunset or after dark had set in. They certainly wanted to be sure no one followed them, I guess.

"At first they had a spotted burro only, which they drove before them loaded with supplies. On one of their trips out, one of the *Americanos* offered to buy a spotted pony from my father, a very good little saddle horse. From a buckskin *talega* or pouch full of gold nuggets, my father was offered a large nugget for his pony. But always ignorance is a great drawback. Not knowing anything about gold my father refused and insisted on being paid one hundred dollars in coined money.

"'Then you will have to go with us to Mora for your money, but you are a big fool not to take the gold. It will bring you more than you are asking,' said the *Americano* who wanted the horse.

"And that's how it was all right. At Mora the gold was changed to money, and, just to show my father, the nugget was weighed separately. It was worth $146.00. The *Americanos* teased my father about this and bought him a gallon of whiskey so he would not feel so badly about it. After arranging for the care of their horse and burro, the *Americanos* left for Las Vegas and father, borrowing a burro from his *compadre* Benigno, returned to the sheep camp.

"It was the custom of those two *Americanos* not to return to the mine until they had spent all their money. They would visit several towns—Taos, Las Vegas, Raton, and others—on these spending sprees, so that many men were anxious to find out where they were getting so much gold. Many efforts were made to get them to talk and to follow them, but they were very careful and nobody succeeded. These men didn't talk when drinking and kept to themselves when sober. As for my father and his herder, they never thought of following them because these men went well armed, and besides, my father was well content with his life as it was.

"Finally at Raton one of these men killed the other during a drunken argument and disappeared to avoid the authorities. He never returned and the mine has never been found. Padre Guerín of Mora spent much time and money trying to locate the mine, but in vain. It must have been a rich placer because father said the gold resembled the placer gold of the Moreno Valley. After realizing in later years how rich the mine must have been, he wished God had granted him courage to follow those men one night. He might have been lucky to have escaped alive, and we might have been rich today. *¿Quién sabe?*, one does not get more than he is supposed to in this world.

"Look at Juan Mondragón. He fell into the richest mine yet, one might say, but died a poor man and denied himself the riches which God wished to give him. He was herding sheep for the Garcías from Santa Fe on the eastern slope of the Truchas Peaks. One of his milk goats fell into a hole and couldn't get out. Going to her rescue, Juan finished caving in the dirt and pole covering of an old mine. After rescuing the goat, Mondragón investigated, and next time he came home he brought back some very rich ore containing much gold. He also brought some very crude tools, homemade and very rusty. The Garcías, his patrons, offered him half of their three thousand head of sheep and two horses if he would show them where the mine was. But he was an ignorant one and refused. I think he was afraid he would be killed after he revealed the location of the mine."

"That man was a *tonto* ('fool')," broke in Donaciano's wife Eulalia, who had been listening all the while as she patted out tortillas for the evening meal. "Don't you know he was always fighting with his wife when he was home. He never let her go to the river for water, and he wouldn't take her to the dances. With the company's permission he was a *pendejo*. Who was there to watch his wife while he was gone? That is the way all these jealous ones are. And didn't he try to hang himself three different times? Twice his poor sister Tonita came running for my father to cut him down, and once, my father not being home, Tonita and I held him up by the knees while his wife, standing on a bench, cut the rope. That time he almost went. The rawhide rope was pretty tough, the knife was dull, and I think the wife didn't use all her strength. I don't blame her either. He sure had a sore throat for a long time after that."

"Sí, a very foolish man," I said. "He didn't have to show anybody this mine. Why didn't he stake out his claim and work it himself?"

"In those days there was nothing known about that," was Donaciano's explanation. "Time after time different parties came to see Juan offering to pay him, to make him rich, promising him anything and everything if he would disclose the location of his mine, but his fear of being killed kept him from doing so. Strange that a man who tried to kill himself should be so afraid of death at the hands of another, no? For many summers the slopes back of the Truchas Peaks were full of strangers looking through every valley and corner of the hills for Juan Mondragón's mine, but I guess no one has found it up to now.

"This Juan belonged to *Los Hermanos de la Luz* or the *Penitentes*. At one time due to the persuasion of the *difunto* ('deceased') Higinio Tórrez, Juan agreed to show the Brotherhood the location of the mine. The mine was to be worked by all, share and share alike, and a certain percentage to go to the *morada* fund. Only Higinio Tórrez could have persuaded Mondragón to agree to this arrangement; *tenía una labia muy suave* ('he was a smooth talker').

"After a *velorio* ('wake') at the *morada*, the party was to set out. This *velorio* was in honor of Santa Inés del Campo, the patron saint of those who live out in the open, also the saint to be prayed to for recovery of lost stock, lost persons, or anything lost out in the hills or plains. So after the night of the wake these men set out for the hills.

"Now you will see what happened. It is useless to go against God's will. The first night, while camping at the Brazos of the Rio Medio, four of the younger fellows were talking apart. One of them said, half jokingly, 'as soon as we know where the mine is let's start a fight over the amount to be given to the *morada*. Then we can get rid of these old men and the mine is ours. We can pretend some *Americanos* killed them. Who can deny our story when we get back?'

"He was cautioned by another not to speak so loudly, but too late, for Mondragón, always suspicious, had overheard and next morning refused to go any farther. The young men, really angry, then threatened to hang Mondragón from a tree until he would consent to lead them on. But not even those threats would make him change his mind. The older men advised returning and waiting until later while they tried other inducements on Mondragón. The truth is that they were a little afraid of the younger fellows. Gold brings many bad consequences even before it is in one's hands.

"Later Mondragón used to go secretly and bring back gold and very rich ore, taking with him his nephew Filogonio, who was then about twelve years old. This nephew always said his uncle did not take him clear to the mine, but that he left him at a certain spot while he went on, returning later with his gold. But I think Filogonio knew very well where it was, but, like all Mondragóns, he was very stubborn and would never disclose anything. At different times he would be gone for two or three days and here three years ago he bought all that land across the river. Also there was that land he bought in Truchas.

"You know in Filogonio's last sickness a year ago how well that Spaniard took care of him? Well, after Filogonio died the Spaniard admitted that Filogonio had promised to show him the location of the mine in case he recovered, but he was quite sick then. The Spaniard also said that Filogonio had given him some signs to go by and that they will be found this summer. Maybe so, but ¿quién sabe?

"And what a time Filogonio took to die! Such a long time he was sick. You know a Penitente will not lie down in bed when he is sick. He must be kept sitting up. Also they believe that no matter how sick they are they will not die until their feet touch the ground. Filogonio's sister-in-law from Truchas, seeing him so sick, said, 'Why do you keep that poor man suffering so? Can't you see he is marked for death? Let his feet down on the ground.

"So she helped the wife turn him sideways in bed, letting his feet touch the earth floor, and that was the last of Filogonio and maybe of Juan Mondragón's mine. *Sea por Dios.*" (79)

The lure of buried riches charmed Hispano and Anglo alike. In 1938, Brown knew several gambusinos *near Santa Fe.*

Gambusinos is the name given to placer miners, who roam the hills seeking scattered pockets or deposits of gold, mostly working over country which has already been worked on a large scale, trying to retrieve what others have left or overlooked. For the most part, their efforts are poorly paid, but they are a contented lot, and there is always the possibility of a large strike to lure them on.

Near Santa Fe, at Cerrillos in fact, which is near the old Ortiz Grant, the greater part of the population are *gambusinos.* At one time a thriving, bustling city because of the coal mines at Madrid, and because Cerrillos itself was the natural center for the other activities which surrounded it, the people did not lack for employment. The smelter, the Cash Entry Mine and others to the north, the big mill at Waldo, the mines at San Pedro, and the gold diggings on the Ortiz Grant all contributed to the prosperity of Cerrillos. The best known was La Real de Dolores, from which the little mining settlement on the Ortiz Grant took its name. So, with all of the sources of wealth surrounding it, added to the fact that it was on the railroad, Cerrillos was known far and wide for its gaiety, its gaming tables, and its night life—a typical mining town.

But now Cerrillos falls into the classification . . . of those towns which are scattered all over the Southwest known as "ghost towns." There is very little livestock raising in the vicinity and no agriculture to speak of. The mines of Madrid still contribute to some activity at Cerrillos, but the greater part of its one-time numerous population have left, and the few who remain live surrounded by the false fronts and gaping windows of its departed glory.

The once productive mines on the Ortiz Grant have been closed down because of litigation. In seeking for a means of subsistence, the remaining men of the town, remembering the large quantities of gold which formerly had been taken out of the grant, became *gambusinos* with rude, homemade dry washers. They would filter into the grant on the sly and wash the dirt they scraped out of the gullies and washes. In stating that they filtered into the grant, I should explain that the company which laid claim to the grant had prohibited entrance to all seekers of gold. These men thus had to enter the grant on the sly, making of them a closemouthed and secretive clan.

The absence of the men of the town was especially noted after a rain, for then they knew that the gold was washed down from the hillsides and slopes into the gullies and arroyos and, collecting in the pockets or depressions, gave better promise of profitable returns for their efforts. *Gambusinos* usually worked in groups of three or more, for one of their number must be posted to watch for the approach of the grant's caretaker.

Once in a while a rich strike would be made. Two years ago, one of these men found a nugget which brought him a little over three hundred dollars. Another one of my acquaintances amongst them located a rich deposit quite out of the bounds where gold was supposed to be. He very quietly moved in with his family to help him, informing his inquisitive neighbors that the whole family was going piñon picking. He succeeded in working the deposit and taking out close to three thousand dollars worth of dust before he was discovered by a group of his skeptical neighbors. Since the grant was forbidden territory, he could not keep his discoverers from sharing in the rest of the gold left on his claim. I have reason to believe his story because, as I knew then and as his neighbors attested, after his return he bought a car and furnished his house with new store-bought furniture to replace the homemade benches and tables which had served him previous to his fortunate discovery.

There is one old miner, who has lived all his life in that section

Lorin W. Brown, graduation picture, Sterling, Kansas, High School, 1918.

Frances Juanita Gilson Brown, graduation picture, 1927–28.

The Brown children and their mother in front of Aunt Alice's studio, Sterling, Kansas, 1919: left to right, Amy, Bascom, Cassandra, Vincent, Floy, Roy, and Lorin.

San Antonio de Padua del Pueblo Quemado Chapel, ca. 1935. (Photo by T. Harmon Parkhurst; Photo Collections, Museum of New Mexico, Santa Fe)

Interior of the San Antonio Chapel as it appeared when Brown wrote his description. (Photo by T. Harmon Parkhurst, ca. 1935; Photo Collections, Museum of New Mexico, Santa Fe)

Brown's maternal grandparents, Vicente Ferrer Martínez and Juanita Montoya de Martínez of Taos, and his mother, Cassandra. (Erie Photo Co., Pueblo, Colorado, 1870s?)

Lorin W. Brown, Sr., at his printing press, ca. 1890.

San Gerónimo Day at Taos Pueblo, early 1890s. Lorin W. Brown, Sr., is seated in the wagon with daughter Amy on his lap.

Lorin W. Brown, Sr.

Cassandra Martínez de Brown at approximately age seventeen.

The Brown children (l. to r.): Floy Violet, Amy Crawford, Vincent Ferrer, Roy Douglas, Lorin William (front), and Bascom Howell. (Photo by E. K. and W. D. Porter, Sterling, Kansas, ca. 1904)

Animal musicians carved by José Dolores López, who sold these intricately carved toys at the annual Spanish Market in Santa Fe. (Collection of the Spanish Colonial Arts Society, Inc., in the Museum of International Folk Art, a unit of the Museum of New Mexico, Santa Fe; photo by Charles L. Briggs)

Screen door carved by José Dolores López, possibly for his own home. The artist's initials and home village dominate the design, while chip-carving and floral inserts increase its complexity. (E. Boyd Memorial of the International Folk Art Foundation; Museum of International Folk Art, a unit of the Museum of New Mexico, Santa Fe, New Mexico; photo by Charles L. Briggs)

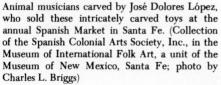

A kneeling José Dolores López displays his carvings. (Photo Collections, Museum of New Mexico, Santa Fe)

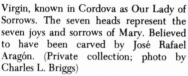

Virgin, known in Cordova as Our Lady of Sorrows. The seven heads represent the seven joys and sorrows of Mary. Believed to have been carved by José Rafael Aragón. (Private collection; photo by Charles L. Briggs)

Michael the Archangel, with sword and scales, by José Dolores López. Note the doweled joints, the careful modeling of the head, and the chip-carving on wings, sword, and scales. (Lepard Family Collection; on loan to the Museum of International Folk Art, a unit of the Museum of New Mexico, Santa Fe; photo by Charles L. Briggs)

St. Anthony of Padua, patron saint of Cordova, probably carved by José Rafael Aragón. José Dolores López repaired the image's fingers, repainted the head and hands, and painted his initials and the saint's name on the base. (Private collection; photo by Charles L. Briggs)

Cordova and the San Antonio Chapel viewed from the west, ca. 1900.

Cordova and the Quemado Valley viewed from the southern edge of the valley, 1977. The San Antonio Chapel appears to the left of center. (Photo by Charles L. Briggs)

Twenty-two Cordova residents, identified by Brown as members of the congregation of the Presbyterian Church, early 1900s.

Brown's mother Cassandra in later years, when she was married to Margarito López of Cordova. (Photo by Brooks Studio)

and who has been actively connected with all the mining ups and downs of the grant, who is the only one allowed free ingress and egress to the grant at all times. The reason for this is that he possesses knowledge of the location of a rich vein of gold-bearing ore. The owners of the grant hope that some day he will lead them to the location of this vein. But he is a very crafty and wise customer, and when conscious of spying eyes he will confine himself to washing very poor paying dirt out of the arroyos or the bed of the little stream which is found close to Dolores. He makes his camp within the ruined walls of what used to be the stone mansion of one of the owners of the mine when it was a thriving camp. Here he grinds the ore, which he has secretly brought in the previous night, in a large, old-fashioned mortar with a pestle shiny from much use. The resulting powdered rock he carries down to the stream where he washes out the gold in his pan. He is still making a very good living from his hidden gold vein and as yet the company has not been able to find out its location. It was this man who conceived the idea of washing the adobes from the abandoned houses in Dolores and securing much gold from them. I would name him the king of the *gambusinos* because he enjoys more privileges than the rest and has made a much better living from the hills of the Ortiz Grant than the others. (63)

> Honra y provecho no caben en un saco.
> (Honor and wealth seldom go together. [Literally:
>   "Honor and wealth do not fit in the same sack."]
>
> En la casa de la rica, ella manda y ella grita.
> (He who marries wealth may be sure she'll wear the
>   pants. [Literally, "In the rich woman's house, she
>   gives orders and screams"].) (100)
>
> El dinero es como sal en l'agua.
> ("Money is just like salt thrown in water.") (101)

Cooperation was more important than treasure, however. The old Spanish institution of compadrazgo *helped assure a close network of concerned relatives and neighbors.*

An institution that is peculiar to Latin Catholics and which exists here in New Mexico in full force is that of *compadre* and *comadre*. There is no English equivalent for these two words . . . which denote a relationship existing between individuals as a result of participation in different ceremonies of the Catholic Church. In every case this participation consists of sponsorship or assumption of supervision for the future welfare of a third party or parties. To illustrate: there are three types of compadres, to wit: *compadres de pila* ("of the baptism fount"), *compadres de primera comunión* ("of the first communion"), and *compadres de boda* or *casorio* ("of the wedding ceremony"). (42)

Three events that eclipse all others in the life of a villager of New Mexico, with the exception of his birth, are his baptism, his wedding, and his death. In the first and the last he is the center of attraction, while in the third he must share the spotlight with his future wife.

Baptism, one of the obligatory rites of the Catholic Church, is the occasion for much festivity, and preparations are begun from the very day of the baby's birth. However, in the case of a sickly babe whose hold on life seems to be very precarious, little or no preparation is made for celebrating the event. A mortal soul is in danger, and the hastily summoned *padrino* and *madrina* ("godfather" and "godmother") convey the child to the nearest priest, next door perhaps, or ten or twenty miles over mountain roads. But when there is no pressing need for haste, how different! First of all, the godparents must be decided upon and notified of their impending honor. It is esteemed an honor and one which is never refused, although entailing a little expense to the recipients.

In the case of a firstborn child, the selection of godparents is automatically fixed by custom. They are the paternal grandparents if the child is a boy, the maternal grandparents if the child is a girl. In accord with the belief that the child will develop the traits of his *padrino* or of her *madrina*, one can conceive of no worthier models for the child's future behavior than his or her own grandfather or grandmother. In the majority of cases this is fortunately so, but, even though human nature and behavior are what they are, the implication conveyed in not asking the grandparents to stand as sponsors at their granchild's christening is not risked. In requesting godparents for succeeding children this belief governs the choice to a great event. Favored in this respect are the brothers and sisters of the parents and the local *ricos* are frequently called upon to serve, thereby accumulating *compadres* and adding to their prestige and influence in party circles. In most cases the local *rico* and the political boss of a community are one and the same person, and they in time have bound the people of the community to them by so many economic and social ties that they are secure in a position of dominance for an entire lifetime.

On the day of christening, the baby, decked out in all of his new finery donated by the godparents, is transported by his *padrino* and *madrina* to the parish priest. If the latter is at some distance, an early start is necessary. (29)

I know of one case in which the baby was lost on the way to his christening. It was a cold morning and the godparents set out in a wagon from Cordova to Trampas. The godparents, riding on the one seat of the wagon, were wrapped to the ears in blankets and woolen mufflers, while the baby rode in an improvised bed on the floor of the wagon. The road was rough and the wagon pitched and jolted as it rode over the frozen ground. During one of these violent lurches the baby bounced out and was not missed for quite a distance. On missing the baby, the team was turned back and urged to a faster pace while the anxious couple kept their gaze on the road ahead. Great was their relief upon finding the baby by the side of the road, crying lustily but otherwise unhurt. The cocoon of blankets in which it was wrapped had protected it from injury. (42)

The departing trio leave behind them a household busily engaged in preparations for their return. Adobe bake ovens, resembling beehives, have been lighted early in the morning. When the wood with which they have been plentifully stoked has burned down to a heap of coals glowing within their interiors, the women of the household appear with the bread, cakes, and cookies which have been molded and prepared for baking. The coals are raked out, the smooth clay floors are swept as clean of ashes as the pulsating heat will permit. One of the women tests the heat of the oven with a piece of wool held on the wooden paddle-like shovel which is used for placing bread in the oven. If the wool ignites and burns to a crisp, the cookies and sweet breads are baked first. They required a hot heat and a quick one. In a few minutes these are baked to a golden brown, and their place is taken by the round loaves of bread that can be left safely in the slightly cooled oven for their required length of time which their greater bulk needs for proper baking.

The tantalizing odors that emanate from the smoke hole of the oven draw the children to its vicinity to hover there until the contents are withdrawn, after the large flat stone which sealed the door has been shoved aside, tentatively at first to permit a hurried glimpse, then with finality when the bread is ascertained to be ready for removal. Indifferent to excited and exasperated commands to remove themselves from underfoot, the youngsters with shining eyes plead for a cookie or a *bizcochito,* or with nimble fingers snatch any which happen to roll off the shovel onto the ground, fleeing with it, dandling it from one hand to the other because of the heat it still retains. The one who has snatched the tempting morsel makes off pursued by the rest, much like the chick that has found a worm but must eat it on the run from the rest of the flock of persistent brothers and sisters. Bread baked thus, next to the clay floor of one of these earthen ovens, without benefit of a tin or iron pan or plate, has a succulence and earth-imparted flavor found in no other product of the baker's art.

While the bread has been baking, the older sisters and perhaps the young aunts of the babe have been appointed to decorate the house. This they have accomplished with the aid of lace curtains, embroidered scarves, and paper flowers whose bright and glowing colors would put the originals to shame. Gaily colored dishes hold candy, raisins, and smaller cakes and cookies—store-bought cookies with vari-colored frosting and the traditional *bizcochitos,* those ubiquitous cookies, rich and speckled with anise, dusted with sugar and cinammon, found on the refreshment tables of all Spanish feasts and without which a fiesta is sadly lacking in completeness. Bottles of soda pop, wine, whiskey, and *mistela* stand at attention beside these. (29)

After the christening the feast awaits the godparents at the home of the child's parents. Here the baby's name is disclosed and friends and neighbors are called in to help celebrate the occasion. Guests are courteously escorted to the decorated tables. The healths of the baby, godparents, and parents are drunk. Then everybody's health is drunk in turn and soon drinking is the order of the day without thought of healths or health.

In one corner are the village musicians improvising and singing couplets in honor of everybody present to the accompaniment of a couple of guitars. The singer is very skillful in his improvisation, using the name of the party honored in a rhymed stanza full of personal praise or sometimes bringing in personal allusions understood and applauded by everyone present. As each person is honored in song he or she cheerfully drops a donation in the hat placed by the musicians for that purpose. "Let us enjoy ourselves, tomorrow we may die," is the general sentiment on such occasions, and an impromptu dance may prolong the festivities until the first roosters crow.

These christening feasts deplete the family purse. In the case of a poor man it may mean the mortgaging of his little home to the local money lender or pledging the results of three months' labor. *Pero no le hace*, but never mind, the feast was enjoyed by all and the child was given a good send-off into life.

Now the relationship between the godparents and the parents of the child is that of *compadre* with the men and *comadre* with the women. The godparents have undertaken the moral and material welfare of the child until his maturity at least, and in many cases throughout life. . . . The new *compadres* treat each other by that title from then on and by no other, even though they are brothers. This new bond is more sacred and supersedes all others. A new ritual of courtesy takes place in all their contacts, both social and business. Intimate knowledge of each other's affairs is never disclosed. This is truer about the *compadres* than the *comadres*, for there is a saying which shows that women are the same everywhere: *Cuando las comadres se 'nojan sale la verdad* ("Truth will out when *comadres* quarrel").

When a child reaches the age of seven or thereabouts, godparents are solicited to be sponsors at his first communion when he is accepted into the church. Previous to the ceremony his future godparents see to his instruction in the catechism and afterwards undertake supervision of his spiritual and moral welfare.

Yet another set of *compadres* is the couple asked to stand up with the bride and groom when they are married. This couple is chosen by the bride's parents. They attend the young couple at confession, before the altar, and enthroned on a platform at the marriage dance. Their obligation thereafter consists in giving advice and counsel and patching up quarrels and the temporary separations seemingly inevitable to married life.

The most highly regarded and most strictly kept *compadre*

relationship is the one of the christening ceremony. In earlier years these relationships of *compadre* and children to godparents made for a very respectful and obedient society. The younger folks were very careful of their behavior and speech before their elders, and before their godparents especially. Disagreements or disputes arising between families of *compadres* were usually settled peacefully after a gathering of the elders of both sides. The issue was discussed at length and a compromise or decision was arrived at.

Politically, the father of a large family may be quite a power purely through the number of his *compadres*. Many *políticos* cultivate *compadre*-ships, I might say at every opportunity, as a means of strengthening their popularity throughout their bailiwicks. A very popular doctor in Taos used to delight in acquiring godsons wholesale. By paying the nominal fee exacted by the Catholic Church for first communicants, he would stand as sponsor for as many as ten children at a time. His admiring *compadres* were scattered all over Taos County. This custom colored the social life of a community, tending to make for an orderly and peaceful existence through its observance. (42)

Community concern was also evident in the treatment of abnormal villagers.

A belief common among the Spanish-speaking population in New Mexico colors the treatment of congenital idiots, imbeciles, or mental cases of any kind. They are regarded in the same light as an infant, insofar as their conception of the difference between good and evil is concerned. According to them, when an infant dies there is no cause for grief. His parents and friends know that heaven has gained one more *angelito* ("little angel"), and the body is accompanied to the grave by musicians playing gay and lively airs instead of sad and doleful *alabados* as in the case of an adult. In such a light are idiots or imbeciles regarded. No matter how long they live they are *inocentes* or innocents, and their unquestioned assurance of a place in heaven is acknowledged by all.

Onésimo was such as these, and he lived in a remote mountain village in northern New Mexico. One of several brothers and sisters all afflicted in the same manner, he was the only survivor when I first knew him and his native village. The others had succumbed to a diphtheria plague a few years before, which had taken two out of every ten children in the stricken village.

Not only was Onésimo an idiot, but his body was grotesquely misshapen, hunchbacked, with terribly twisted hands and feet. He was a pitiful figure to behold. Owing to his deformities, the clothes he wore were all too large for him. Overalls had to be bought for him large enough so they could be drawn up so the bib came close under his chin to be sure that the suspenders would not slip off his rounded back. With shoes several sizes too large for him, the only kind that would fit over his feet, and somebody's cast-off hat on his bullet-shaped, shaven head, he was easily a figure to frighten anyone not used to him.

Yet even the children from infancy became used to him and never mistreated him. This shambling figure could be expected to enter any home at any time, for he ran at large through the village. Thus it was that the children were early imbued with the idea that he was a *pobre inocente* who should be treated kindly. If he entered a home while the family was seated around the table, the children were taught to carry a piece of tortilla and a dish of food to the corner in which he sat. For he was an *inocente,* and his presence safeguarded the home village from harm and violence. Good fortune and a favorable entry in the recording angel's books were the reward for kindly acts toward Onésimo. So it was that he was made room for and accepted with good-natured tolerance wherever he appeared. He would take his place at any and all gatherings—at mass, at a wake, or with the Penitentes as they made the pilgrimages to Calvary or the village church. He would be the only male attending the vesper services of the Niñas de María during the month of May.

Onésimo was a great handshaker and gave cause for amusement when, holding up his precariously hanging overalls with one hand, he shuffled up to the priest while he was saying mass and insisted on shaking hands with him. As a confirmed handshaker, he appointed himself official greeter for all newcomers or visitors to the village. Being from a village which attracted many tourists, Onésimo was kept busy greeting them whether they liked it or not. No sooner did a Harvey car or any other vehicle stop and its passengers start to alight than Onésimo would advance in his usual form, left hand aiding his suspenders and right hand extended in greeting. Many were the involuntary shrieks and shrinking retreats, but Onésimo insisted on shaking hands with each and every one. Then, grimacing and bowing, he would wave his right hand and repeat over and over again *"all' está."* Whatever he meant by these words was not known, and, although they can be translated as "there it is," they did not always suit the occasion. The only other intelligible words he ever spoke were *"qué bonito, ¿no?"* These he would ask when he was playing on his violin, which consisted of any two sticks he would happen to pick up.

Onésimo's love for music was very great. He never failed to accompany the musicians as they circled the narrow streets, playing as they went to let the people know that there would be a dance that night. This form of invitation to a dance was called *sacando el gallo,* or bringing out the rooster. The origin of the name I do not know, but the procession would form at the home of the fiddler, who, because he was lame, rode a led horse. The donors of the dance followed close behind the musicians, with a group of shouting boys behind them. They would wend their way around the town and wind up at the dance hall. Thus the town folks knew which dance hall to go to that night, whether *la sala de arriba o la de abajo* ("the upper or lower dance hall").

As I said, Onésimo was part of this procession, all the while playing his mute violin. No doubt he thought he was contributing as much as the fiddler or more, and he would pause only when someone would shout *"baila Onésimo,* dance!" Then he would stop and with right arm encircling an imaginary partner, execute a few steps in good time with the music. Then at a rambling, shuffling pace he would catch up and resume his role of musician.

At the dance that night Onésimo would be found sitting on the platform with the musicians, playing with them. He seemed to have a great admiration for the lame fiddler and would always sit beside him. Perhaps it was because this fiddler showed Onésimo more kindness than others. He it was, being the town barber, who always cut Onésimo's hair and shaved him. He also kept Onésimo fairly decent by supplying him with shirts and overalls and seeing that his wife kept Onésimo's clothes washed. Perhaps the fiddler, being lame, felt a stronger bond of sympathy for that misshapen lump of humanity than the rest. Also, being a gambler, the fiddler was superstitious enough to keep on good terms with good fortune by treating this unfortunate *inocente* as he did.

So it was that Onésimo enjoyed nothing more than presiding over the musicians' platform at a *baile,* leering and grimacing at the dancers as they swept by and often bursting into wild laughter as the tempo of the music increased. He was an institution at a dance, and his contribution to the merriment was accepted by all.

After the dance broke up he would shuffle along with the musicians to the dingy little pool room. Here, while they would drink up part of their night's pay, Onésimo was not forgotten and came in for his share in the form of a can of sardines and a box of crackers.

If, as usually was the case, gambling followed the dance, Onésimo would sit in a corner by the fire. There, barely distinguishable in the shifting shadows cast by the eager players as they hovered and stooped around the gambling table, he would squat gibbering and talking to himself. He was a strange god of chance to be given small gifts in the form of candy, cigarettes, pop, or cookies by the fortunate players. His beneficent influence was wooed with the same gifts by those whose luck had turned against them. Every so often the monte dealer would gather his cards to him or turn them over to a helper and leave his place at the table for a drink at the little counter which served as a bar. He would get his drink but never failed to give Onésimo a dime or some other coin or a gift. Onésimo did not know the value of money but treasured these shining pieces of metal in his pockets. His widowed father would search his pockets and put to good use the coins which Onésimo received from tourists, gamblers, and others.

Onésimo's life was not one of any hardship. He was fed and clothed and treated as one who could withhold the evil hand of misfortune from both the individual and the community. In the winter he crept into the warmest corner of any dwelling he chose, and in summer he would be seen sleeping in the shade of some tree or dwelling with his pockets stuffed with pieces of tortilla and bread, contributions from all over the village. Awakening from a nap, he would sit up and start munching on some of his provisions. Later he would join the children at play or wander down to the river for a swim with them.

Everything remained peaceful in the little village, with no untoward happening out of the ordinary. But about five years ago Onésimo sickened. He crawled into his bed at home and seemed just to give in to his strange sickness. No ministrations helped him. The neighbors were more helpful in his case because he was Onésimo and because his helpless father knew little about household tasks and had learned less during his widowed life.

Dios se acordó de Onésimo, God remembered Onésimo. He was carried to the graveyard with an accompaniment of music, for was he not an *inocente* destined to go straight to heaven?

Shortly after Onésimo's death there was a killing in the place.

True, neither the man killed nor the killer were of the village, but it gave the place a bad name, linking it with its neighboring villages in Rio Arriba County which were notorious for the killings committed in them with appalling frequency. Also the crops failed for two years, and work outside in the sheep and railroad camps became very scarce. People would say, "Since Onésimo died we are having bad luck; money is scarce, work is not to be found, and now this killing in our town."

The lame fiddler brooded more than anyone else over the death of his mascot. We might say his lucky talisman was dead. He took to drinking more than usual, and in this state his inflamed mind became more alive and suspicious of the indiscretions of his pretty and flirtatious wife. In a moment of insane fury he caught the object of his suspicions and, dragging him to the floor where he could discard his crutches and use his powerful arms, he cut his victim's throat. Onésimo's death had removed a kindly protection from the village and loosed a malignant spirit that bred discontent and hatred with fatal results. (72)

> Mucho vá de Pedro a Pedro.
> (There is wide difference between man and man.
>> [Literally, "There's a wide gulf between one Peter and another."])
> Uno come la fruta con gusto, al otro le da dentera.
> (One man's meat is another man's poison. [Literally,
>> "One man eats fruit with pleasure, another gets a toothache."]) (100)
>
> En la tierra de los ciegos el tuerto es rey.
> ("Among the blind the one-eyed is king.") (1)

Besides fiestas, bailes, *horse racing, and gambling, village men also enjoyed playing ball games.*

This game is similar to ice hockey and is known as shinny among English-speaking school boys. It has been played in New Mexico for many years and is a favorite competitive sport between rival villages and between rival groups in the same village, e.g., between the married men and the single men, the fat men and the lean men, and so forth.

I have seen a game between the men of Taos and the Indians of the Taos Pueblo which lasted for four consecutive Sundays. The goals were the Taos square and the river which divides the Taos Pueblo. A marker was placed at the spot where sundown found the ball, and the following Sunday the game was resumed from that spot. In this case the Indians were successful in driving the ball across their goal line early on the afternoon of the fourth Sunday, thus winning for themselves the purse which had been bet collectively as well as many individual bets of ponies, sheep, blankets, and so on. The spectators who followed the course of the game across fields and over hills and rivers were as greatly exhilarated as the players themselves, for it took a good pony to follow a fleet Indian. With braids streaming behind him, the Indian would bound after the ball, giving it further impetus as he overtook it on its flight toward the Pueblo.

The game is played with curved sticks shaped something like a hockey stick. These sticks are fashioned from green oak or wild chokecherry (*capulín*) branches. The curved end is shaped by inserting the end of the stick into a fire and bending into the desired shape while it is still hot. It is then firmly tied and, upon being loosened after a few days, will permanently retain the desired shape. The ball is made of rawhide sewn all the way around except for an opening through which wool is stuffed into the ball, after which it is sewn up. The ball is seldom round but usually has a semi-oval shape.

To play the game, the players are divided into two teams. The ball is placed on a "tee" between the two goals. There is no set measurement for the distance between goals; this is determined beforehand by the players themselves. The leaders of the two teams stand over the ball with their *chuecos* ("shinny sticks") poised over their shoulders. At a given signal, each strives to knock the ball toward his goal and the game is on.

A player may pick the ball up in his hand and bat it toward his goal line if he has the time and opportunity, but usually the opposition is so close on his heels that the best he can do is take a hasty swipe at the ball and follow in its wake. Another reason that the above method is not practiced is that it results in badly bruised knuckles or shins. Another good rule to follow is to keep on your own side of the ball because your opponents have full authority to strike you on the shins if they catch you trying to drive the ball from the wrong side. Hence the saying "shinny on your own side."

This is the reason that a lefthanded player does not care for *chueco*.

As in ice hockey, the side making the most goals in a previously determined period of play wins the match. (37)

Children imitated their elders in play. The younger ones enjoyed simple circle and central person games.

Gallinita ciega ("the little blind hen"). This game may be played by any number of children, one of whom takes the part of the little blind hen. She gropes around as if blind and imitates a hen scratching for food. The rest circle around her and ask these questions:

All: *"Gallinita ciega, ¿qué andas haciendo?"* ("Little blind hen, what are you doing?")

Hen: *"Ando buscando unos cunquitos."* ("I am looking for some cornmeal grounds.")

All: *"¿Pa' quién (Para quién)?"* ("For whom?")

Hen: *"Pa' mis pollitos."* ("For my little chicks.")

All: *"¿Y me dará uno?"* ("And will you give me one?")

Hen: *"No."*

All: *"Pues piérdete."* ("Get lost then.")

At this time all the rest of the children scatter and the "little blind hen" chases them. Whichever child she catches becomes in turn the "little blind hen," and the game continues anew.

El florón ("the large flower"). In this game all of the children except one seat themselves in a row and one of their number hides some small object such as a ring or button in his hand. He extends his clenched hands for the other to guess which holds the hidden object and all recite this verse:

El florón anda en las manos	In these hands the flower is hidden
En las manos del Señor	Hidden in the hands of the Lord,
El que no lo adivine	He who does not guess where it is
Se queda pa' tontón.	Is still a big, big fool.

If the guesser does not hit on the hand holding the ring, the next child in line hides the ring, and so on until the one in the center hits out the hand holding the ring. He then trades places with the one in whose hand he discovered the ring, and the game continues (74)

Infants were lulled with songs like the one Brown collected from Mrs. Zoraida V. Montoya of Taos:

El camarón. A whimsical nonsensical song whose words and tune lent themselves to a widespread use as a lullaby.

En el mar en donde andaba	In the sea where I did stay
Bajo del agua	Far down below the waves
Cerca de un mes	For a month and a day,
Vide unos pescaditos	Some tiny, tiny fish I saw
Tan chiquitos	They were so very tiny
Como la punta de un alfiler.	As small as the head of a pin.
Ay! cómo quemaban	And oh! how they could sting.
Agua por Dios pedía	For water I did pray
Y un camarón dijo	A simpering shrimp did say:
"Yo le serviré café."	"Some coffee I will bring." (120)

Another popular pastime was riddling and posing problems to anyone interested in matching wits.

¿Quién es?

> Mi madre es una criatura
> Que no tiene entendimiento.
> Ni luz ni conocimiento,
> No puede hablar porque es muda.
> Y para formarme a mí
> Hicieron mi sepultura.

Respuesta: La tierra. Cuándo Dios formó a Adán de un puño de tierra, dejando un pozo la cual explica la referencia a la sepultura.

What is it?

> My mother is a creature
> Who has no understanding.
> Neither light nor knowledge,
> She cannot talk because she is dumb.
> And to form me
> They made my sepulchre.

Answer: The earth. When God made Adam out of a handful of dirt, leaving a hole which explains the reference to the sepulchre.

Redondito, redondón, sin agujero, sin tapón. El huevo.
("Round and large circle without a hole or cork. The egg.")

Rita, Rita, que en el monte grita y en su casa calladita. La hacha.
("Rita, Rita, on the mountain it roars and at home is quiet. The
    axe.") (3)

Pregunta:

Allá en el alto veloz
Te pregunto con anhelo
Antes de Dios y la luz
¿Quién entro primero al cielo?

Question:

Up there in the infinite heights
Eagerly I ask you
What first entered into heaven
Even before God and light?

Respuesta:

Si estudias con gran anhelo
Escucha compositor
Antes de Dios y la luz
El Divino Resplandor.

Answer:

If you've thought diligently
Hear me my poet
Before God and light
The Divine Radiance entered there.

Pregunta:

En argumento capaz
Le pregunto al más agudo
¿Qué cosa quiso hacer Dios
Quiso pero no pudo?

Question:

Reasoning most intelligently
I will ask the most brilliant
What was it God wished to do
Would have but could not?

Respuesta:

En el Río del Jordán
Vide a Cristo de rodilla
Bautizándolo San Juan
Porque El mismo no podía.

Answer:

On the banks of the River Jordan
I saw Christ on one knee
Being baptized by Saint John
Because He could not baptize Himself.
    (4)

Problema:

Seis saltos de un perro
Equivalen a cuatro de una zorra;
De la zorra dos saltos
Equivalen a nueve de un mono;
Un salto del perro,
Dos del mono y catorce de la zorra
Componen cien varas;
Lo que salta cada uno lo ignoro.

Problem:

Six leaps of a dog
Equal four of a fox
Two of the fox
Equal nine of a monkey;
One leap of a dog
Two of a monkey and fourteen of a fox
Total a hundred *varas;*
But 'tis the distance each leaps I
    would know. (98)

*Storytelling was also a favorite amusement. Brown recorded a
number of folktales, among them a version of "El caballo de siete*

colores" from his mother (33) and "El león y el hombre" from
Santiago S. Mata of Santa Fe (76). His most compelling narrator
was the recognized wise woman of Cordova, Tía Lupe.

One of the most beloved characters in Cordova was known to
young and old as Tía ("Aunt") Lupe. Guadalupe Martínez was her
formal name, but she was aunt to the entire village, a great-
hearted, simple, understanding soul to whom all turned for advice
or consolation. Her vast store of wisdom and knowledge, gained
through a long life rich in experience, was for anyone who needed
it, and she dispensed it with humor, grace, and tolerance. It was
her skillful blending of these, whether for spiritual or physical
need, that made her the counselor, guide, and healer of the
community.

When Tía Lupe was long past seventy, her small, slender frame
was still erect, and her bearing was that of authority derived from
inner integrity. Her small, finely shaped hands were gnarled by
many years of washing wheat in ice-cold water, working in the
fields, sewing, spinning—all the countless tasks in which those hands
had been busy, whether in her own home duties or helping
neighbors garner their harvest or keep their homes in order. Her
fine features, straight nose, and generous mouth above a firm chin
gave evidence, even when full of wrinkles, that she had been a
beauty. Her light complexion proved her a *rubia*, as redhaired
women are called. But it was in her clear, sparkling brown eyes
that she was known for what she was, so alive they were, so full of
the zest and joy of life, always alight with interest and ready to
show concern on hearing of someone's distress, the light leaping
higher when hearing of another's good fortune. She was a picture of
neatness, from her center-parted hair, brushed back and gathered
in a smooth knot, to her small feet encased in soft black shoes. And
her voice! That was as full of light as her eyes, and her laugh was a
joy to hear because of its infectious quality.

Tía Lupe was all things to all people. She had a youthful quality
and an understanding of the young that drew them in groups to her
door. A recalcitrant child changed into an obedient and loving one
under her care. She knew all ages and sympathized with them, and
her breadth of understanding seemed to encompass all situations
and all phenomena.

Tía Lupe was left an orphan when she was six. She was born in

Cordova, where her parents died in a smallpox epidemic. She was adopted by Don José Chávez and his wife, Doña Carmel, of Chimayo. Don José was wealthy, reckoned by standards in those days, and maintained a large household of servants and various employees. He was engaged in the overland trade with Mexico and was absent from home three to four months at a time. Lupita, the little orphan, soon became a favorite with her foster parents, and during Don José's long absences she was Doña Carmel's inseparable companion. Before long she was loved by them as dearly as if she had been born to them, and she was treated as their own child.

Lupita moved happily and helpfully through the activities of that large establishment, gaining firsthand knowledge of life in the home of a *rico* of that period. A large number of servants was necessary to the smooth management of so large a household; many of these were Indian slaves bought outright by Don José or acquired through barter. Those engaged in domestic duties were under the watchful eye of the mistress. Some of the servants worked in the fields, some tended stock, those working out of doors being supervised by a trusted *mayordomo* who managed the estate while the master was away. Lupita learned that the relations between master and servant were almost those existing between parents and children. The older servants, especially, treated their master and mistress with great familiarity, although there was a point of propriety beyond which they never went. Don José and Doña Carmel regarded the servants as part of the family, keeping them after age and illness rendered them no longer able to work. Their attitude was one of paternalism throughout. . . .

The years in that fascinating household were full of wonder, but they were few in number, for at fifteen Guadalupe fell in love with Agapito Martínez and married him. It was a tragic experience. Agapito was so possessive in his feeling for her that his jealousy made him mistreat her, and she led a very unhappy life. Agapito threatened her life many times. Finally, in desperation and unable to endure her misery any longer, she left her home and husband and went to Santa Fe, where she found work in the home of a pioneer family named Staab. She became so much a part of this family and so endeared herself to them by the faithful and efficient way she worked, that she came in time to be treated as one of them.

There was much excitement in Santa Fe in those days, for

merchants in the Midwest were exploiting this market and finding it profitable. Lupita saw the gaily decorated drays that brought the first bock beer of the spring into the town; saw the high-stepping horses with beribboned, shiny harnesses; saw the high-hatted driver perched atop the pyramided kegs as the horses clop-clopped over the rutted, dusty streets and pulled up in front of the old Exchange Hotel.

After eight years in Santa Fe, Lupita moved to Cordova and settled in the little adobe room close by the church where she lived so many years. Its almost austere neatness and cleanliness was relieved by the cheerful glow in her fireplace with its escalloped guard wall. The fire that always burned there typified the warmth and love in Tía's heart, at both of which flames people came to warm themselves.

It was fitting that one so highly regarded should be entrusted with the keys to the church, should be responsible for the cleaning and dusting of the interior. To her, more than to most, it was the actual dwelling place of God, and it was her joy and satisfaction to see that all of its appointments were furbished and free of dust. She lavished special care on the various images of the saints, whom she loved and with whom she carried on a loving, though familiar conversation. Each was a distinct personality to her, and she knew the responsibilities each had assumed. She would tell San Antonio, as she gave the child in his arms a loving pat on the cheek, "Be careful with that child; do not let him fall, good San Antonio." She would promise the Virgin a new dress because the old one she wore had a spot of melted wax from the taper that stood by it. San Miguel, with the writhing serpent underfoot, would receive the most enthusiastic and admiring praises for his courage and heroism in subduing the monster, and he would also be admonished: "¡Ay, ten ese feo, no lo dejes ir!" ("Keep that ugly one underfoot; do not turn him loose!")

Then she shook an admonitory finger in the face of Santa Inés and said, "¡Mira! ('Look!') I will not make you that new dress if you do not help my nephew Manuel find his burro so his family will not lack wood." At this an unobserved witness chuckled, whereupon Tía Lupe turned with an exclamation: "¡Válgame Dios, qué rebato me dites!" ("God save me, what a fright you gave me!") Then, "How long have you been watching?" When reassured, she was asked, "Are you not afraid of the good saint's anger if you treat her that way?" And Tía Lupe said charmingly, "No, I didn't mean it, and Santa Inés knew that I didn't." Just the same, Tía Lupe made haste to light a fresh candle in front of Santa Inés, whose aid is sought in locating animals which have strayed or in finding lost objects. Then she continued. "The saints can and will punish us if we do harm to them or to any of God's children."

Just then Manuel and Shon, on one of their periodic sprees, reeled past the church door arm in arm. "See that Shon?" demanded Tía Lupe. "His grandfather was one of the best *santeros* in the country. One day I was helping Shon's grandmother winnow some wheat. Shon's grandfather, *el difunto* Antonio—may God give him peace!—had stood three large *santos* out in the patio to dry, having just finished painting them. A pair of no good *borrachos,* just like those two, came by. One of them glanced over and saw the saints. He called his friend's attention to them with a wavering finger and remarked: 'Look at those infernally large saints!' The other looked in that direction, then, greatly perturbed, commanded his friend to whisper, saying: 'Keep quiet! Don't let them hear you! Don't you know that the saints are the very devil for punishing one?' "

Laughing heartily at her own joke, Tía Lupe stepped from the church and rolled and lighted her corn husk cigarette, her face still wreathed in smile wrinkles. With her the saints were human beings, of exalted station and with great power for good, but with human failings that endeared them, perhaps much more on that account, to her. Many were the tales she told of the saints. . . . When the tales were about their righteous and charitable acts, she was always careful to point out the precept or moral and emphasize it with some recollection of an experience of her own or that of another. When the tale would provoke a laugh at the expense of the saint, she would say *"Sí, los santos son gente como nosotros, no más que tienen el oído de Dios para rogar por nosotros."* ("The saints are human like the rest of us, except that they have access to God's ear and so can intercede for us.") (116)

Saints' legends, such as the one about Santa Rita which Brown collected from sixty-year-old Amalia Kahn of Santa Fe (114), and anecdotes about the vagaries of family santos were popular subjects of conversation and narration. Tía Lupe often told about St.

Christopher acquiring his name and about St. Peter losing the keys to heaven.

How San Cristóbal Came By His Name:

"*Mira qué bonita medalla de San Cristóbal,*" said Tía Lupe as she pointed proudly to a medal of St. Christopher above her mantel. The medal was the one usually carried in automobiles by those desiring the protection of this patron of travelers. It had been given her by one of the couriers. "And do you know how San Cristóbal came by his name?" she asked. "No? Well, this is how it was:

"One day a little child was playing on the banks of a mighty river. This was in a country on the other side of the sea (*el otro lado del mar*). While the child was playing, a strange man came up and spoke to him. The child replied without fear because there was something, a light, in the stranger's face that made the thought of fear impossible. The man was *un hombre muy bonito!*

"The stranger said, I am *Cristo,* and I want you to carry me to the other side of this river.'

"The child thought there was nothing strange about this. The man perched on the little lad's shoulders—how that could be I do not know—and the child stepped into the stream. The water was very swift and strong, but the little boy had been given superhuman strength because of the sanctity of his burden. Nevertheless, in midstream, the current tugged harder than ever and he found his burden great.

"He called out, '*¡Cristo, válgame Dios, cómo pesas!*' ('God save me, but you are very heavy Christ!')

"The man heard, but His only answer was to urge the child on. Several times the boy called out in the same words: '*¡Cristo, válgame Dios, cómo pesas!*' When he finally reached the other side and his passenger once more stood on land, he was addressed thus: 'For this deed and for the words you spoke to me on the way over, you shall be known as Cristo-val, Cristóbal. You shall be very strong and carry many people across this and other rivers, and you will come to dwell with me as one of my saints.' "

Tía Lupe continued: "San Cristóbal, you know, earned a saint's crown by helping people across raging torrents. He was a giant compared with other people and carried them on his shoulders, sometimes breasting waist-high torrents with them. At other times he carried them in his arms. What miracles God can work if He only wishes! Who could believe that a small child could carry a grown man across a river? *Pero alla 'sta quien* ('But there is the source of all power')," and she pointed eloquently upward.

"It is a true tale," she said with conviction, "because to God all things are possible."

How Saint Peter Lost the Keys to Heaven:

One day St. Peter was sitting outside the gates of heaven. There were not many people coming in; all of them seemed to be going the other way. While he was sitting there thinking and watching the great crowds that descended toward the great columns of sulphurous smoke that marked the entrance to the pit, an elegantly dressed gentleman approached him. This visitor was clad in a fine black broadcloth suit with a gold watch chain across his vest. He was very suave and engaging and St. Peter gladly listened to him. He had nothing else to do; all the souls seemed to be lost ones; nobody bothered him to open the gates on that day.

Finally, after a long and interesting conversation, the stranger handed St. Peter a fine cigar. St. Peter accepted the cigar, in the lighting of which he employed both hands. In doing so, he left the keys to heaven lying loose on his lap. This was evidently what the stranger wanted, for he snatched the keys and vanished in a cloud of smoke, leaving a strong stench of sulphur behind him. It was then that St. Peter realized that the fine gentleman was none other than Satan himself. Desperate with grief and rage St. Peter railed against the Devil, but it was useless.

Fearing what God would say to him when the loss was made known, St. Peter went back to earth. Seated on a rock by the side of a road, he began to weep bitterly at the plight in which the Devil had placed him. An old woman passed and asked what his trouble was.

"None of your business, old woman," was the saint's exasperated reply.

"Tell me, maybe I can help you," offered the crone, undaunted by the saint's rudeness.

"How can an old woman, *colita de ratón* like you, help me?" The poor old dame's braids did resemble rat tails, they were so thin and meager. ("Just like mine," Tía Lupe said with a laugh.)

Then St. Peter became ashamed of his behavior and told her how he had lost the keys.

"Take me with you to the gates of heaven; it may be that I can help you."

St. Peter took the old lady with him as she had requested. On their way to heaven they were overtaken by a terrible storm and arrived very wet and bedraggled. There were many saved souls awaiting St. Peter, seeking entrance to heaven. The old lady walked up to the gates and opened them with ease using the crucifix of her rosary. St. Peter gladly let her pass in, knowing that she must have been sent by God to help him in his plight and to teach him a lesson in humility. As the old woman walked through the gates, she was transformed into an angel, and then St. Peter knew that God had sent her to help him, and more than ever he repented his hasty and angry words. (116)

Brown recorded a visit with Tía Lupe which illuminates her treatment of the saints' images and the depth of her faith in their efficacy.

Strolling aimlessly through the most deserted streets of the little village of Cordova one afternoon, I stopped in the open doorway of Tía Lupe's one-room adobe home. There was a storm coming up, one of those sometimes violent electrical mountain storms following a spell of hot weather.

I was shocked and surprised to see this pious old lady engaged in a sacrilegious act so contrary to my knowledge of her simple and sincere love and veneration for the saints. With a very blunt butcher knife she was endeavoring to slice a portion lengthwise from the side of a *bulto* or a wooden figure of Santa Bárbara. This battered figure showed signs of previous mutilations of like nature, and a rich resinous odor was released in the little room by this recent operation, which had been successfully concluded before I had gotten over my surprise. . . .

¿Qué tiene Tía? What are you doing with poor Santa Bárbara? She will punish you for mistreating her so."

"No, *hijo*. Come in and I will show you what I am doing."

As I stepped in through the door the storm broke outside, and a flash of lightning lit up the little room.

"*María Santísima y Santa Bárbara nos libre,*" was Tía Lupe's audible prayer. "See, now I will protect my little *casita* and all in it from lightning."

So saying the old lady stooped over and placed the sliver of wood from the saint's figure in the fireplace. The bed of coals already there ignited the rich pitch pine sliver, making a bright little blaze. Making the sign of the cross while her lips moved in silent prayer, Tía Lupe next seated herself on a wooden bench in the fireside corner. After she had rolled a corn husk cigarette she made the following observations:

"Santa Bárbara should be prayed to in time of storms, but in the way I have shown you she is more sure protection. For many years I guarded myself and my *casita* in times of storms in the way I have shown you. When Padre Ramón told me to remove Santa Bárbara from the altar to make way for a new santo given by Don Matías, I brought her home. I told Santa Bárbara how I was going to use her and ever since she has been my sure protection."

That was the explanation I received for that seeming irreverent treatment of the saint's image.

"But don't the saints punish us sometimes?" I asked, wishing to hear the other side of this interesting question.

"The blessed saints do punish as well as protect, so we must be careful how we speak of them and treat them," was her answer. (117)

The lessons which Tía Lupe gleaned from the lives of the saints provided her with perfect examples of personal conduct. Brown's description of the esteem in which Cordova held Tía Lupe suggests that the saintliness of her charges must have been contagious.

Throughout her life in Cordova, Tía Lupe earned the gratitude of the whole village by her willingness to help in any time of distress. She was the first to offer aid to an overburdened mother or to the ailing and infirm, so it was not strange that during the last years of her life she never lacked for food or wood. There was always some loving neighbor who would leave a load of neatly split wood on her doorstep at night so that when she awoke it would be the first thing she saw. If she knew or suspected the identity of the donor, she would hasten to his or her home to help at whatever tasks needed doing. Her friends wanted her to rest for the few years left to her long life, but she would and did pay or try to pay for everything she received, although her rich store of anecdotes and sprightly conversation would have made her welcome whether she had turned a hand at helping or not.

When a pinch of salt thrown out on the wind in the form of a cross was of no avail in turning aside a threatening hail storm, Tía Lupe knew that some sinner in the community had brought down this punishment from heaven as a reminder of the power of God's wrath. At these times, Tía Lupe would say humbly, *"Más merecemos, tatita Dios"* ("Even greater punishment have we deserved, our Father"). Her use of the child's name for father, *tatita,* showed clearly her attitude toward God and all His works, which was that of a child trusting in the omnipotence of the father who sees to all its needs with loving care, yet is stern and just in the face of disobedience.

When the *turistas* began coming in their cars to Cordova, Tía Lupe became a great favorite with the young ladies who acted as guides in charge of tours sent out to places around Santa Fe. Her stories, interpreted by the couriers, were so interesting that her home was made a regular stopping place on these visits. She was given many a handsome tip by these sightseers.

When she would show these tips to a friend and offer a manufactured cigarette that was also a gift, she would say, *"¡Ay qué gente tán rica! Son de los estados me dijo la señorita"* ("What people! So wealthy! The young lady tells me they are from the States"). The only name Tía Lupe knew for the rest of the United States was the old one of *"Los Estados,"* the designation for that part of the country that had been American territory before this southwestern area had been added. "And why is it that all *Americanos* are rich?" she would ask. "They must have asked for the gift of making money when God was handing out gifts to the different races, while we, *tontos* ('fools') that we are, all we asked for was love and large families."

There were a few envious ones in the village who coveted Tía Lupe's lucrative position as caretaker of the church and possessor of the keys. They made every effort to have her removed and eventually succeeded. The woman who took her place belonged to a family who did not mingle with the rest of the village in the same wholehearted manner that members of the community showed each other.

Poor Tía Lupe grieved over the loss of her guardianship. Who could take care of her saints as she had? Her many years of companionship with them had made their care an essential part of her life, of her very being. She tried not to show her grief. She attended all of the religious services as usual, but the critical glances she cast toward her former charges were quite obvious. A look of indignation or solicitude crossed her face if she detected dust where it should not be or a tiny embroidered skirt awry.

Tía Lupe failed perceptibly and finally succumbed to a bad cold, it was said, but it was a grieving heart that caused her death. She died fully conscious that the end was near and accepted death with complete resignation, just as she had accepted the trials life had brought her after she left her brutal husband. Those who knew her know that she died in the hope that she would rejoin her friends in heaven. (116)

Tía Lupe tended the santos *in the Cordova church, but almost every home had its own altar or* nicho *with the family's special holy objects and figures.*

Nichos—the word suggests our English one, "niche," and such the *nicho* was in very truth at first—purely a whitewashed niche carved or hollowed out of the adobe walls of the native homes of New Mexico. These arched niches with their decorations of little lace curtains and paper flowers held the home's most precious treasure, the image of some favorite saint, before whom votive candles were ever kept burning.

Later however, as more leisure was acquired, the native craftsman bent his efforts toward evolving a more fitting abode for his beloved image. Little chapel-like *nichos* of delicately carved wood were the result. The image, more impressively garbed in silk and beads, was moved into its new home amid much rejoicing.

When glass and tin were available, the craftsman turned his clever workmanship to these materials. *Nichos* then were made of tin on which were stamped and punched many beautiful designs. Square or gabled tin *nichos* with plain or painted glass sides now held the saint, perhaps a Santo Niño de Atocha seated on his little chair, who looked down on the busy household from behind the little glass door which kept dust from settling on the little figure and the flowers placed so reverently around him. (84)

Tía Lupe cared for chickens as well as santos.

Someone had given a villager a little pullet which grew up into a grey, bright-eyed little hen of an indefinite breed. She became quite a pet and pulled through the winter by appropriating for herself a corner in the woodshed. A very busy, bustling bunch of feathers—it was astonishing the amount of noise she could make as she proudly announced that there was a newly laid egg in the nest she had made in a dark corner under the woodpile.

Along in May she became broody and it was decided to "set her." Knowing little or nothing of the process involved, the villager also decided to consult Tía Lupe, who was wrapped up in the care of a dozen hens and a rooster which she housed in a curious structure resembling a small two-storied log cabin. The upper story of this unique hen house was reserved for the laying hens. By some means Tía Lupe knew which hens would lay during the day, and these were imprisoned in the upper story to fulfill their duty by their owner, while the rest of the flock were released to wander through the village.

Tía Lupe had a name for every one of her flock and could often be heard talking to them as if they were children. One hen she would scold for laziness, another for gluttony, while the rooster came in for his share of scolding for his arrogance and pride. Yet, if any dog or cat menaced any one of her brood, Tía Lupe would be after it brandishing her straw broom, naming the so-and-so in such searing terms that it was fortunate that the offending animals could not understand. Bystanders were greatly amused at these performances.

So to Tía Lupe for help. Oh yes! She would help.

"How many eggs are you going to set her with? Thirteen? *¡Bueno!* Quite a few for such a small hen, but we shall see."

First the nest should be made soft and comfortable, but above all two pieces of iron should be placed under it in the form of a cross.

"Why is this?" she was asked.

"That is to protect the eggs from being spoiled during a thunderstorm."

Two narrow strips of scrap-iron were found and placed to Tía Lupe's satisfaction under the nest. Next the eggs were carefully laid in the hollow place prepared for them.

The little grey hen had been underfoot all this time as if she

understood the significance of all this activity. Being shoved toward
the nest, she finally settled herself on the eggs after many
experimental turnings and querulous clucks.

"*Ahora falta nomás en comendarlos a San Lorenzo* ('Now we
must commend them to San Lorenzo')." So saying, Tía Lupe
recited this verse:

San Lorenzo barbas de oro	San Lorenzo of the golden beard
Te voy a pedir un favor	I am going to ask as a favor
Que esta gallina que he hechado	That this hen which I have just set
Saque todas pollas y un cantador.	May hatch all pullets and one songster (rooster).

"Now, time is all it takes. In this way you will have all pullets
but one, and you can have fresh eggs next winter."

Leaving the little grey hen peacefully settled on the nest, the
neighbor left, knowing there would be twenty-one days of waiting.

Tía Lupe evinced much interest as time progressed and was
present when the first chicks started pecking their way through
their shells. It would be hard to say who was prouder of the perfect
hatch of thirteen chicks—the little grey hen or the little grey
woman. And sure enough, later it was found that the brood
contained twelve pullets and one cockerel. (116)

*Tía Lupe had two favorite stories which she told to appreciative
audiences.*

Dame Fortune and Sir Money:

Dame Fortune and Sir Money were so infatuated with each
other that one was not seen without the other. Sir Money was
always following after Dame Fortune, so much so that public
criticism made them decide to get married.

Sir Money was a fat, chubby fellow with a round head fashioned
of gold from Peru, a torso made of Mexican silver, and legs shaped
from Santa Rita copper. He wore wooden clogs imported from
Spain. Dame Fortune was an eccentric person of unaccountable
whims and fancies, mean, and blinder than a mole.

No sooner had they partaken of the wedding cake than the pair
was at odds. The bride wanted to be the master, but Sir Money,
who was stubborn and proud, did not agree. Since both wished to
be the more powerful, they decided to put the matter to a test.

"Look," said the wife to her husband. "Do you see that dejected and hang-dog fellow seated in the shade of yonder cottonwood tree? Let us see which can bring to him the best good fortune."

The husband agreed. They headed toward the cottonwood tree, he waddling like a frog while she reached it in one leap. The man, an unfortunate creature who in his whole life had never seen either of them, opened his eyes in amazement when these two celebrities appeared before him.

"May God keep you," was Sir Money's greeting.

"And you also," replied the poor man.

"Do you not recognize me?"

"I do not know your Grace, but I am at your service," replied the poor man.

"Have you never seen my face?"

"Never, as God is my witness."

"Well then, have you no possessions?"

"Yes, my Lord. I have six sons naked as door bolts, with gullets as gaping as old socks, but as to possessions, I boast of only a 'have and eat' whenever I can get it."

"Well, why do you not work?"

"That is good! Because I cannot find work. I have such accursed luck that everything turns out as crooked as a goat's horn for me. Since I have been married it seems that everything goes wrong with me. The other day a property owner set me to digging a well on a contract, promising us two *doblones* when we should have reached water, but he would not turn loose a penny beforehand; that was the agreement."

"And well for him that he did so," was the sententious reply of Sir Money, "for the old saying, 'money paid in advance, excuse for broken arms,' is very true. On with your story, my good man."

"We put our whole souls into the digging of the well, for even though your Grace sees me as an apparent wreck of a human being, I am a man."

"Yes," said Sir Money, "I believe you."

"As I was saying, for all that we dug and dug as deep as we could, not a drop of water did we find. It seems as if the center of the earth had entirely dried up. Nothing did we find, Sir, from first to last, except a shoe cobbler."

"In the bowels of the earth, a cobbler?" exclaimed Sir Money, indignant that so lowly a neighbor should be found so near to his ancestral castle.

"No, sir," replied the poor man, "not in the bowels of the earth; rather on the other side. A country inhabited by other peoples."

"What peoples, man?"

"The antipodes, sir."

"I wish to do you a favor, friend," said Sir Money, as he pompously slipped a dollar into the poor man's hand.

At this the poor man thought he was dreaming, but he started off at a run so swift it looked as if he were flying. Joy lent wings to his feet, and he arrived almost immediately at a bake shop where he bought a loaf of bread. When he went to draw the dollar from his pocket he found only a hole there, through which the dollar had slipped without so much as a by-your-leave.

The poor man began a frantic search for the lost coin, but what hope could he have of finding it? The fat pig destined for the wolf's maw—not even San Antonio can save it from its fate. After losing his coin, he lost time in his vain search, and after much time lost, he lost his patience and began to curse his bad luck with all of the most fearful maledictions he could think of.

Dame Fortune doubled over with mirth while Sir Money's face became, if possible, more yellow with rage. He could see no other remedy for the situation except to reach into his pocket and give the unlucky one a gold piece.

The poor man was so overjoyed at this that his eyes almost popped out of his head. This time he did not go to the bake shop but to a store where he bought some cloth with which to give his wife and children at least a pretense of covering for their bodies. But when he offered the gold piece in payment the merchant flew into a rage, asserting that the gold was counterfeit, that its owner must be a counterfeiter, and that he was going to denounce him to the officers of the law. The poor man, upon hearing this, became utterly confused, and his face became so red that piñons could have been toasted upon it. He fled the store and went to tell Sir Money, crying because of this new misfortune.

Upon hearing his tale, Dame Fortune nearly split her sides laughing, and Sir Money almost suffocated with rage. "Here," he said to the luckless one, as he handed him two thousand *reales,* "You have had back luck, but I am going to stand by you and better your fortune, or truly prove myself of little power."

The man left so transported with joy that, until he ran into them headfirst, he did not see a band of footpads, who left him stripped of everything, even his ragged clothing.

Dame Fortune ridiculed her husband unmercifully while he jumped up and down in anger and mortification.

"Now it is my turn," she said, "and we shall see which is the master, skirts or trousers."

She drew near to the poor man, who had thrown himself to the ground and was tearing out his hair in his grief, and passed her hand over his head. At this, he found his lost dollar under one of his extended hands. Something is better than nothing, he thought to himself. I will go and buy some bread for my children, who have had only a half penny to spend the last three days and their stomachs must be as empty as the lid of a pot.

As he passed the store where he had bought the cloth, the merchant called him inside and said that he wished to apologize for his previous treatment of him. He had really thought the gold piece to be counterfeit, but an assayer had tested it and found it to be genuine and to weigh even more than it should. He had the coin there and also the cloth which the poor man had selected and which he was giving to him as a gift to make up for his groundless suspicions.

The poor man accepted the apology as well as the cloth, and, as he crossed the town square, he saw a squad of city police conducting the men who had robbed him to the *juzgado*. And the judge, who was a just judge as God has commanded there should be, restored to our hero the money of which he had been robbed.

The poor man invested his money in a mine with his *compadre* as partner. They dug scarcely three yards into the ground when they discovered a gold vein, also one of lead and one of iron. Very soon after this, the poor man was addressed as Sir, then as Your Lordship, and in time became Your Excellency.

Since that time Dame Fortune has her husband completely under her power in the toe of her slipper. She continues to be more impudent, more erratic than ever, distributing her favors without rhyme or reason, willy nilly, here and there, fall where it may, by God's good grace, to the just and the sinner, like the blind flail.

The Priest's Cats:

Santiago sang at the top of his voice as he half ran and half walked home. He was so happy and excited over his good news that he was hurrying home to tell his mother and have her rejoice with him.

Reaching their little home, he jumped inside, startling his mother with the exuberance of his entrance. *"Madre,"* he shouted. *"El padrecito* has given me work at his home. I am only to help around the house; just help the cook, bring in wood and water, and help in the garden. And *mire usted, cinco pesos* every month and maybe some clothes!"

"Qué buena suerte, hijo," said his mother. "And the cats? Will you have to take care of them too?"

Santiago's smile diminished somewhat at the mention of the cats. Everybody knew of the many cats the old priest kept and which he thought so much of. They were the bane of his housekeeper's existence, and he had had several housekeepers because of these infernal cats. The old *padre* demanded as much care and solicitude for their welfare as he asked for himself, and more even, so that one housekeeper after another left him in disgust after putting up with the pests as long as they could. Naturally, all the village was acquainted with these facts, and Santiago's mother was quick to call to his attention the task that undoubtedly would be his now, because it was also known that the new housekeeper had threatened to leave if she had to take care of the swarm of pets.

Now Santiago was reaching the age when *bailes* and the *señoritas'* smiles began to interest him. But bare feet would be laughed at at a *baile,* and besides shoes, he should have new trousers and a silk scarf so that he could vie with the best for the dancing partner of his choice. So he was not going to let any cats keep him from the money which meant all these things to him.

"O madrecita. Those cats, I will take care of them. I will soon cure *el padrecito* of his love of cats. You'll see."

"You do not know of what you speak," said his mother. "Many housekeepers have tried that, but the cats are still there—and where are they?"

Next day, Santiago started. He enjoyed the work in the cool, shady garden and, above all, the substantial and varied meal he ate at noon in the kitchen with the cook. As he anticipated, the only chore that spoiled his work for him was the feeding of the cats. Three times a day they would congregate in a large room, gathering there from all over the house and grounds. Here Santiago would have to bring their food and apportion it into various vessels amid a squalling and spitting which daily became more trying. At first the *padre* supervised the feeding of his pets, making sure that his new helper would fully realize the importance of their welfare. Satisfied that Santiago was a conscientious lad and that he would take good care of the cats, he finally left him alone at his task.

Soon after this, the *padre* left for Santa Fe for a week on some church business, after first commending anew to Santiago the care of his cats. This was Santiago's opportunity to try out a plan of his, one he thought would rid him forever of his obnoxious charges.

Santiago provided himself with a long whip, and, at the regular mealtime for the cats, instead of feeding the creatures he shut them up in the room and proceeded to lay on the whip. The poor cats could not understand such treatment as they received the cruel bites of a whip instead of food. Also, Santiago would cry *"Ave María Purísima"* at the top of his lungs all the time he was plying his whip. This treatment of the cats continued all during the week the *padrecito* was absent. Santiago fed his charges but once a day and only after whipping them around and about the room. As always, he kept crying *"Ave María Purísima,"* so that in time the cats associated those words with the punishment inflicted by the whip.

The day before the *padre* was to return, Santiago rehearsed his unwilling actors for the last time. This time he entered the room without his whip, but he did cry out *"Ave María Purísima"* time after time as he moved around the room. The effect was the one he had hoped for. Instantly the room was filled with leaping, snarling, spitting forms jumping frantically toward the ceiling, up the walls, clinging momentarily to the beams or the door jambs—anywhere, anyplace to evade the presence and the whip which they had learned to associate with that presence and those words. Satisfied, Santiago smiled to himself and then gave them a final taste of the whip just to make them remember their lesson for the morrow.

Next morning after mass, the priest's concern for his pets was evident, as the first order of the day was to summon Santiago and inquire after them. Santiago's averted face and faltering answers caused the priest to fear that something was wrong.

"¿Qué pasa, muchacho? Haven't you been taking care of my cats?" he asked.

"Sí, padrecito, but there is something the matter with them. I

think they are possessed of the Devil." Here Santiago crossed himself.

"*Tonto*, what do you mean?" thundered the usually calm-voiced *padre*.

"*¿Quién sabe?, padrecito,* I don't know. But if I mention the Blessed Virgin's name the cats go wild like devils. They spit and snarl and try to run away from me. But you come and see for yourself."

"Let's go see what *tontería* this is of which you speak," said the priest, rising from his chair.

Following closely behind, Santiago wondered if his plot would succeed. When they got to the room where the cats were, Santiago said, "As we go in the door I will call on the Virgin Mary, and if you will do so also, then you will see if I am telling the truth or not."

So, opening the door, they both stepped in, Santiago calling on the Virgin Mary in a louder voice than that of the priest. The bewildered priest saw his forty-odd pets transformed into a varicolored whirlwind of snarling, yowling creatures, leaping and blazing eyes and jumping frantically away from him, full of hatred and terror. This exhibition finally convinced him that the Devil had possessed them, especially since they showed such fear and hatred of the Virgin's name and of him, a man of God.

After trying vainly to exorcise the devils that possessed the cats, the *padre* retreated through the door, ordering Santiago to close it and not to let any of them out. Later, he gave the order for their wholesale execution, a task which Santiago gladly undertook.

Thus did a wily lad rid himself of an annoying task. Today, he is still gardener in the same house. Several priests have lived there and gone on, yet Santiago stays. He enjoys the peace and quiet of the place more than ever now, and he laughs gleefully when he tells this story. (116)

Witches and witch tales also inspired concern and speculation.

Manuel Trujillo was busy making a pair of *teguas* or cow-skin moccasins and had only ceased plying his awl while he gave me a good day. Seating myself in his doorway, I talked first of this and that as I watched him at his work. He was acknowledged one of the best moccasin makers in the village. I could well believe this as I noticed the efficiency with which he worked and the neatness of the escalloped edges where the sole was stitched to the uppers.

The soles were made of well-softened cowhide used hairy side out. When new, they gave the wearer the same effect as walking on a deep-napped rug. Deer hunters keep a pair of these moccasins in reserve because they render their footsteps noiseless in the woods. Before factory-made shoes and boots were introduced into this country moccasins were commonly used for everyday. Any shoes or boots acquired through trade with Mexico were very carefully saved for feast days or other great occasions. In those days a good moccasin maker never lacked for work and food for his household as he was paid in produce, money being almost unknown.

Suddenly, the tolling of the bell broke in on our conversation.

"Must be that José Dolores has died," said Manuel. "He has been quite sick, but let's see."

Stepping outside, he lifted his old eyes to the bell tower. All the patios of the village were full of people after the same information, and the bell toller was straining his voice to make himself heard above the reverberations of the bell. Since everybody was asking the same question, he kept repeating "Commend to God the soul of Teodorita Garduño."

"They are tolling for Teodorita, who died in Taos, may God have mercy on her soul," was Manuel's comment.

"Oh yes, I remember her," I said. "She seemed to be a very good woman. I remember she was the one who always rang the bell for vespers during the month of May. She was so old it must have been a real sacrifice to climb that long ladder every evening of the whole month."

"Yes, she kept that up until her granddaughter took her to live with her in Taos," answered Manuel. "But I happen to know how she took on that duty. That and other seeming pious acts of hers were just to make us believe she was a good Christian and were done through fear. I happen to know she was a witch and that she was made to beg for forgiveness in public twice, and even for her life. Maybe she really repented before she died. God only knows. But I will tell you:

"The first time was when José de la Luz Chávez's wife claimed before the *alcalde* that Teodorita was trying to bewitch her or her baby and swore that she had proved her a witch. She testified that she had tested Teodorita once when she called at her home. After

Teodorita was inside she had secretly placed two needles in the shape of a cross over the door-frame. Teodorita tried to leave the house several times, but she would get only as far as the door and return. She tried this several times and became desperate at her inability to go through that door. Finally Luz's wife, taking pity on her, removed the needles and showed them to her. 'Now I know you are a witch, and I want you to promise never to harm me or my family,' she told her. But Teodorita rushed out the door and in her anger cursed Luz's wife and threatened her baby and herself with unmentionable evils. This was the testimony sworn to before the *alcalde*. Whereupon, the *alcalde* named two men to accompany Luz to punish Teodorita. They were empowered to whip her if she did not confess and promise to refrain from harming Luz or his family.

"In those days the *alcalde* was the law and what he ordered was carried out. One of these men was Salvador Martínez who helped kill that witch in Chimayo. Because of some harm done him by witches when he was younger he had a very great hatred for them and would gladly kill one. And this time he had the authority given him by the *alcalde*. When they reached Teodorita's house and read the accusation, she at first denied everything, but when Salvador approached with a lariat to tie her she knew she could expect no mercy. His reputation was too well known to her. Throwing herself on her knees she begged for mercy, confessed herself a witch, and promised to repent and not to harm Luz or his family. She did not get off so easy because she was made to pray the rosary with her bare knees resting on gravel taken from ant hills. That is very painful, I know very well.

"I doubt if she ever did quit even if she did appear to be so saintly. Many times we noticed those balls of fire bounding down the hillside as if from Truchas. Reaching Teodorita's house they would disappear as if down the chimney. And the owls used to hoot always in the trees near her house. I doubt if she ever reformed. At any rate everybody in the village was afraid of the old woman and would cross themselves on meeting her. Very few people ever ate anything she prepared and she never had any visitors except those who came through the air.

"At another time a group of our brethren were going on a visit to Chimayo. As we were going along singing we noticed a ball of fire rolling along the top of the ridge just to the right of us. Juan Mondragón was with us; you know a Juan can catch a witch no matter what shape she is in. So Juan stepped over in front of this ball of fire and, making the sign of the cross, drew a circle in the air with his finger, more or less around or in the path of the ball of fire. And there was Teodorita with her little eyes glaring at us in the lights from our lanterns! She was very mad and implored Juan to let her go. We would not let him do so until we had made her pray with us and accompany us, barefoot, to Chimayo and back again to Cordova. Then it was that she promised again to behave and perform good deeds in penance for her years of being a witch.

"I have seen many strange things on those night visits to other *moradas* made in company with others of my brethren. When we had a visit to make to Alcalde we did not go by way of the road, but we would cut across through the hills by way of the *Sentinela.* Twice after leaving here and getting to the Cañada Ancha we were joined by departed brethren. *Amiguito,* the flesh of our bodies would crawl and creep when these ghosts joined us, even though we knew they meant us no harm.

"Before we knew it, they would be with us and they would accompany us until we started down toward the first houses in Ranchitos. The lights from our lanterns seemed to shine through them, and we could see their ribs and the bones of their arms as they walked along with us. They were all hooded; some were flagellating and others dragged crosses. How strange to see those *disciplinas* fall on those ghostly, scarred backs and to see those heavy crosses dragged along without a sound. And when we stopped to pray, our brethren from the other world stopped with us, crossing themselves at the proper times, but never making a sound.

"You may be sure we were glad when they would leave us, and we waited until daylight to make the return trip. These were undoubtedly brethren who had made vows while on earth to make some penance or pilgrimage and had neglected to do so while alive. They had been sent back to fulfill their promises before being able to enter heaven. *¡Pobrecitos!* May God have given their souls rest before this." (115)

Dos alesnas no se pican.

("Two awls will not pierce each other.")

Aunque la mona se vista de seda, mona se queda.
("Although the monkey dresses in silk, she remains a monkey.")
(1)

A Taoseño was known for his ability to tell tall tales.

Common to all races and languages are the purveyors of tall
tales. Usually in every community there is one man who is
unanimously acclaimed the best. Such a one was José María Tafoya
of Taos, who had bested all the rest in the art of drawing the long
bow. As a result of this proficiency he was given the nickname of
Guashi, a name really of no meaning but thereafter affixed to any
improbable tale so that any such were laughingly dismissed as a
Guashada by the hearer. Even his family was known by this name,
so you never heard their family name. His wife was known as *La
Guasha*, the children as Guashitos, or, when in need of clarity as to
which, as José Guashito or María Guashito.

Like all who attain perfection in any art, Guashi had many who
would have liked to have occupied his position by displacing him.
So it would happen that at wakes or while taking the sun seated
against the sunny side of a building, or at the cantina around a
bottle of wine, or any hours of leisure when men gathered in
groups, competition induced fearful drains on imaginations, to the
delight of a noncompeting audience. But through many years
Guashi continued the acknowledged champion.

Guashi had his own flock of sheep which he attended accompanied by one or the other of his two sons. Gossip had it that no
sooner was he out of sight of the town with his flock than Guashi
threw himself on the ground in a comfortable spot. Leaving his son
to take care of the sheep, he set himself to the more serious business
of thinking out his *Guashadas*.

One time, so Guashi relates, he had to take his sheep out to graze
by himself, neither of his two sons being available. He had his burro
with him on this occasion to save himself a lot of walking. At noon
when the sheep had eaten their fill and had bedded down as usual
during the heat of midday, Guashi also retired to a shady nook for a
siesta. He had slept a very short while when he awakened because
he was being shaken insistently by the shoulder. Opening his eyes,
he was astounded to see that his awakener was a bear. And not only
one bear; nearby was a mother bear holding a cub.

"*Amigo,*" the bear said, "I want you to do me and my wife a favor. We are going to christen our little son and want you to honor us by being his *padrino.*"

"My mouth was so dry I could only nod my head; I was so afraid and astonished at hearing a bear speak," said Guashi. "But the big bear helped me to my feet so gently that I took courage, especially after the she-bear proudly held out her baby for me to admire. I tried to show no fear and smiled as I patted the cub on the head.

"'Well, let's go, *compadre.* The *padre* is waiting and all my *amigos* also over in my cave,' said my strange *compadre*-to-be.

"So I went along between my two so-strange friends. My knees were kind of weak at first, but they talked so kindly with me, asking me about my family, how many children I had, and so on, that I began to think that bears were not so bad as they were painted. Soon we came to a cave in a ledge of rock overlooking a small stream. I could see three old-looking bears sitting outside, who seemed to be talking together about the weather or of the prospects for good hunting. As soon as they saw us one of them bolted inside to tell the rest I guess, and Holy Mother if there weren't about twenty bears who came rushing out to meet us.

"'*Amigos,* I bring here the *padrino* for my son. I introduce to you Don José María,' said the big bear, whose name I might as well tell you was Gorgonio.

"I shook hands all around and really was received most politely. On entering the cave, two bears inside started playing a guitar and a violin. Then I saw the *padre,* a great big silvered bear, much larger than the rest.

"'Well, friends, I am proud to have Don José María christen my son because then I know he will be like his *padrino* and have a tame herd of deer to watch, and he will never go hungry,' was the announcement made by Gorgonio.

"So with my *ahijado* or godson in my arms I stood before the *padre* bear and the baby was baptized. *Seguro,* I had him named José María after myself.

"After the christening we feasted awhile; then we started dancing. I danced first with my *comadre,* Gorgonio's wife, in a *valse redondo.* All the bears danced every piece, stomping their big feet on the floor and clapping their paws together until their claws clicked when they wished the music to continue. The cave was large with a rock floor. I asked for a polka and, seizing a young she-bear, I showed those bears how a polka should be danced. They were very good at the polka, but you fellows know that they had to go some to beat me.

"And the feast! *Hombre*, what a good feast! I ate of everything, but I liked their wild strawberry wine best. Ay! what a wine, very strong, and soon I was feeling very good and felt as if I had known these bears all my life. You should have seen those bears dance the *cuna* and *varsoviana*. Don't ever let anybody tell you the bear is not a graceful animal.

"Once I asked to sing the verses for a *valse cantado*. Here I had a chance to honor all my friends, the bears. I sang a verse first in honor of both my *compadre* and *comadre*, then one for my godchild, to whom I gave my horsehair hatband for a collar. It was all I had to give him. As I sang each verse I was offered a glass of wine, so that by the time I had reached the last one I was feeling very happy. By that time also, it was beginning to get light and I said I had to get back to my sheep.

"I was heartily embraced by both my *compadre* and *comadre*, and after giving my godchild my blessing I said goodbye to the rest. Two young bears took me to the top of a ridge and told me I would find my sheep in the little valley below. And thanks to Santa Inés I soon found my burro and nearby were my sheep.

"But the country was strange to me. I thought I knew every part of the mountains around here, yet I could see no familiar landmarks. Maybe it's the wine, I thought, so I just followed along after my sheep as they grazed, hoping to locate myself soon or to recover from the effects of the wine, if that were the cause. I soon began to feel hungry and could find only a few cold tortillas in my lunch sack. So I killed a fat lamb and built a fire on which to roast some meat. I remembered to save the rennet for my wife, who had told me she needed some to make cheese.

"Feeling thirsty, I started looking for water. I found a spring, *amigos*, but what a surprise to see that it ran milk instead of water. Just the same, I stooped over and took a big drink of it; it was cold and quenched my thirst very nicely. As I got up from taking my drink, the rennet, which I was still holding in my hand, fell into the spring. The spring was deep, and I couldn't recover the rennet, especially after the milk began to curdle. Well, I thought, it looks like the good God wants me to help my wife out on the cheesemaking. So I set to work and soon had a large number of cheeses made and hung up to drain on willow shelves.

"Feeling drowsy, I built up a big fire and went to sleep. I must have slept a long time, for when I woke up the fire had crept up and under the cheese. It was hanging in long threads; you know how cheese gets when it is heated. This made me pretty mad, but what could I do?

"Thinking I might have to spend a few more nights out until I found out where I was, I wondered how I could keep warm. So I made a loom like the Navajos use and wove those cheese threads into a large white blanket. That night I slept very comfortably under my new blanket.

"Next morning I ate breakfast and, getting on my burro, tied the blanket on behind me and started after my sheep. They seemed to know where they were going and I just followed them. Soon we were in country I knew and by evening we were home.

"I was anxious to show my wife the blanket I had woven and to tell her about my friends the bears, so I jumped off my burro and thought I would untie the blanket. All I found were a few threads which had caught on the saddle. Somewhere back on the mountain a thread must have caught on a limb of a tree or some stump, and the blanket had unravelled as I rode along. Now I had nothing with which to convince my wife as to where I had been, so I went very sorrowfully into the house.

"I never could find that spring again, and, as for my godson, I once saw a bear that looked like it had a collar on. It must not have been he, because when I tried to get closer he ran away. No godson of mine would treat his *padrino* in that manner." (66)

Less elaborate but similar stories were told about places like El Potrero (now part of Chimayo) with its famous healing shrine, El Santuario.

The peak overlooking the Santuario, called El Cerro de Chimayo, has near its top a cave called La Cueva del Chivate or Billy Goat Cave. Legend has it that mountain goats used to disappear in this cave when hard pressed by the hunters. Some hunters who ventured in after these animals were lost in the cave and never seen again. There is a belief that if one were to follow this cave through to its end one would come out into daylight again somewhere in the vicinity of the Pueblo of San Ildefonso. *¿Quién sabe?* (35)

The miller Eusebio recalled the exploits of hunters he had known.

"Not one of these Romeritos, or Ysidro, who have always claimed to be such good hunters, has ever killed a bear. At least, I have never heard of them doing so."

By the diminutive appellation applied to the Romero brothers, I could judge Eusebio's opinion of them. I had been leading him on to a discussion of the hunting and the best hunters of this vicinity, more particularly of the time when he was young.

Stamping his foot and shaking his head, he continued: "But my father, José Rafael, killed eighteen bears during his lifetime and deer without number. In every kind of hunting he was of the best. And mind you, with the old muzzle-loading rifle, not these modern rifles. I'd like to see Matías kill a bear or even a deer with one of those old rifles. If it was a bear he would get cured of his rheumatism pretty quick if he missed his first shot and had to reload."

Matías, to whom he referred, was the youngest of the Romero brothers, and I knew that the irascible Eusebio was still smarting over a horse trade in which Matías had bested him. So I thought I would change the subject and get some light on something I had heard about another oldtimer who was reputed to have been one of the best deer hunters yet.

"How about the *difunto* Manuelito Romero?" I asked. This word *difunto*, meaning deceased, is used in conversation whenever referring to any person who has departed this life.

"Oh, but with him it was different. He couldn't help being a good deer hunter because he had a stone."

Quite at a loss, I very innocently asked how Manuelito could have had any notable success killing deer with a stone.

"Don't be a *pendejo* ('fool' or 'chump'). It wasn't just any old stone, but a stone he took out of a special deer and which gave its owner a special power. You know, but no, you don't know anything. I am going to tell you, but wait."

Here, after letting me know he realized my ignorance, Eusebio had to cut the conversation short in order to adjust the hopper of the old grist mill which all this time had been busy turning the village grain into flour. Two sets of millstones nearby, worn so thin as to be no longer serviceable, attested to the age of this old mill.

Returning, Eusebio continued: "Every once in a while a hunter would come back from the hills very excited and very mad too. He would tell a story about seeing a *gargantillo* buck and usually would tell about wasting all his ammunition on him without any results. And, as nearly all the hunters in town had had the same experience, they would make fun of him, and for many days ask him if he had finished drying the meat from his last kill.

"These *gargantillo* bucks are so called because they have a white mark around their throats. They are very large, but only once in many years is there a man lucky enough to kill one. These are enchanted animals and carry a stone. This stone is found in the center of these animals' foreheads. Anyone possessing one of these stones can kill all the deer he wishes. No one but the owner must ever see this stone.

"*El difunto* Manuelito told me how he had come to kill this deer. He said he was returning from an unsuccessful hunt, and near the Llano Bonito he saw a large buck. Slipping in behind a tree, he started creeping up closer in order to get a sure shot. In his excitement he stepped on a dry limb and it broke, making a lot of noise. He thought he surely had scared him and stepped out of cover to see him go. There was the deer looking straight at him and not moving at all. Then he could see that he was a *gargantillo*.

"The deer gave him time to raise his rifle and shoot, but he missed that first shot, he was so excited. He swears that the deer moved up closer toward him, seemingly asking to be killed. Well, he did kill him and right away looked to see if he could find a stone. He found it and from that day on meat was never lacking in his house, and *el difunto* Manuelito never lacked money.

"It looked like the deer followed him asking to be killed after he became owner of this lucky stone. When he hunted on horseback he would carry it in the bottom of his rifle scabbard, and at other times in a little buckskin sack hung around his neck. But only when he went hunting would he carry it because, since he liked his liquor, there were those who, seeing him drunk, would have taken advantage of the fact to see what this stone looked like. And that would have destroyed its power.

"So all he had to do when he wanted money was to take two or three burros to the hills and load them with venison to be sold in Santa Fe or Española. What luck some people have! Yet he was goodhearted and many is the time he would bring in two or three deer and give them to the poorest families in the town.

"One time Romero rode up to a camp in the hills and, as is the custom, was asked to get down and have a cup of coffee. He unsaddled his horse near the fire and turned him loose to graze. He had left his saddle too near the fire and turned in time to see one of his friends pick it up to remove it from danger. This fellow picked the saddle up in such a way that the mouth of the scabbard hung down. Seeing the danger, Romero shouted, *¡Cuidado hombre!* Leave my saddle alone!' But it was too late. The stone rolled out of the scabbard and as quickly disappeared from sight.

"And that was the last of Romero's deer hunting days. He started going to Wyoming to the sheep camps and returned once a year for a big celebration with his *compadre* Shon. And there he died three years ago, and there he was buried. *Que en paz descanse.*" (70)

Santa Inés was the patron of the outdoors beyond the village.

In the backyard of a home on the south slope of Santa Fe Canyon, this side of the first reservoir, there is a small shrine dedicated to Santa Inés del Campo. She is the patron saint of all followers of outdoor pursuits such as sheepherders, cowboys, woodsmen, trappers, and so on. Also, she is the saint whose aid is invoked for the recovery of lost or strayed animals, lost articles of any kind, as well as children who have been lost in the hills or mountains. So it is that often the passerby will see one or more candles burning before this shrine, and he may be sure that each candle represents some lost article or strayed animal for the recovery of which its owner has made a pilgrimage to this shrine. After a prayer to the saint and after leaving a candle before the image of Santa Inés, the suppliant and distressed owner withdraws from the shrine with full faith that with Santa Inés's aid that which he has lost will be restored to him. (107)

The following *alabado* is one sung in honor of Santa Inés (Saint Agnes). . . . Shrines to her are usually rude affairs of a sylvan nature, made of willows and roofed with boughs and exposed to the elements, in conformity with the fact that she is the patron saint of those who must live outdoors. The wording of this *alabado* is very simple, but the tune that accompanies it is singularly beautiful and must be heard to be appreciated.

Santa Inés del Campo	St. Agnes of hill and plain
Tus milagros bellos	Your wondrous miracles I know,
Por los que te aclaman	For those who plead with you
Ruego a Dios por ellos	Intercede with God for them.
Tus milagros bellos	Of your wondrous miracles
Yo mil veces canto	A thousand times I sing
Libra al que te aclama	Guard him who thus calls on you
Santa Inés del Campo.	Saint Agnes of hill and plain.
Con este tu nombre	With this, your beloved name
Al demonio espanto	I will the devil dismay
Mira a tus devotos	Look down upon your devotees
Santa Inés del Campo.	Saint Agnes of hill and plain.
Pasastes tú tormentos	You who tortures underwent
Sin número tanto	Too numerous to recount
Por librar al hombre	In order to free mankind,
Santa Inés del Campo.	Saint Agnes of hill and plain.
En una cuevita	A little hidden cave
De aquel llano santo,	On those blessed plains of old
Fue tu habitación	Was your holy habitation,
Santa Inés del Campo.	Saint Agnes of hill and plain.
A los caminantes	Pilgrims of trail and road
Los mereces tanto	Stand ever in need of you
Que la acompañasen	And of your holy company,
Santa Inés del Campo.	Saint Agnes of hill and plain.
Aqui cantaremos	Praises here we sing
Este nombre santo	To your holy name
Postrados a tí	Prostrate here before you,
Santa Inés del Campo.	Saint Agnes of hill and plain.
Postrado de rodillas	In all humility I kneel
Ofrezco yo mi llanto	In supplication before you
Y tú nos consueles	Grant us consolation,
Santa Inés del Campo.	Saint Agnes of hill and plain.
Adios Santa Inés	Farewell St. Agnes,
Adios Madre Mía	Farewell beloved mother mine,
Con tu gran poder	Through your gracious favor
Seas nuestra guía.	Be our strength and guide.

En fin Santa Inés	And so Saint Agnes deign give ear
Te ofrezco yo mi canto	As this hymn I sing to you
Por que nos perdones	And grant us pardon one and all,
Santa Inés del Campo.	Saint Agnes of hill and plain. (20)

The hymn to Santa Inés del Campo is one of the most beautiful of all the *ababados*. It is a favorite of the people of the rural and sheep-raising sections of New Mexico. For these people, who still follow their flocks from one pasture ground to another and who must of necessity spend much time in the hills, appreciate and understand the sentiments expressed in this hymn. (107)

Brown's most detailed and extended piece describes the dangerous, lonely life of the proud pastor, *Basílico Garduño.*

It was late afternoon when I approached the campsite in the shadow of El Cerro Redondo ("Round Peak"), near Jemez Hot Springs. The sheep were still grazing, although all had their heads turned toward the wooded base of the peak which dominated this upland pasture. The meadow, stretching as far as I could see, encircled the peak. I knew enough of sheep habits to go in the direction in which they grazed, for there would be their *majada* ("bedding ground"), and close by would the camp of the *pastor* ("shepherd").

A curling blue column rising from a cluster of fir and spruce indicated the spot I sought, and three nondescript dogs gave warning of my approach. Then Basílico's squat, broad figure emerged from the patched and weatherbeaten one-pole tent. He was clad in bib overalls of denim, over which an old, ill-fitting jacket of the same material was worn. This was buttoned over his shirts (the weather determined the number worn). A battered felt hat and homemade shoes completed his costume. A low, muttered command to the dogs quieted them, and a circling motion of his arm sent them racing around the edge of the flock to urge on lagging members toward the *majada* and make the group more compact.

"*Buenas tardes,*" I said, and added praise for the well-trained dogs.

My greeting was returned in a low tone, strange and hesitant, the reluctant, inhibited speech of one used to living alone. "*Llegue, amigo* ('Come in, friend')," said Basílico, his wind-reddened, bloodshot eyes glaring into mine as if he were angry. Years of squatting over a campfire had given him this baleful look.

I seated myself on a block of pine while he poured a cup of coffee, the *pastor's* first act of hospitality. A blackened coffee pot is always present on the edge of the campfire. Ground coffee and water are added as needed. Some of the essence of the first potful made in each camp remains until the camp itself is removed.

The beat of many hooves accompanied by the throaty bleating of the sheep and the quicker blats of goats announced the arrival of the flock at the salt troughs scattered near the bedding ground. I looked up to see the sheep clustered in shoving, butting groups along the length of the slightly hollowed logs that held the coarse rock salt. This salt had been brought from the natural salt deposits of the Estancia Valley.

A ten-pound lard pail huddled in the coals near the coffee pot, its nail-punctured lid emitting jets of vapor which I hoped might come from beans and fat mutton cooked together. Without saying anything more, my host set an iron spider on a bed of coals and put in two spoonfuls of lard to melt. From the tent he took a sack of flour and rolled down the edges until a mound of exposed flour was formed. Into this he poured a cup of water, then added the melted grease. Stirring the mixture in the sack, he soon lifted out a ball of dough, which he placed in a small pan. All the flour that had come in contact with the water and grease had become incorporated in the ball of dough, the rest remaining dry. Evidently baking powder and salt had been added beforehand, making the mixing of a batch of dough a quick and simple process.

Pinching off small portions of dough, Basílico rolled them quickly into small balls, then flattened them into round cakes a little thicker than tortillas. These were *gordas* ("fat ones"), the bread commonly made by the New Mexican sheepherder. Soon six browned gordas were taken from the skillet and stacked on a cloth spread across a water keg. The pail of beans was dragged out of the fire and its lid pried off.

Just as Basílico was about to seat himself on a log close to the bean pail, one of two goats that had approached quite familiarly to the fireside bleated softly. Taking down a small pail that hung from a tree branch overhead, Basílico approached the two goats, seized one of them by a hind leg, and milked her. The other was treated likewise. Tossing the two a piece of old bread, he set a cupful of milk down on the keg holding the *gordas*, first straining it through a piece of thin cloth, part of an old salt sack. The goats' milk was almost as thick as cream.

Basílico needed no spoon. Each mouthful was picked up with a split *gorda*, bent between thumb and forefinger. Meat was enfolded in a piece of the *gorda* and eaten with it.

A muffled drum of hooves caused me to look away from the fire. The dim forms of burros loomed up, and I realized that it was growing late. Their feet were hobbled, and the two leaders were belled. One of the *almanaques* ("almanacs"), as Basílico called them, was obviously a pet. He asked for a tidbit in the intimate, demanding tone that pampered animals use. The herder rose and fed them the remnants, and while they ate he removed their hobbles.

"Aren't you afraid they will stray away if you loose them?" I asked.

"No, not at night, and scarcely ever in the daytime either. At night they stick very close to where I sleep, as you shall see."

I realized then that I was going to spend the night at the camp. It was just as well, since I had not yet even mentioned the purchase of the *cabrito* ("kid") for which I had come.

I picked up the hobbles that were thrown in a heap close to where I sat. They were homemade, and I was curious about their construction. They were about three feet long and as many inches wide, the inner side lined with cowhide on which the hair had been left to give more protection from chafing. The wide straps fitted closely around a forefoot, just below the fetlock. After several twists, which took up slack and looseness between the two front feet, each end of one fitted into a slot cut into the end of the other, a neat and efficient fastening which, since the leather was soft, would not be difficult to fasten or unfasten with benumbed fingers on a cold, damp morning. I appreciated this feature because of my experience with store-bought hobbles of heavy, thick leather straps linked with chains and secured with heavy buckles. There is no agony equal to that of trying to unbuckle one of these manufactured hobbles wet and stiff from snow. Awkward, unmanageable, and perverse, they inevitably produce torn fingernails and bad tempers. These seemingly crude hobbles of Basílico's were a vast improvement. Later on, I saw Basílico use them as a tie strap to secure a pack and for other purposes by linking five pairs together.

The burros did stay close to the fire, except when Basílico slaughtered a lamb and they moved over to the scene and looked on. The lamb had been seized and carried from the bedding ground to a convenient tree, then suspended by a hind leg from a lower branch that was just high enough to be within easy reach. Basílico's left hand held the lamb's muzzle and bore its head back and down against the bole of the tree while his right hand drew a sharp butcher knife across the taut throat. This stroke was followed by a sharp cut down the underside from tail to severed throat. Incisions up the length of each leg connected with the central belly cut. From this point on, Basílico had no more use for the knife. He tossed it aside and started ripping off the skin with his hands. One hand held the carcass away and against the pull of the other. In separating the pelt from the sides and back, he used his fist in a knuckling, rolling fashion, neatly separating the pelt from the carcass while rending the paper-thin tissue that held the two together.

The pelt, flesh side up, was stretched out on the ground. The smaller portions were laid on it, the quarters being hung on limbs to cool. The dogs sat around with lolling tongues and cocked ears, deftly catching each offering that Basílico tossed them. They did not fight over each other's share but gulped their own and resumed their eager, expectant attitude.

"Hey, don't throw them all of that," I called out excitedly, as I saw Basílico start to apportion the liver amongst the expectant circle. "I should like some of it for breakfast."

"Here's something else we will have for breakfast," said Basílico as he held out the lamb's head for my inspection. From the way he kept his eyes fixed on my face, I knew he was trying to get my reaction to this novel breakfast dish. He had not neglected to save a piece of liver as well.

"*La cabeza es del matador,*" I said. My saying that the head belonged to him who killed the animal evoked a pleased smile. I had given him to understand that I knew what a delicacy roast head was considered, especially that of a lamb or *cabrito*.

Digging a hole in the spot from which he had cleared the coals of the campfire, Basílico deposited the head therein, after first throwing a little water on it and on the sides and bottom of the hole itself. He placed a tin lid directly over the head and covered the whole with hot ashes and glowing coals.

"In the morning it will be done to a hair," he said, "but for now I will make some *burrañiates*. Do you know what they are?"

I pretended not to know in order to allow him the pleasure of introducing a new dish. Taking a chunk of leaf lard from around the kidneys, he gave it the form of a wiener. Around this he wrapped a good length of the milk intestines, which had first been stripped of their contents with thumb and forefinger.

With greedy eyes I watched to see how many of these delectable bundles he would make. Six—three apiece—I thought to myself as he handed them to me saying, "You roast these while I make three or four more *gordas*, and don't forget to salt them when they are just about done."

"Leave them to me," I answered, pleased that he thought I could be useful. Folding a *gorda* in the center, I placed my *burrañiates* inside, sandwich fashion. The filling had just the desired crispness, having body yet with no greasy taste as might be expected. The surrounding forest was quiet, its silence unbroken except for the occasional sound of the cowbells as the burros cropped the grass nearby.

"And why do you call your burros *almanaques*?" I asked as Basílico was fixing a pallet for me near the fire.

"Oh, they are the almanac of the *pastor*. I can tell of sudden changes in the weather by watching their actions and hearing their braying at unusual hours of the day or night." That was new to me. I had heard them called many things, some of them unprintable, but never almanacs.

My bed consisted of three woolly sheepskins next to the ground, a blanket over these, and another with which to cover myself. Additional warmth, if needed, would have to be supplied by the "poor man's blanket," the fire, wood for which stood neatly stacked close enough so that I could throw an occasional stick on it without getting up.

My friend, as I thought of him after those *burrañiates*, lay on a pallet similar to mine on the opposite side of the fire. Both of us had lighted cigarettes, and I talked to him about the stars. He had interesting names for some of the more familiar constellations. The Pleiades he called *Las Cabrillas* ("herd of little goats"), the Great Dipper was *La Carreta* ("the cart"), and he pointed out to me what seemed to be one star but which was in reality two, he said, if your eyesight was good enough. He said the Indians used the phenomenon to test the eyes of their young men. I took his word for this; all I could see was one star. *La Estrella del Pastor*, as the morning star was called, according to him received its name from the fact that the shepherd is supposed to be up when it appears. He added drily that all the stars might so be called since a *pastor* sees them all nearly every night, sleeping as he does with one eye open, especially when on the summer range in the high mountains.

The moon appeared over the top of El Cerro Redondo. He said it promised wet weather because its points were tilted so that it would not hold water. He told me he could figure in advance the different phases of the moon for months ahead. This knowledge he found very useful in caring for his flock. For instance, a full moon was of great advantage at lambing time. He therefore figured out the exact day to turn the rams (*carneros mesos*) in with the ewes so that the lambs would begin to drop while there was a full moon to light the *pastor's* labors. A full moon was also to be desired when the sheep were driven from summer to winter range or back again.

Basílico also claimed to have a method of predicting the weather for a year ahead by means of *las cabañuelas*.

"And how do you do that?"

"It is very simple," he replied, then launched into a very complex account. I was soon lost in a maze of *primeros, segundos* ("firsts" and "seconds") and *cuarto días* ("quarter days").

Boiled down, the method was based on an average of the weather for the first twenty-four days of January, called *las cabañuelas*. These twenty-four days were paired to make twelve units, using the first and last together, each pair determining the weather for one month. For instance, the second and twenty-third days of January represent February; the third and twenty-second days March; and so on. Then there are *los pastores*, the succeeding six days of January, which do not enter into the calculation of *las cabañuelas*. These are divided into quarter-day units, twenty-four in all and, as in *las cabañuelas*, are paired, the second and twenty-third entering into the calculations for February, and so on.

"*Y el último día de enero* ("and the last day of January") . . ." I was very drowsy by this time but gathered that the last day of January also entered into this complicated system. Vaguely I heard Basílico explaining that the twenty-four hours of the last day were paired in the same manner as the two-day units of *las cabañuelas* and the quarter-day units of *los pastores,* and that they entered into and figured in the calculations for the weather for the months of the year in the same sequence. I recall dreaming something about Einstein and pairs of sheep darting off in different directions, and the next I knew Basílico's voice was urging me to breakfast.

The coffee pot was hissing and the table was laid, my cup and saucer on one keg, his on another. The baked head of lamb lay on a pie tin, skinned, and broken into convenient pieces. The brain pan had been opened, exposing its steaming contents. Basílico had baked several loaves of *pan de pastor* ("shepherd's bread"), round loaves made of the same dough as the *gordas* but baked in a Dutch oven. This bread keeps, and sheepherders bake supplies of it when time cannot be spared to prepare *gordas* at every meal.

The Dutch oven sat close to the fire with hot grease smoking inside. "I left that for you to fix your liver to your own taste; I know nothing about that," said Basílico as he handed me the chunk of liver and a sharp knife. Like most of the rural people of New Mexico, he would not eat liver, professing not to know even how to prepare it. (Some think this prejudice is based on the fact that sheep liver is susceptible to disease.) I sliced the liver, which was soon fried, and, heaping my saucer, joined Basílico. The meat of the jaw-bones of the sheep's head had a sweet, nutty flavor, and I also sampled the brains.

The sheep were beginning to move slowly out of the *majada*, the vigilant dogs posting themselves on the outskirts of the flock on higher points where they could catch the warmth of the sun. Basílico had already prepared his lunch. It was wrapped in a white flour sack, strapped to his waist with the long straps of the sling he carried, and fitted close to the small of his back.

"I am going to graze the sheep toward El Rito de San Antonio (St. Anthony's Creek), where they will water, and I can get water for the camp also. Do you want to come along?"

Two burros, already saddled and with water kegs hanging on each side, grazed close by. Basílico handed me a flour sack which bulged with a quarter of lamb. "Here is something for you." I could not refuse the gift, nor could I now say that I had originally come for a *cabrito*.

Since the small stream lay for a distance along my own route back to the springs, I followed the slowly moving flock. I noticed that the ewes were heavy and mentioned the fact to Basílico.

"Yes, we'll be lambing about San Domingo Day. Come and visit

my camp at that time, if you wish to see us then. We will be on the
north slope of El Rito de los Indios ('Indians' Creek') where there is
better shelter."

The dogs kept the sheep moving in the desired direction. I
commented on their training.

"Do you remember that *melada* ('goat') I milked last night? Well
she is the foster-mother of my two youngest dogs. I take young
puppies, newly born, before their eyes are opened, and suckle them
to a nanny goat. In this way I get dogs that think they are part goat,
I guess, because they soon learn to love these animals and take care
of them. They take care of the sheep also, but treat them with
contempt, just like these *mocosas* ('snivelers') deserve, for they are
a very foolish animal."

We came to a saddle in the low ridge along which we had been
walking. Here Basílico and his flock would cross and go down the
lefthand slope, while I continued along its length for some miles
more. As the dogs turned the flock, pressing in on its right flank, its
leader, a patriarchal billy goat, swung the first of the woolly wave
over and down the slope. We stood to the left and a little higher,
like commanders of an army watching it pass in review. Basílico
scanned the flock closely, seeming to take notice of each individual
mutton.

" '*Stá bien*,'" he said to himself as the last sheep passed over.

"You didn't count them, did you?" I asked.

"*Sí y no* ('yes and no')," he replied. "I counted my *marcadoras*
('markers'). They were all there, so the rest must be." These
marcadoras, he explained, were the black sheep in the flock, about
one of these for every hundred of the others. Any *corta* ("stray
bunch") would be almost certain to include one of the black sheep.
So if all the black sheep were accounted for he assumed the whole
flock would be intact.

Many *pastores* cannot count beyond the number of fingers on
both hands and must use counters to overcome this handicap. The
old Spanish saying, "*Carnero entregado, peso contado*" ("Wether
sold and handed over, a dollar counted out"), applied to them as
well as to others with the same disadvantage. This means that the
price is paid for each animal as it is sold because of the seller's
inability to reckon the total.

A full tally of the sheep is usually made by the owner or *patrón*
on one of his periodic visits to the sheep camp. At that time the

pastor may hand his *patrón* a tobacco sack full of pebbles. Some of these will be larger than the rest and are usually black in color. In this case the *pastor* has made a count of his *rebaño* ("flock") some time prior to his *patrón's* visit, and his count is recorded in these pebbles. The black pebbles show how many hundred there were; the white ones how many tens; the remainder are either committed to memory or shown by notches cut into the shepherd's staff. To account for sheep killed by wild animals or dead from any other cause, the *pastor* skins and saves the pelts, ears and all, against the day when his *patrón* comes to count his sheep, because he is responsible for every one.

"Why don't you come over to the Springs to visit me?" I asked. "I shall be there for a week or ten days more."

"I will if the *patrón* sends me a *remuda* ['exchange' or 'replacement'] soon. But, *amiguito*, I have known those springs for many years. In fact, that was where I first started to herd sheep. My father and I both worked for Don Mariano, who first owned those springs, that is, the grant on which they are located. He was *muy rico*, a man of many sheep and much land. We used to lamb in the grassy valley just above the springs and dip the sheep in troughs built just below the main sulphur spring. We used nothing else except the very water from the spring to rid the sheep of scab and ticks. It was much better than this stuff we have to use nowadays.

"Don Mariano was a great *patrón*, a great fighter and eater, but of good heart. When he came to visit our camp to count the sheep, my father would always kill the fattest lamb, then open it while it was still warm, even before skinning it, and remove the paunch. This he would place to roast on the *rescoldo*, a big bed of coals prepared beforehand. There was nothing Don Mariano liked better than paunch roasted thus. When it had roasted sufficiently, he would cut it open with his *daga*, empty the half-digested contents, cut up the paunch, and eat it. He said that besides his liking it very much, it was very good for a stomach trouble from which he suffered. *¿Quién sabe?*"

By *remuda* Basílico meant a herder sent up to relieve him. On holidays Basílico usually took all his burros and stopped at his *patrón's* house, where he left them. He then went about his own affairs. With many *pastores* these leaves meant drinking sprees or women until, funds exhausted, they were rounded up by the *patrón* and set upon the sobering trail which led back to camp. With the

married ones, while it might also mean a spree, in most cases there
was a reunion with wife and children. As far as I knew, Basílico had
never been married. He was very reticent about what he did on
these leaves. His *patrón* confided that Basílico would go to Santa Fe
and return on the appointed day, with never a word as to his
activities.

I shook hands with Basílico, assuring him I would return at
lambing time if possible. He promised to have ready for me upon
my return a pair of *teguas* ("moccasins") which he had offered to
make for me. I had seen *teguas* worn by other *pastores*, but they
were hybrid affairs with handmade soles and uppers salvaged from
some pair of store shoes or boots. Basílico's were his own handiwork
throughout, being made of cowhide with the neatest of stitching,
close fitting, and undoubtedly very comfortable; he wore no other
kind.

He was a master in working leather. He could braid quirts, belts,
hat bands, *reatas* ("ropes"), and those long, braided, tapering whips
known as blacksnakes. His neatest job, next to the *teguas*, was the
hondas ("slings") he made, like the one he now carried. They were
shorter than those I had when a boy. The egg-shaped piece that
carried the stone was larger also, and on the end of each swinging
string was a lash which cracked like a pistol shot after each throw.
He was amazingly accurate with it: he would never hit a sheep or
goat, but would sling a stone to strike in the vicinity of a straggler
and thus startle it back to the flock.

Basílico's attire, on those rare Sundays when he was in a
settlement varied from his everyday clothing only by being newer
and perhaps a little cleaner. It was topped by a brand new black
hat, brushed for the occasion. This hat was kept at his *patrón's*
house in town for just such rare outings, and was the *patrón's*
annual bonus to his faithful servitor, a gift added to his wages. Each
year the holiday hat was taken over for workdays, and soon became
the battered affair that Basílico doffed as we parted there on the
ridge.

I returned to Basílico's camp the day before San Domingo Day.
True to his prediction, there was a full moon in the sky that night,
and, soon after its appearance, the thin bleats of newborn lambs
sounded. Basílico, with three extra men who had been in camp
since the first of the month, worked from the time I arrived until
morning. He and his helpers would appear at the campfire, singly

in most cases, to drink a cup of coffee and then return to their labors.

I wandered over to the corral that had been built a few days before for *el ganado preñado* ("the pregnant ewes"). The bobbing lanterns revealed the whereabouts of the men. Spotting Basílico, I drew close to him and found him skinning a stillborn lamb. Its mother stood close by bleating incessantly in that stupid manner so characteristic of sheep.

"Surely you don't have to save the skins of such as those for accounting to the *patrón?*" I asked.

"No, no. I am fixing it so this *tonta* may have a foster son, tomorrow perhaps. There will be some ewes that will die tonight, leaving *pencos* ('orphan lambs'), and others that will have twins. I will take either a *penco* or a twin lamb away from its mother, tie this skin to his back, and fool this *vieja* ('old woman') into adopting him. The ewes recognize their lambs by scent at first, and through this trick we save many lambs that would die otherwise."

Several diminutive pelts hung around the corral, separated from each other so the scents would not be mixed. In the midst of confusion and noise and the constant blatting and bleating, the herder and his helpers moved from one birth to another. I asked one man how he could pair up the right ewe with each lamb pelt; they all looked exactly alike to me. He said there were differences of appearance, and besides, each ewe had a different note to her bleating, by which he could fix her in his mind. Listening to the bleat of one particular ewe, I was finally able to distinguish her baaing from the medley which arose from the corral. There were not many of these adoptions to be arranged. Basílico's flock had wintered well, and the ewes had reached the lambing season in very good condition.

It was close to four in the morning when I returned to the campfire. Above the commotion from the corral the shrill yapping of coyotes could be heard. They seemed to know what the sounds issuing from the corral meant. I could imagine their slavering jaws and burning eyes as they pointed their slender noses to the sky.

In the morning I accompanied Basílico in a round of inspections of the corral and the *chiceros* ("small brush pens"). At the corral, we picked up the carcasses of the lambs that had been skinned the night before and tossed them over the side of a nearby bluff. At the *chiceros*, where the newborn lambs were kept while the flock grazed, Basílico paused to count again the lambs that huddled together for warmth. He chuckled with satisfaction as he commented on their number and general sturdiness. As we stood there, one of the extra men appeared with four more lambs. From time to time throughout the day more lambs were added to the *chiceros*.

One of the men drove a small group of nervously bleating ewes close to the *chicero* where the orphans and twins were segregated. With a lamb clothed in one of the pelts removed the night before, Basílico would head for one of the ewes. Sometimes a good deal of persuasion was necessary to induce the ewes to allow the lambs to suckle. They would be held and forced to smell this odd-looking lamb with the legs of its strange covering dangling from its sides. The lamb on its wobbling legs would be butted and shoved aside, but it persisted in satisfying its hunger, bringing its mouth again and again to the ewe's side in spite of all rebuffs. When after many attempts accompanied by strong language on the part of Basílico and his helper the lamb was accepted by the ewe, it would kneel to receive the milk, while its tail wriggled ecstatically just below the lifeless one of the lamb whose place he was taking. After the lamb had finished, the ewe would move off to graze, still eyeing dubiously this mysterious creature that had the scent of Esau but the voice of Jacob.

That evening I left the camp after negotiating for a kid, which I held on the saddle before me. Also tied to my saddle were the *teguas* that Basílico had promised me. Somehow, during the busy days of preparation for the lambing rush, he had found time to make them. Basílico's helpers would depart in a few days, leaving him to the solitude that he seemed to prefer. I said I would try to get back again in a few days. "Yes, come back after these other ones have gone; then we can talk." As I rode away, my cargo awakened the echoes of hillside and canyon along my return trail.

The next time I saw Basílico was by chance. I was out riding around the hills below the lambing camp and on the slopes of the mountain that led toward the settlement on the Rio Grande. Entering an open park, I happened onto a flock of sheep obviously on the move from one camp to another, for burros loaded with camp equipment grazed at the edge of the flock. I recognized the animals as Basílico's and rode to the rear of the flock in search of him. I met him carrying a lamb in his arms; it had played out some time back. Its excited mother alternately grazed in erratic pauses close to Basílico's footsteps, then dashed toward him baaing in a stupidly inquiring manner, evoking plaintive responses from the lamb.

"Where are you going with your *ganado?* Is it that your *patrón* has sold it and you are taking it down for delivery?" I asked, for a movement of a flock from the summer range to winter range country at this time of year was unusual.

"*No, nada de eso* ("no, nothing like that"). The *patrón* has a shearing shed down here a little way, and I am driving the sheep there to be sheared."

As we crossed a small stream Basílico stooped to pluck a green feathery plant which grew under the overhanging bank close by some violets.

"What is that?" I asked, as he thrust the fern-like wisps into his mouth.

"It is *plumajillo,* very good for the stomach. Try some?"

It was bitter to the taste and should have rated very high in the locality, where the efficacy of any medicine is measured by the strength of its flavor. Basílico asked if I would bring him some *hediondilla* from the vicinity of Socorro the next time I was down there. I confessed that I did not know what that was, but from the name, which means "stinking," it could not be anything pleasant. I learned later that it was the creosote bush, popular remedy for kidney ailments, and that he had need of it.

"You know much about herbs, no?"

"Yes, every *pastor* knows about *yerbas del campo* ('wild herbs'). It is well that he does, he is alone so much. Knowing them, he can treat any disease that might strike him while out alone with his sheep. Only a broken leg holds any terror for a sheepherder. I can name you a great number of herbs and the particular benefits of each, but that would take a long time. Some other time I will give you some of each and directions for what ailments to use them for."

After the sheep had bedded down, as we sat smoking our aftersupper cigarette, Basílico talked about herbs. He recited a list that would put an herbalist's catalogue to shame. The most prominent was *oshá,* which is so highly regarded by native New Mexicans that it is considered virtually a cure-all. Others were *altamisa, chimajá, chamiso, orteguilla, poleo, yerba buena, amole, canaigra.* The only way one could fix this list of names in mind would be, he suggested, to get a sample of each and record its properties in detail.

While on the subject, Basílico also mentioned *pinque* ("Colorado rubber plant") and loco weed, from which the *pastor* must guard his sheep. *Pinque* is most destructive in the month of October, or after the first frosts. It is more resistant to frost than grass and stays green and tender after the latter has begun to dry up. For this reason the sheep turn to the *pinque,* and great losses result. The symptoms are salivation, nausea, depression, and weakness. The careful *pastor* will keep his *rebaño* away from a region infested with this weed during that critical period.

Loco weed causes losses in the months of February and March. Stock that feed on it go "crazy." Having tasted it once, sheep cannot leave it alone; it affects them like a drug. Eating nothing else, they stagger along, their actions extremely erratic. Finally they die from lack of nourishment.

In the morning the shearing crew arrived in a cloud of dust in a small truck piled high with bedding rolls and other equipment. They were a noisy band of itinerants, shearing sheep on a commission basis all over the state and into Colorado. Basílico would have nothing to do with them except during shearing time when they were kept constantly occupied.

To prepare the sheep properly for shearing, he would drive about a hundred of them at a time into a small adobe room which had only one opening. There, closely confined, the warmth of their bodies caused the "sweating" that made shearing easier. To get them into the room, he made use of the oldest and wisest billy goat, the patriarch of the small herd he kept with his sheep. It was amusing to see how well the bearded old rogue knew his business. He no sooner entered the door with the sheep close on his heels than he stepped aside close to the exit. He knew that he must get out again and be ready for the next bunch. His whole demeanor showed his supreme contempt for the victims of his guile and his wish to escape close confinement with such idiots.

The sheared sheep, looking more foolish than ever in their nakedness, were held by the dogs in a corner of the hills while Basílico took care of doling out the others to the shed as required. I watched the shearers deftly turn their victims, the wool clip rolling off in a soft mat. As each was finished, a cry of *"¡Uno!"* brought the boss, who acted as inspector. His *"bueno"* permitted the shearer to release the animal as properly sheared. A metal disk was handed the worker to be used at the end of the day in computing his pay.

The crew of shearers would be in the neighborhood for several

days since other sheepowners had requested the use of the sheds for
the shearing of their flocks. I knew Basílico hated to remain in their
company any longer than necessary. He lost his temper under the
bantering of the shearers, who treated all *pastores* with contempt.
The crowning insult was that they persisted in calling him Basil
Loco (literally, "Crazy Basil"). I left that evening atop a load of the
huge sacks into which the wool was packed after shearing.

Basílico and his flock were again at the shearing sheds when I
next saw them. The flock now seemed much larger. I thought at
first more sheep had been bought, but I soon discovered that it was
the spring lambs that made the increase. They were large now,
weighing seventy to seventy-five pounds, a good average for this
type of sheep. I was surprised to see what sturdy, fat fellows they
were.

Basílico's *patrón* had ridden in with a helper to aid in castrating
and docking the lambs. In the first process the lamb was upended
and held with his head away from his captor. Sometimes, in the
case of a particularly vigorous lamb, the forefeet were tied. Both
hind legs were held in encircling arms with hooves caught in the
sheepman's armpits. The right hand held an opened clasp-knife to
sever the tip of the lamb's bag, which was held in the left hand.
The tip of the testicles showing was seized in strong teeth and
withdrawn with a jerk of the head, to be deposited in a pan or pail
close by. The men worked singly as a rule, scarcely making a sound,
perhaps because of blood-smeared faces. The stain spread down the
front of their overalls. An element of rivalry entered into this task,
each worker trying to outdo the other in the number of lambs
altered.

At this time too, the ears of the lambs were marked with the
patrón's distinctive crop or slit, or combination of both, and its tail
was docked to within an inch of its base. The poor creatures, after
undergoing this three-way treatment, stood dripping blood from
many parts of their bodies, bleating disconsolately and shaking
their heads vigorously, sending thin sprays of blood through the air.

At supper that evening I received my introduction to the
so-called "Rocky Mountain oysters"—a big Dutch oven-full which
had been fried and a pile on a lard can lid that had been roasted
over the coals. Both ways I found that they deserved their fame as a
seasonal delicacy.

"Yes, we had a very good *hijadero* ('lambing season'). About half
and half ewes and males, about ninety lambs of every hundred

ewes, and very little loss. We will sell nearly eight hundred lambs, and the *patrón* has had me cut out very nearly three hundred old and toothless ewes. These he is going to pasture on his home meadows, selling them to Indians of the Pueblos and his poorer neighbors. They are good for nothing else but meat now."

Basílico went on: "I will stay here until it is time to turn the rams in with the sheep. This we will do the first of the month of the dead (November). I will winter with my sheep on the chamiso-covered flats between here and the Rio Grande.

"During the month of December I have for many years taken the part of *El Diablo* in *Los Pastores,* that old play that deals with us shepherds, our life in camp, our language. It is directed by my *compadre* Higinio Costales. I make a very good *Diablo,* wouldn't you think so?"

"Wonderful," I said, smiling and taking in his great dark head, wild hair, and angry-looking eyes under heavy brows.

"Come down to see me do it in the month of *Noche Buena* ('Christmas Eve')."

I resolved to do so. *Noche Buena* was the month of *luminarias,* those small fires still lighted in New Mexico on Christmas Eve in commemoration of the shepherd campfires long ago outside the town of Bethlehem. In *Los Pastores,* the Christmas play with its scene laid near the town of Bethlehem, I would see this solitary Basílico, who lived all year with sheep, among his brothers. (28)

The Christmas folk play of Los Pastores *was very popular in Hispano New Mexico. Shepherds often acted some of the parts, and groups of players from one village might visit neighboring communities to entertain and be entertained.*

> Onde hablan letras callan barbas.
> ("Bearded sages are silent when confronted with the written word.") (1)

> No firmes carta que no leas ni bebas agua que no veas.
> ("Sign no paper without reading it nor drink water without looking at it.") (100)

Manuscripts for these and all folk dramas were cherished by their owner. Brown obtained and transcribed three such cuadernos *with texts of* Los Pastores:

(1) From Antonio Gallegos of Agua Fria.

A certain Valentín Flórez from Old Mexico first brought this version of *Los Pastores* to New Mexico about the year 1856. In his troupe he enlisted four Escudero brothers—Miguel, Francisco, and two others—of College Street in Santa Fe. After Valentín Flórez left, the Escudero brothers, since deceased, continued putting on the play in Santa Fe and neighboring villages. One of their troupe, Eliseo Trujillo, acquired a copy of the play when he was twelve years old.

After the Escuderos died, *Señor* Eliseo Trujillo, in company with Pablo Griego, organized a troupe and put on *Los Pastores* in Santa Fe and outside villages as far north as Alcalde and south to Madrid. In Santa Fe they played to audiences in the old Museum, St. Michael's College, St. Catherine's, and in the old San Francisco Hall. This last-named hall was located at the junction of Agua Fria and Water Streets, the present site of Purdy's Bakery. Of the last named company of Griego and Trujillo, only *Señor* Eliseo Trujillo is alive today. He is sixty-six years old and lives at 717 West Manhattan Street, Santa Fe, New Mexico.

The Agua Fria version is a copy of the original as copied from the Old Mexico version by *Señor* Trujillo, with the exception of the introduction of the Indian character in the last part of the play. This character is the creation of some New Mexican author who thought it seemly to have an Indian come and worship the Christ-Child also, giving this version a unique New World touch. (90)

(2) From Gregorio Chávez of Leyba, "who copied it from a book in the possession of Sr. Pablo Madrid of Duran, New Mexico. Sr. Pablo Madrid's copy was one handed down to him from his father and one that was brought from Galisteo when his father left Galisteo to settle in Duran." (91)

(3) From Ysidro Mares of Santa Fe.

Don Ysidro, sixty-nine years old, knows for a fact that this copy belonged originally to his *padrino*, the late Nasario Rivera. This *padrino* died when Don Ysidro was fifteen years old and had used this copy to produce *Los Pastores* in Santa Fe, Agua Fria, Tesuque, Cienega, and other adjacent towns. This original, then, must be all of seventy-five to ninety years old that we know of. How long Nasario Rivera really had it in his possession and where he obtained it could not be ascertained.

The present owner, Don Ysidro Mares, has had this copy in his possession since "Governor Larrazolo was in the Capitol" and directed a production of Los Pastores for the first time then. "And my Lucifer was the very devil," he related. "When he was banished to the infernal regions he would go and hide amongst the ladies of the audience." Since that time, Don Ysidro has directed Los Pastores and has taken his troupe to Cerrillos, Agua Fria, Cienega, Nambe, Pojoaque, and other places near Santa Fe, and in Santa Fe has shown it in different sections of the town. (92)

Productions of Los Pastores were only a part of the Christmas festivities.

Christmas Eve or Noche Buena as observed in New Mexico among her Spanish settlers was somewhat different before the era of American influence. The giving and receiving of gifts was not then the uppermost thought in the minds of the native people. True, there were gifts, but mostly for the children. Enjoyment of the Christmas season was so great and looked forward to with such anticipation that the month on which the celebration falls was not referred to as December but as el mes de Noche Buena, or the month of Christmas Eve. (In like manner June was el mes de San Juan or the month of St. John, and July was el mes de Santiago or the month of St. James.)

For some time before Christmas the youngsters were kept on their good behavior because of the fear instilled into them by repeated threats of: "Si no te sosiegas, llamo el Abuelo" ("If you don't behave, I'll call in the Grandfather"). The Abuelo was the bogeyman of those times. In his grotesque makeup and mask he would make his appearance sometimes a week before Christmas. His blood-curdling cry would sound out on the frosty air at dusk as he approached the door of some dwelling. The door would be opened and in he would stride to find a cowering group of children staring at him, bug-eyed and trembling, utterly terrified by this terrible figure with the long rawhide whip which was a never-absent part of his costume. Cracking his whip, he would roar: "¿Han sido buenos muchachos estos?" ("Have these children been good?")

The speechless children could only bob their heads in pitiful eagerness to placate as their eyes besought their parents, asking them to intercede for them. Simulating a like fear of this awful figure, the parents would hasten to assure the *Abuelo* that their *niños* had been very good and that he should not carry any of them away. *"Pues que recen y se acuesten"* would likely be his next order, let them say their prayers and get in bed. Prayers would be hastily said and little heads would burrow under the covers to shut out the sight of their enemy the *Abuelo*. After receiving a glass of wine or some other refreshment, the *Abuelo* would leave to visit the next house.

Now the *Abuelo* is a character who has his part to play in the dance of the Matachines. He is the masked figure of the long whip who harries and carries on a mock fight with *El Toro* or the character who in his horn-decorated mask plays the part of a bull. The *Abuelo* also keeps the spectators at bay, making sudden terrifying dashes at different children in the crowd. Yet as I have related, he had another part that he played in the life of the community even before the Matachines made their first public appearance. His ululating cry was enough to break up any game near evening and send a frightened, home-seeking bunch of children hurrying to forgotten chores. Having done these in a surprisingly short time, no child would venture out of doors again that evening.

Having rehearsed privately, the Matachines made their first full-costume appearance or *Ensayo Real* the afternoon of Christmas Eve. This beautiful dance, portraying in its characters and movements such a mixture of Indian and Spanish legend, was an annual feature of the Christmas festivities. Any village that put on this dance was sure of a crowd of visitors to help make merry and upon whom the sacred rites of hospitality could be exercised.

After the Matachines the crowds would disperse to their homes, the men to build and light *luminarias*, those cheerful and appropriate bonfires built of pitchy, resinous sticks of wood laid log-cabin fashion. These bonfires, several in front of some homes, lit up the village in a most beautiful way. They imparted to the frosty air a tang of strong smoke which, more than tinsel or holly, spells Christmas to me whenever or wherever I get a whiff of it. These twinkling lights flaring up throughout the village have a most delightful significance. They are to light the way for the Christ Child so that His small feet find their way back to earth, to His Church and into the hearts of His people on this His birthday.

Emboldened by the lights from the *luminarias* and by the

presence of their elders, the children would risk or forget the
menace of the *Abuelo* and gather in gay groups around these
bonfires. This made fine hunting for the *Abuelo* and suddenly he
would appear, his shadow enlarged to giant proportions by the
firelight. Cracking his whip, he would scatter the little groups
toward home, some sobbing and stumbling in their fright, others
laughing hysterically as delicious chills of apprehension chased up
and down their spines.

In the meantime, the womenfolk had been busy frying and
baking. The fat hog killed in anticipation of this event had been
converted by their art into delicious stuffing for *empanaditas,* those
tasty and filling turnover pies made of minced pork, raisins, and the
meat of the piñon nut. There would also be *buñuelos, bizcochitos*
and *chicharrones.* These last, chitlings to you, are to my taste
almost as good as the rest if I can eat them sizzling hot, wrapped in
a hot tortilla sandwich fashion, plentifully salted, and with a good
glass of wine to wash them down.

Supper is an easy problem to solve with all the food cooking.
Everybody eats whatever they most like, and the children are
constantly warned and threatened with the *Abuelo* for being too
greedy. All this time neighbor women are coming in to bring gifts
from their kitchen and, after visiting awhile, they leave knowing
that they too will receive a similar gift from this neighbor and that
one. This exchange of gifts is a great occasion to compare and
discuss the culinary skill of the different housewives. You may be
sure the opportunity is not wasted; women are the same everywhere.

Suddenly a new sound is heard outside the door—several voices
raised in a sort of chant:

> Oremos, Oremos
> Angelitos semos
> D'el cielo venimos
> A pedir Oremos
> Si no nos dan,
> Puertas y ventanas quebraremos.

The door is opened and in troops a bunch of youngsters, neighbor
children old enough to have lost their fear of the *Abuelo.* In their
chant they have proclaimed themselves angels from heaven asking
for gifts. In the last line of their chant they threaten to break down

doors and windows if they are turned away without a gift of some kind. This last threat is regarded laughingly, and the children are treated to food and sweets. As they leave each is given a gift to take with them. What the origin of this *Oremos* custom is I do not know, but it has been explained as a reminder that the stranger outside our door should not be forgotten, for he might be the angel of the Lord in disguise, and he might visit some punishment on the home which so far forgot itself as to turn the homeless away empty-handed.

It is now nearing time for *La Misa del Gallo* or midnight mass. Nearly everyone attends this solemn ceremony celebrating the birth of Christ. The mass closes with a file of communicants going forward to partake of Holy Communion at the altar rail. The crowd is pervaded with awe and religious quiet when they first leave the church, only to burst into joyous enthusiasm as they gather at their homes. There the traditional spread of chocolate, *buñuelos, empanaditas,* and wine is served.

The usual breakfast dish for Christmas morning was one called *principio,* which means the beginning or we might say the send-off, a dish of boiled beef, onions, and raisins. It was supposed to be very efficacious as a restorative for excessive drinking, loss of sleep, or overeating rich foods such as were served at the midnight supper. It was not the only dish served but was the main one for the reasons I have given. Breakfast over, the rest of Christmas morning was spent watching the Matachines and visiting.

A dance at the neighboring Indian Pueblo would draw some the crowd away, to return for the night's performance of *Los Pastores* as rendered by a group of visiting players. This play, somewhat similar to the morality plays of England, is vastly amusing to the rapt villagers. It depicts the story of the birth of Christ, bringing together the shepherds, angels, the Holy Family, and all of the characters from that far-off time. It also has its comic characters whose remarks cause much merriment. Thus would end a usual Christmas season in any of New Mexico's villages before the advent of Santa Claus and his sleigh full of gifts. (85)

Sometimes other folk plays were produced around Christmas. Los Tres Reyes, *"another religious play which deals with the visit of the Three Wise Men of the East to the manger at Bethlehem" was "sometimes given in Taos during the Christmas season."* (94)

Special songs were also sung. The following alabado *honors the "trinity" of the Holy Family:*

Daremos gracias con fe	Grateful praises we sing
Y crecidas esperanzas	And hope renewed confess
Cantando las alabanzas	As hymns of praise we sing
De Jesús, María, y José.	To Jesus, Mary, and Joseph.
Este es el raro prodigio	To us this marvel is given
Que a nuestros ojos se ve	Our eyes are blessed in seeing
Esta es la Sagrada Familia	This is the Holy Family
De Jesús, María, y Jose.	Of Jesus, Mary, and Joseph.
Por Providencia Divina	Through Providence Divine
El Verbo encarnado fue	The Word took human form
Sin manchar pureza	And left the purity intact
De Jesús, María, y José.	Of Jesus, Mary, and Joseph.
Canten bellos serafines	Sing out ye Seraphim
Que en Belén nacido fue	For in Bethlehem is born
Jesús, el Fruto Bendito	Jesus the Blessed Fruit
A Jesús, María, y José.	To Jesus, Mary, and Joseph.
En tan feliz nacimiento	Attendant on this blessed birth,
Una mula y un buey fue	Were an ox and a humble mule
Los que hicieron compañia	They were the only company
A Jesús, María, y José.	Of Jesus, Mary, and Joseph.
Los tres Reyes del Oriente	Three Magi from the East
Por grande dicha se ve	With great good fortune we see
Que adoran en el portal	Worshipping arrive before and kneel
A Jesús, María, y José.	To Jesus, Mary, and Joseph.
Dulces acentos oyí	The sweetest music I heard
Y con júbilo escuché	And rejoicing heard that they
Que las Glorias entonaban	Glory, glory sang in unison
A Jesús, María, y José.	To Jesus, Mary, and Joseph.
De los antiguos profetas	The scribes of old foretold
Todo el deleite se ve	The glories of this day
Ensalzar la castidad	And praised the immaculate purity
De Jesús, María, y José.	Of Jesus, Mary, and Joseph.
Salve Divina María	Mary Divine, all hail
A quién siempre invocaré	Whom I always will invoke
Salve Rosa Matutina	Hail, O Morning Rose,
De Jesús, María, y José.	Hail Jesus, Mary, and Joseph.
El sentido más tapado	Every ear however deaf
Oye con voz de la fe	In faith will harken joyfully

Alabar los Santos Nombres	To praises of the Holy Names
De Jesús, María, y José.	Of Jesus, Mary, and Joseph.
Hasta la lengua más muda	A tongue however mute
Desenmudece y se ve	But what will speak to sing
Muy libre para alabar	And voice the praises of
A Jesús, María, y José.	Jesus, Mary, and Joseph.
En toda tribulación	Amidst all tribulations
Aclamamos con gran fe	With faith we'll ever sing
A los dulcísimos nombres	The praises of the Holy Names
De Jesús, María, y José.	Of Jesus, Mary, and Joseph.
Cantan en su son las aves	Birds sing in joyful harmony
Mejor de lo que pensé	Much sweeter than I thought they could
Declaran las alabanzas	They raise their song in praise
De Jesús, María, y José.	Of Jesus, Mary, and Joseph.
Adios aquella vista hermosa	Goodbye enchanting scene
En el cielo gozaré	Which in heaven I will join
Adios Familia dichosa	Goodbye, O gracious Family
De Jesús, María, y José.	Of Jesus, Mary, and Joseph. (11)

Special customs were observed on December 28, the Feast of the Holy Innocents, and on New Year's Day.

The custom of which this sketch treats, that of borrowing some prized possession from someone and then making them redeem it, has been practiced for many years in New Mexico by the native people. The origin of the custom has been explained as the act of the children of Israel before their flight from Egypt. It will be remembered that they were instructed to borrow everything of value that they could from their Egyptian masters and thus recompense themselves for their many years of slavery. Another explanation is based on another historical incident. This has to do with the St. Bartholomew massacre. Here also the intended victims were despoiled under the pretext of borrowing. Which explanation is authentic I could not say.

In the latter part of this sketch there is reference to the serenades which are accorded to those persons named Manuel by their friends. This custom is followed on New Year's morning, just as the Antonios are serenaded on the 13th of June, the Santiagos on the 25th of July, and the Lorenzos on the 10th of August, and so on. Thus, according to this custom, regardless of their actual birthday, an individual's day to celebrate is the saint's day whose name corresponds with his own.

o   o   o

Just a few days after Christmas, Isabel was touching up her fireplace with *tierra amarilla* (a yellow, micaceous dirt used decoratively) and otherwise putting her little home in order. They had had many visitors during *Noche Buena*, and her white walls and usually spotless floors showed some after-effects from the company. Yes, she thought as she worked, she would have to whitewash her front room before New Year's, for wasn't her husband's name Manuel and wouldn't his friends be around early on New Year's morning to celebrate the day of his saintly namesake. But today she would rest for it was only three days since Christmas and she was still tired from the strenuous activities of the day and the preparations for it. So she was thinking when she heard a light rapping on the door.

"*¿Quién es?*" she called out.

"Shonita, *madrina*," a child's voice replied.

"*Entra* Shonita," was Isabel's answer, upon which the door opened to let in a bright-eyed girl about eight years old.

"*¿Como está, madrina?* How nicely you have cleaned up your room and I sure like the smell of that *tierra amarilla*. When it is wet like that it makes me think of the smell in the air after a shower on a hot summer day."

"*Cómo hablas,* how you talk, Encarnación," answered Isabel, calling her godchild by her full name instead of the diminutive Shonita. "How is my *comadre?*"

"She is well, and *madrina*, she wants to borrow your shawl. She is going to the chapel to light a candle she had promised to San Antonio and her shawl has a big stain on it. Some whitewash got spilled on it a little while ago and she wants to go to the chapel right now."

"*Bueno*, Shonita, but tell *comadre* to be careful with my shawl and not get any wax on it. Your mother is very careless."

Isabel was undoubtedly tired and out of sorts or she would not have spoken of her *comadre* in that manner or called her godchild by any other than the fond diminutive Shonita. But my *comadre* is careless, thought Isabel as she went to get her shawl out of her trunk. And she did begrudge lending her beautiful *tapalo;* it was her most prized possession with its rich black folds and long silken fringe. It had been a present from her husband along with the other bridal gifts that the bridegroom presents to his bride at the betrothal ceremony. So, wrapping it up carefully, she handed it to Shonita with another warning to be careful.

Closing the door rather sharply on her retreating godchild she went on about her tasks, but an angry energy had replaced the indifference of a short while ago. She had barely finished the fireplace when there came another rapping on the door. This time she recognized it to be Shonita.

"Entra, Shonita, *¿qué quieres hora?,* what do you want now?"

Shonita slipped in, eyes dancing with barely suppressed merriment. *"Aquí mandó mi manita."* ("My mother sent you this.") So saying, Shonita handed her *madrina* a diminutive straw broom tied with a little red ribbon and darted out of the door again.

"¡Mil diablos! ¡Inocente, día de los Inocentes, y me hizo inocente esta mi comadre!" ("A thousand devils! Innocent, day of the Innocents, and this one my *comadre* has taken me in, fooled me!") Such were Isabel's exclamations as she gazed on the little broom, which she finally threw into a corner of the room.

The reason for Isabel's dismay and consternation at the sight of the harmless little broom must be explained. Her *comadre* had taken her in or fooled her on this day of the Innocents, which falls on December 28th. You should be careful on that day not to lend anybody anything, especially some article you value highly, because if after you do you receive such a little broom you must redeem your loan. And the price of redemption is in direct proportion to the cost of the article or to the value you are known to place on it.

"Madre Santa, what will Manuel say? Oh, this one and that one of my *comadre,* she's a sly one all right." And so, muttering several uncomplimentary remarks about her *comadre,* Isabel waited impatiently for Manuel to come back from the hills where he had gone for wood.

As she rolled and fashioned the tortillas she handled them with a violence that spelled anything but pleasure with her *comadre* next door. But that one, a lighthearted creature, was smiling to herself, well knowing how angry her *comadre* would be at her but little caring. Isabel shouldn't take such jokes so seriously. She surely had taken her in though, and she would insist on a suitable *desempeño* ("redemption") before she would return the shawl.

As soon as Isabel heard the clatter of the wood as it fell from the burro's back she rushed out to tell Manuel of her misfortune. A movement of the curtains in the window of her *comadre's* house sent her back inside. Her *comadre* should not have the pleasure of overhearing her tale of woe to Manuel.

But Manuel, once inside, had to listen and bear the storm of her protests. Finally he spoke: *Calla mujer, no es pa' tanto ¿Y quién te manda ser tan simple?"* ("Quiet, woman, it's not so serious as all that, and who asked you to be so dumb anyway?") We will give a dance and redeem your shawl. *Mira*, look! On New Year's Day, my saint's day, they will be coming to serenade me. We will have to receive and treat guests so just tell *comadre* that we are giving a dance here on that day as her reward and for her to bring all the family and her friends and we will invite our friends. In that way we will discharge two obligations at once. You make more *bizcochitos* and pies than you had figured on. I will buy more wine and candy, hire the musicians, *y all' está* ('and there you are)." So Manuel, a fun-loving soul and practical too, found the solution.

Isabel showed her acceptance by going to the door and calling "Shonita, Shonita" at the top of her voice. The promptness with which Shonita appeared was suspicious. She eagerly listened to Isabel as she said, "Shonita, tell *comadre* that I'm redeeming my shawl by giving her and *compadre* a dance here in this house on New Year's Day, to bring all her friends and my shawl too."

On New Year's morning, as was the custom, Manuel was serenaded early in the morning, as were the other Manuels in the village. He smilingly received the musicians and his well-wishing friends, listened proudly to the verses sung in his honor, and joined in those sung in honor of Emanuel, his namesake and saintly patron. He was generous in his rewards to the musicians and with the sweets and wine which he had provided just for this occasion.

As this group of merrymakers started to leave for the homes of other Manuels, their host cordially invited them to his home again that afternoon for the feasting and dancing. He also spoke to the musicians for their services at the dance. *"Bueno*, Manuel. *Seguro*, Manuel. You are such a fine fellow that we cannot charge you anything on this your day," was their enthusiastic response. Well they knew that the generous Manuel would voluntarily give them more than they would ever think of charging.

So Manuel's home was a merry place that New Year's Day, and

Isabel enjoyed herself immensely after all. She was secretly glad that Shonita had taken her in but resolved that the little broom should sweep away her gullibility and prepare her for next year. Maybe she could catch her *comadre* napping next year and ask her to lend her Shonita to run an errand. If so, it would take something really wonderful to redeem her. *Ahí veremos el año que viene* ("Next year we shall see"). (56)

> El que presta lo que ha de menester el diablo se ríe de él.
> ("He who lends that of which he has need is laughed at by the devil.")
>
> Más vale algo que nada.
> (A half a loaf is better than no loaf at all. [Literally: "Something is worth more than nothing"]) (100)

Perhaps the most important time of the year was Holy Week, especially Good Friday. In most villages, Lenten and Holy Week observances were sponsored by the local morada *or chapter of the Brotherhood of Our Father Jesus, a pious confraternity of laymen dedicated to mutual aid, community charity, the spirit of penance, and the Passion of Jesus. Brown's description of Brotherhood rituals and social importance appears in his earlier publication,* Echoes of the Flute *(126). While on the Writers' Project he was also able to transcribe and translate hymns from a* cuaderno *("notebook") "loaned by a member of the Penitente Order of Rio Arriba County, New Mexico." The following brief example is identified as an "alabado sung during the rite of [simulated] crucifixion" on Good Friday.*

Oh Jesús, por mis delitos	Oh Jesus, for my faults
Padeciste tal dolor;	You suffered so much pain;
A tus pies arrepentido	At your feet you see me
Me ves, dulce Redentor.	Repentant, Sweet Redeemer.
Agonizante en el huerto	We meditate upon Your agony
Contemplemos al Señor,	In that garden of old, Our Lord,
Postrado en tierra su rostro	With His face bowed to the earth
Con un sangriento sudor.	Covered with bloody sweat.
En el pretorio le vemos	In the Pretorium we see Him
Azotado con furor;	Suffering furious scourges;
Es de cadenas cubierto	Chains are loaded on Him
Por los hombres el Señor.	Our Lord is treated thus by man.

Con afrentas y dolores	With affronts and cruel blows
Ciñe la tropa feroz	These fierce troopers bind
Una punzante corona	A cruel crown of thorns
En la frente de su Dios.	Upon God's holy brow.
Al cordero manso cargan	They make the Gentle Lamb
Con el leño del dolor;	Carry a cross, emblem of pain;
Su pesada cruz a cuestas	With His cross upon bent shoulders
Marcha el dulce Salvador.	Our Saviour marches to Mount Calvary.
A Jesús en cruz clavado	Look, oh sinner, on the Christ,
Contémplale, oh pecador;	Jesus nailed to the cross;
Ve al hijo del Eterno	Look on the Son of the Eternal
Expirando por tu amor.	Expiring for love of you. (15)

Feast days of special saints were also observed. In the spring, most farming communities honored St. Isidore, patron saint of farmers.

"San Ysidro Labrador" is the title of an *alabado* or hymn sung in honor of Saint Ysidro the husbandman, beloved patron saint of the farmer and, next to San Antonio, the most popular saint with the rural inhabitants of New Mexico. The image of San Ysidro is to be found in nearly every village church. It is a quaint and sometimes amusing figure for sometimes the saint is depicted in top hat and dress coat, yet he is always shown with his yoke of oxen hitched to a miniature plow.

In the little valley town of Valdez north of Taos, or San Antonio as it used to be known, San Ysidro Day, May 15, is celebrated in this manner: On the eve of this day a procession of the villagers, who are all farmers, carry San Ysidro in state to the farthest farm up the valley. Here their host, the owner of this farm, awaits his saintly visitor. In the field near his farm he has prepared a *jacal* or little hut made of willows.

When the procession arrives, San Ysidro is placed within this miniature farm house. Candles are lit around the figure and bonfires built outside. This is the wake or *velorio* of San Ysidro, and the whole community make themselves comfortable around the bonfires. The hymn to San Ysidro is sung as well as other *alabados* interspersed with the praying of the rosary. With all reverence, a good time is had. Gossiping groups take advantage of lulls in the singing and praying. The opportunity for flirtatious interludes is not neglected by younger members of the group.

Near midnight the owner of the farm, who is proud of the honor of having San Ysidro as an overnight guest, summons the group to supper. First, the old folks and the leaders in prayers and singing make their way to the well-laden tables, to partake of the meal amid decorous and dignified conversation. It is a different story when the young folks come to the table. Hilarity and laughter prolong the meal until elder authority asserts itself and the younger ones reluctantly return to the group around the *jacal* or shrine of San Ysidro.

When the rays of the rising sun first show themselves over the mountains on this, San Ysidro's own day, his hymn is sung with renewed vigor. With San Ysidro carried at the front the whole body of people wends its way down the river, following lanes and through fields so that San Ysidro may bless the crops, insure fertility, and grant a bounteous harvest in the fall.

Slowly the procession follows the winding river, chanting and praying as it goes. Near noon they reach the last farm at the other end of the valley, where the pleased owner awaits them with great quantities of roast mutton, oven-baked bread, pies, and coffee. San Ysidro is temporarily neglected as the crowd scatters to the shade of the cottonwoods to feast on the bounty which has been provided.

On his return to the village San Ysidro is carried through the fields on the opposite bank of the river, so that none should fail to receive the blessings that his passing would bring them. His near approach to the village is heralded by the clear tones of the church bell. It is a tired but happy people who, after ensconcing San Ysidro in his own place in the church, disperse to prepare for the dance that night, confident that their fields would again yield bounteously this year. (106)

San Ysidro Labrador,	Saint Isidore, Husbandman
Patrón de los labradores,	Saintly patron of the farmer,
Que nos libre tu favor	May your favor grant us protection
De langostas y temblores.	From locusts and temblors dread.
Por la gran misericordia	By virtue of the mercy shown
Con que te ayudó el Señor,	By the Lord to you of yore,
Derrama paz y concordia	Grant that peace and sweet accord
Entre todo labrador.	Dwell with the farmers evermore.
Pues que fuiste designado	Since 'tis you who has been chosen
Por patrón de la labor,	As saintly patron of the farmer,
Siempre serás adorado	Hymns of praise shall e'er by them
Del devoto labrador.	Be sung in honor of your name.

Cuando el Señor por castigo	When our Lord as punishment
Nos manda mal temporal,	Sends adverse winds and hail,
Con tu bondadoso abrigo	We on your kind protecting grace
Nos vemos libre de mal.	Rely to save our crops from harm.
Del ladrón acostumbrado	From the arrant thief who steals
Que nunca teme al Señor	With no fear of God's wrath,
Nos libres nuestro sembrado	Oh grant protection for our fields,
Te pedimos por favor.	We ask it of your grace.
El granizo destructor	Hail, our most destructive foe,
Que no nos cause su daño,	Oft lays our harvests flat,
Te pedimos con favor	Its wrath withhold, and grant to us
Tener cosecha este año.	A bounteous harvest this coming year.
En tus bondades confiado	Confiding in your kindly heart
Te pido de corazón	I ask with all my own
Le mandes a mi sembrado	That you will deign to bless
Favores y bendición.	And grant fair weather to my fields.
Adios, Oh Santo glorioso,	Farewell, Oh blessed saint
Escogido del Señor	Until the coming year,
Hasta el año venidero,	Thou chosen one of the Lord
San Ysidro Labrador.	Saint Isidore, the Husbandman. (19)

Velorios for a saint involved processions, hymns, prayers, and a midnight supper. The wake for San Luis Gonzaga on June 21 differs, however.

San Luis Gonzaga is the patron saint of the dance. His day falls on the 21st of June. In some places a vigil is held in his honor. This in itself is not so unusual, but the nature of the ceremony is different from the usual vigil in honor of any special saint. For since he is the patron saint of the dance, a dance is given in his honor.

The saint is seated between the musicians, usually a guitar and a violin player. San Luis's hymn is sung and, after praying the rosary, dancing is the order of the night. Instead of singing couplets in honor of the different dancers, the musicians dedicate their verses to San Luis Gonzaga, coupling his name with some one of the dancers on the floor. The individual so honored is expected to give the musicians a coin in acknowledgment of the honor. The dance lasts until daylight, when the saint is joyfully carried back to the church. (105)

Sometimes, feast day celebrations included the exciting gallo race.

October 22 is the date of the annual feast day observed by the villagers of Galisteo in honor of their patron, Nuestra Señora de los Remedios. A feature of the day's celebration is a *corrida de gallo* or rooster pull, a very lively and spirited contest in which two competing bands of horsemen take part.

A live rooster, buried in the sand with only his head and neck showing, is the prize for which the two groups compete. The riders take turns in swooping down on the buried bird, leaning perilously from the backs of their speeding mounts as they endeavor to snatch him from his sandy prison in passing.

When after several trials one of the riders is successful in seizing the rooster, he makes off with it with the rest of the horsemen in furious pursuit. The fortunate fellow's teammates surround him, fending off the opposing team's efforts to secure the hapless rooster. The rooster is freely used as a weapon to belabor anyone who rides in close and tries to seize him. The object of the chase is to see which team still has possession of the rooster at the end of a stated period, usually sunset. (50)

Most villages held gallo *races on June 24, San Juan Day. The following description of one such race held at Pecos is based on a nine-stanza ballad collected and translated by Brown.*

A rooster pull was a favorite amusement and test of strength, of horsemanship, and of horseflesh. Challenges to a rooster pull were common between villages at the time of which this ballad treats.

It seems that the folks of Pecos had challenged the Galisteos to a rooster pull on San Juan Day. This challenge was given and taken at some midwinter fiesta where the two groups met. Now it happened that Galisteo and vicinity had a very dry spring. No moisture meant poor grazing and consequently weak horses. So the Galisteos wrote to Pecos asking a postponement of the meet, citing the condition of their horses as reason.

Pecos refused to accede to this request, accusing Galisteo of cowardice or fear of the outcome. They so taunted Galisteo that it was finally decided to hold the contest as agreed upon originally. Pecos had been able to winter feed their horses and were confident of winning over the Galisteos with their weak ponies which had to depend solely on grazing for sustenance.

Don Ambrosio Pino, leader of the Galisteos, had a trick up his sleeve which saved the day for his people. His good friend Federino of Albuquerque had a fast horse which was kept in good condition for racing. He borrowed this horse and entrusted it to his best rider. When Pecos with the rooster in their possession were riding away exulting, this rider on the fast mount came up with the leader, and, wresting the rooster from him, raced back to Galisteo, thus saving Galisteo from defeat and also winning for Galisteo the many bets made loyally in the face of expected defeat.

These facts regarding the condition of the Galisteo mounts and of the horse from Albuquerque I had from my informant Don Augustine Montoya. He was eighteen years old when this contest took place and, although seventy-two years of age, remembers well this incident. The ballad describes the action of the actual contest but does not hint anything of the above facts. Only in the last verse is there any indication of this. In this verse Don Ambrosio Pino thanks his good friend Federino for the help he has given Galisteo in this contest with their rivals from Pecos. (62)

Santa Cruz residents presented the stirring horseback folk drama of Los moros y los cristianos *("The Moors and the Christians").*

This play was brought over from Spain and sometimes enacted at Santa Cruz on the feast day of Our Lady of Carmel, July 16, and sometimes on Santa Cruz Day, May 3. The play is enacted on horseback and depicts an encounter between the Moors and the Christian Spaniards. As near as can be ascertained, the play was based on the victory of the Spaniards over the Moors in the 15th century. It was first given in New Mexico at the dedication of the church built at San Gabriel del Yunque, the first capital. (94)

Taoseños *produced* El Niño Perdido *("The Lost Child") in the autumn.*

This religious play is given in Taos in the fall of the year. It deals with the Virgin Mary's search for the child Jesus whom she lost during the feast of the Jewish Passover in Jerusalem. The characters are the child Jesus, the Virgin Mary, a rich man, the rabbis in the temple, and others.

The child Jesus, who has been lost for three days, stops at a rich man's house and begs for something to eat. The rich man refuses his request, the more so after the Child confuses him and provokes his anger by confounding him in a discussion of the laws of the prophets. From the rich man's door the Child goes still in search of someone who will feed him. He encounters a poor but charitable family who, moved by pity and some instinctive recognition of his divinity, give him food. He tells them that he must go to the temple on his father's business and that if his mother should come there seeking him to direct her to the temple. One of the members of this household has opportunity to tell the Virgin Mary of the whereabouts of her child. She finds him in the temple surrounded by the rabbis and discussing the laws and their meaning with reference to the coming of the Messiah. The end of the play shows Mary leaving the temple with the child Jesus and the rabbis astonished at the wisdom of this child of three and partially convinced of his divine origin.

There are a few songs in this play. In this connection I will say that for variety and beauty of songs no play equals *Los Pastores* in this respect. (94)

Like most Hispano villagers, many Cordovans regarded the annual celebration of saints' days and other observations as integral to the welfare of the community. Nevertheless, these practices proved no less susceptible to modification or neglect than other aspects of village life. Brown described the changes that accompanied the influx of migratory wage labor dollars into Cordova.

The line of flat roofs extending around the square is today broken by upthrusting pitched roofs covered with corrugated iron. These roofs were introduced as a result of the prosperous era of 1919-30, when high wages in section camp, sheep ranch, and mining camp brought into Cordova a surplus of money which was employed in these so-called improvements.

The World War era and the years that followed brought many changes into the village, for the most part in social customs that no longer found complete satisfaction with the peaceful rounds of planting and harvesting crops. Veterans of the World War came back with new ideas and no desire for what they called a humdrum existence. Men began to seek seasonal occupation outside their own village and state. Some left for the sheep ranches of Utah and Wyoming, others for the mines of Colorado and Utah, and still others to the section gangs of Colorado and Kansas.

There was no abandonment of the land, rather, a new order saw the women taking charge of planting crops, aided in part by their children and men too old to seek work outside the valley. Economically, this practice raised the standard of living to a certain extent. During the long summers the women tended their gardens and fields with perhaps more care than even their men-folk would have. Every available fruit and vegetable was dried and preserved. The *dispensa* was filled by these hardworking women, so that when the head of the house returned with six to eight months' wages in his pocket he found that he need buy only sugar, coffee, salt, and perhaps some white flour. This, with a supply of clothing, constituted nearly everything needed to get through the winter months.

The result was a surplus that must be disposed of in some way because, as they say, "*¿Pa' qué se hizo el dinero?*" ("What was money made for?"). This extra money wrought outward and inward changes in Cordova, for instance, the metal roofs and a few automobiles. Also, this abundance has served to increase the stakes in the *monte* game and increase the amount of liquor bought. In a social sense, the excursion of these seasonal workers into other fields is to be noted in the modern dance steps executed on the floor of the *sala de baile* and in the freedom with which the younger people commingle, something that their elders condemn but to no effect.

A virtue that persists is the inherent love of the soil, the land their forefathers fought so hard to reclaim and hold. Although most of these men who work outside the state have lost some of the love of tilling the soil, they still cling to that fierce pride in ownership of their own land. If, as it often happens, the worker's money is spent before it is time to return to his job in Wyoming or Colorado, he can always borrow on his land from the local moneylender. This individual knows that his client will never think of relinquishing his land, no matter if he has borrowed an amount equal to its full value. One man, through an unlucky session at monte, borrowed so much money against his and his father's land that he stayed in Wyoming for four whole years in order to clear the debt against it. The land in question is scarcely capable of three hundred dollars worth of produce a year, but it had been in the family for generations and pride forbade that it go to someone else.

A Cordova father left his two sons about four acres of land, part of which was in fruit trees. Division of the land was made to the satisfaction of both heirs. Soon the younger son lost his share to his older brother, through sums of money borrowed on his inheritance. His propensity for giving dances in his own and neighboring villages was the cause, for he who gives a dance must pay the fiddler. The older brother was strictly conservative and lived meagerly from the produce of the four acres. He never got much ahead, but he was a landowner, and he always looked down on his foolish younger brother because the latter owned no land. The younger one lived much better after he got over the wildness of his early years; he turned his native wit to good advantage. He was a shrewed trader and to some extent a practical politician. One way or another he made more money in three months than his brother made in a year. But the landowner's contempt for his brother's way of life and his feeling of security in the ownership of land never diminished in the face of his brother's prosperity. He always mentioned his brother in a pitying way as *"pobrecito mi hermanito,* he was so thoughtless in losing his land; what is a man without his own piece of land and four walls wherein he may hang his hat whenever he pleases?"* On the day when ditch bosses are elected by the landowners whose fields are irrigated by these ditches, the elder brother would put on an ancient frock coat, symbol of his status as a landowner, and glance loftily at his brother seated outside the polling place, which he could not enter since he owned no land.

With the passing of men like Don José Dolores López and women like Tía Lupe, family life in Cordova lost its strongest bulwarks for family unity and the old customs of respect for elders which made for amicable relations. The sage advice of the oldtimers falls mostly on deaf ears, and new ways are being adopted that destroy the simplicity and charm of traditional manners and customs. Groups of girls arrange parties and go into Española for their permanents.

However, the customs and traditions of centuries are tenacious and hard to eradicate entirely. All of the customary fiestas and saints' days are still observed with the same spirit of reverence mixed with gaiety, and hospitality is extended just as freely to the stranger or visitor as always. The religious parts of these celebrations remain the same; no new or jarring note mars them. Observance of all ritual is still carried out with the same simplicity and devotion as before. *Luminarias* are lighted on *Noche Buena;* the *alabado* is still heard at wakes; and during Lent, with the inevitable accompaniment of the *pito, alabados* are sung by the Penitente Brotherhood.

There is one exception, however. For several years, San Ysidro has not been taken out over the fields and hills to bless the crops. Old men and women of that generation, which is fast disappearing, shake their heads in sad disapproval and aver that good crops cannot be expected if the old rites are neglected. And it is true that the fields have not yielded as in other years; hail has beaten down the beans and oats in the upland clearings, and rain has not come at the right time to bring the bean crop to its fullest yield. Perhaps it is a change in climate; perhaps the soil through years of tilling has become impoverished. Although science might find many reasons for the decreased harvests, the old folks would not accept them. No, it is that San Ysidro is angry; he is offended and will no longer intercede for the farmers.

One innovation has finally been accepted, although it entailed a long and bitter struggle with those who did not believe in interfering with God's will. This is the vaccination of the children by the Public Health Service through its traveling nurses. There were many who refused to send their children to school on the day that the village schoolmaster announced that the nurse would be there to make all the children immune to the dread plagues that used to sweep the village. In some cases, the force of the law was called upon to persuade recalcitrant parents that they must comply for their children's sake. These stubborn ones finally consented, and virulent plagues are things of the past. As recently as 1922, an epidemic of diphtheria struck the village, and the village bell tolled for the deaths of thirty-six children in twice that number of days. The people now realize the great difference that vaccination and inoculation have made.

Through a program fostered by the New Mexico State Board of Education in cooperation with the Work Projects Administration, the village of Cordova is proudly conscious of a new school building. This building is so greatly superior to the old one that they are not to be compared. It is as if the old building had never existed; it was just a shed composed of two small rooms into which some seventy children were crowded by twos on benches designed to seat one. Even so there were not enough school desks, and some of the children seated themselves in a window. The floors of this building were broken, doors and windows were drafty, water for drinking purposes was brought from the river in a pail, and one dipper served the whole school. It was almost impossible for the teacher to keep any semblance of order, what with two children to a desk and these desks crowded against each other in such a manner that no normal child could forego the chance to pull braids and kick shins. It is greatly to the credit of the harassed teachers of other days if even one child under their tutelage learned the alphabet under such conditions.

As in most of the settlements of New Mexico, the first school in Cordova was conducted in a room of a private home. The teacher was paid fifty cents per month for every child sent to him. Each child was required to carry a stick of wood to the school each day to be used in the corner fireplace that alone furnished heat. Backless *tarimas* ("benches") served them as seats and a square of well-scraped hide served as a slate or copybook. A piece of charcoal was the pencil. Instruction was in Spanish and embraced three subjects—reading, writing, and spelling, the last taught in the old manner. Each syllable of the word to be spelled was spelled separately and its pronunciation given immediately after; the next syllable was treated the same, and so on until the whole word was pronounced in its entirety. The entire process, repeated at top voice by a class in unison, made the schoolroom a veritable Babel. All studying was done aloud. It is not surprising that the school term lasted only four months out of the year.

There was a succession of this type of schoolteacher for many years in Cordova. One was a Presbyterian missionary who, it was said, was the most conscientious of all, his pupils making the most progress. Another was a Negro with a wooden leg who drifted into the village; no one knew from whence he came. In addition to teaching, he practiced medicine and busied himself prospecting in the hills around Cordova. Many old diggings and shafts resulted from his efforts to find gold or other metal deposits. Because he could speak English, he was counted better educated than those who could not, so he was accepted as the schoolteacher. This was in the days when teaching was private employment.

One of these teachers, it is said, was very remiss in his duties. An incorrigible gambler, he was especially fond of the game called *palito*. In order to indulge his love for it and still attend to his duties, he would leave the younger boys and all the girls industriously telling their alphabet aloud in the schoolroom, so that any passing parent would be deceived into thinking that education was being administered. In reality, this worthy would be gambling at *palito* with the larger boys outside the building, on the sunny side that was hidden from the rest of the village. But such was the tolerance of the parents that when they learned of this they were more amused than indignant and took no action.

Those teachers who were Catholics taught the children their catechism as well as the three other subjects, but no high degree of learning was possible, of course, under these conditions. To be able to read and write was considered a great attainment, and this was about all that could be achieved.

One of the more enterprising residents of Cordova made arrangements for a tutor for his children. This tutor was a broken-down *Americano* who had drifted somehow into the backwash of this corner of the hills. In exchange for a home, he taught the boys and girls of this family. Stress was laid on his teaching them English, for the shrewd father saw that this would give his children a great advantage; he foresaw the inevitable intrusion of American ways and speech into the whole scheme of their lives. That he was wise in this is borne out by the fact that these sons, with the advantage of speaking English, became the leaders in that section of the county. When the existing public school system came into being, they became the first public school teachers, holding these positions for many years before any of the local youth could qualify as teachers and thus challenge them for the position. From teachers to politicians was a natural step, and these same sons prospered and advanced to responsible positions as the recognized leaders of their communities.

It is a far cry from a scraped hide and a piece of charcoal to the shining expanse of blackboards that line the walls of the new schoolhouse. The first produced black letters on white, the new white letters on black; and the difference in customs, educational method, facilities, and general results are as marked as the difference between black on white and white on black. One link, however, still connects the two eras: two great-grandsons of the man who insisted on his children being taught English wield the rod of authority in the new schoolhouse. (52)

Some ancianos *might complain, like the anonymous Galisteo composer of the following verses:*

Every generation looks on the events of its declining years with a despairing and pessimistic eye. Upon reading this *"Lo que pasa"* or

"What is going on" one might think it had been written today. Yet Mr. Francisco Leyba of Leyba, from whom I acquired this copy, told me he had been left this poem by his father and that as near as he can remember it must have been written at the outbreak of the Spanish American War. His father told him it had been written by a resident of Galisteo, but unfortunately Mr. Leyba did not know or could not recall his name.

Guerras, pleitos sucediendo	Strife and wars impending
Muerte y hambre amenazando,	Menace of death and hunger,
Todos los vicios creciendo	All the vices increasing
Y las virtudes menguando	And the virtues on the wane,
Sin pedir misericordia	Without ever asking for mercy
El mundo finalizando.	The world hastens to its end.
Ya no hay quién trate verdad	There is no one speaks the truth
Ya no hay palabra en la gente	Nobody's word is good any more
En estos tiempos presentes;	In this day and age there is
Ninguna formalidad	No guarantee of faith 'tween men,
Nadie tiene caridad,	Charity is altogether lacking
Segun estoy advirtiendo	From what I can see;
La mentira está rigiendo,	Untruth is in the saddle
La venganza está privando,	Vengeance is on the loose
Por eso se está mirando	This is why we are aware
Guerras, pleitos sucediendo.	Of strife and wars impending.
No hay ninguna educación	Good breeding has disappeared
En niños mozos y ancianos,	In children, youth and ancients,
No hay unión en los Cristianos	No unity amongst Christians,
Ni en pícaros reprensión,	No restraint on rascality,
Sigue la mala intención	Evil intentions rampant
La ley de Dios quebrantando	Break the laws of God
La de María abandonando;	And abandon those of the Virgin Mary;
Por eso se llega a ver	That's why we have come to see
Muerte y hambre amenazando.	Death and hunger menacing.
No hay veneración al Templo	Veneration of the temple is naught
Ni a los retratos sagrados	Or for the sacred paintings,
No hay respeto a los Prelados,	No respect for the Prelates
Y ellos dándonos el ejemplo	Some of them set us an example
Según lo que yo contemplo,	As far as I can see,
Ya el Ante-Cristo reinando	Anti-Christ is arising
Ya sus hijos gobernando	Dominant over his own
Según historia divina,	As prophesied in divine history,
Por eso se ve la ruina	That is why ruins we see
Y las virtudes menguando.	And the decline of virtue.

A los que están caducando
Pregunto si acaso vieron
En los tiempos que vivieron
Lo que hoy día se está mirando,
Los niños que se están criando
Viven sin crianza ni dieta
Porque ya nadie respeta
A los que están caducando,
Todos los vicios creciendo
Y el mundo finalizando.

To those whom age is destroying
I ask if you have ever seen
In the prime of your lives
Such events as of today;
Children being brought up today
Grow without restraint of manners
Because no one has respect
For our failing old men;
All the vices are on the increase
This world is ending.

Antes de ahora se estimaban
Niños, hombres, y mujeres
Que aunque tuviesen haberes
Nada de esto codiciaban
Antes la mano se daban,
Por eso todos tuvieron
Hijos, padres decidieron
El vivir de buena fe,
No vieron lo que hoy se ve
En los años que vivieron.

Before this there was mutual esteem
Between children, men, and women
Nobody's good fortune
Was cause for covetousness
Rather the helping hand was stretched
And prosperity was general,
Sons, fathers of one accord
Resolved to live in good faith,
They did not see what we see today
Those years in which we lived.

Ya se llegó al tiempo fijo
Ingrato, cruel, y cobarde
Ya no hay hijo para padre
Ni padre ha de haber para el hijo,
Mi sentir es más prolijo
Cuando me pongo a pensar
Que este tiempo ha de llegar,
Lo que ellos no conocieron
A los más sabios ancianos
Pregunto si acaso vieron.

Now we come to the present
Ungrateful, cruel, and cowardly;
The son has neglected the father
So the father treats the son likewise,
My senses become tired
The more I think and study
That these days had to come to pass,
Such as they never knew
So I ask the wisest of the ancients
Have you ever seen such happenings?

Ya no hay un hermano leal
Ni el menor es obediente
Con el mayor es valiente
Que hasta lo quiere ultrajar;
Cómo no se ha de acabar
Lo que Dios nos está dando
Así voy considerando
Que no aclamamos a Cristo,
En otros tiempos no he visto
Lo que hoy día se está mirando.

There are no more loyal brothers
The youngest is not obedient
He opposes his elders
Even to insulting them;
Why then shouldn't we lose
Favors which God bestows,
Which makes me consider
That we no longer acclaim Christ,
My eyes had not seen before
Sights like those of today.

Ya no hay por qué preguntar
El origen de todo esto
Habiéndolo Dios dispuesto

There is no need to ask
The reason for all this,
God has brought this all about

Por nuestro modo de obrar,	Because of our way of living,
Pues no queremos guardar	You see we don't try to keep
De Dios ningún mandamiento	Any of God's commandments,
Este ha sido el fundamento	This has been the very reason
De la desgracia y discordia	For all this misfortune and discord;
Sin pedir misericordia	Without even asking for mercy
El mundo va falleciendo.	The world hastens to its end. (78)

Most old people followed their customary routines as long as possible, like the aged Cordova compadres in the humorous anecdote below:

Ignacio Trujillo of Cordova was standing in the open doorway of his home. He had just had breakfast and, having lit his pipe, was watching the sunrise over the mountains to get an idea of the weather promised for that day.

In the next yard his *compadre* Alejandro was saddling his burro. He was grumbling to himself because the little beast had stepped on his foot while shifting around trying to ease the pressure of the cinch. I might say that these old men were brothers but first of all *compadres*. Both were afflicted with deafness, not entirely deaf but quite hard of hearing.

Seeing his brother, Ignacio called out, *"Buenos días le dé Dios, compadre."* ("May God give you a good day, *compadre.*")

Alejandro did not hear his brother but knew the answer. For many mornings through the years this rite had been unchanged. So he answered, *"Y a Vd. muy buenos días le dé Dios compadre. ¿Cómo amaneció?"* ("And to you may God give a good day. How are you this morning?")

Ignacio replied: "I am well. Are you going for wood?"

Alejandro thought he had heard correctly and answered: "No, I am going for wood."

Throwing out his hand in an understanding gesture, Ignacio answered back: "Oh, I thought you were going for wood."

Alejandro climbed on his patient burro and with an *"arre"* and a whack on the side of the beast's neck to turn him into the roadway, left. Ignacio returned inside, wondering where his *compadre* could be going if not for wood. (64)

While some of the old folks regarded with bitterness the decline of their authority and the replacement of old customs by new ones, others responded more positively to the situation. In at least two reported instances harm was turned into advantage, and clever ancianos left their mark on a changing world. Brown relates the significance of the arrival of the first Social Security checks in Cordova.

The blessings of old age relief, where procurable, are evident in Cordova as well as in the other villages of New Mexico. Due to the long-established custom of allotting to each married son his share of the parental lands and so many *vigas* ("beams"—a method of dividing off space in a house) of the family home, parents of large families seldom attain economic or financial independence in old age. Not that the sons and daughters of the native villagers are lacking in filial love and respect—far from it; but the spirit of independence is as much a part of the makeup of these old people in the villages as anywhere else in the United States, if not more so. Theirs is the independence of tillers of their own and their ancestors' land, land which has been in the possession of one family for several generations, a record in that respect longer than most in the United States, for the Spanish colonists here came a generation earlier than the Pilgrims.

Scarcity of water, however, makes these jealously guarded two or three-acre family possessions a vital factor in the family economy. When so small an acreage must be divided among, say, three sons, each son's share must include five or six trees in the family orchard, a strip of the alfalfa patch, and his just share of the best farmland and of the meadow or pasture, if any.

Even after the first son has married, the parents are still in *poder* (literally, in possession) of the other two sons and any unmarried daughters. They can still direct the cultivation of the farm and care of the stock, and they are deferred to by the remaining dependent children. The share of the family possessions allocated to their first-wed son has made no appreciable difference in their authority and obligation to provide and take care of their children.

When the last of their sons has left, and the number of *vigas* has been lessened (by the number of sons multiplied by five or six *vigas*), the old people are left with perhaps but one small room to call their own. There is no voiced complaint when this occurs; it is the way things are done. However, at evening, when one of the sons has questioned some decision of his aging father, his father whose every suggestion has been law, the old ones sit silently by the low flickering light of their corner fireplace. The long silence that ensues is not broken by the old mother, as both puff on their *cigarritos*. Well she knows that her husband is dwelling on the day's rebuff, feeling keenly his loss of dominance in the family, feeling keenly that, having transferred all possessions into other hands, the authority has gone with them. She can appreciate his emotions because Angélica, her youngest daughter-in-law, has steadfastly refused to follow her advice on the proper method of weaning her grandson.

The old ones do not lack for food. The first fruits of the harvest are brought to them. Wood, neatly split, is supplied by first one and then another of their sons. When they venture to help at some task, they are tolerated at first, then kindly but firmly admonished to rest and leave the work for younger arms.

And, as a matter of fact, they do enjoy resting. They like to let the sun soak into their old toil-warped bones, but they crave the deference and importance that was theirs and do not like to be shunted aside as useless. Like old people everywhere, they like to feel necessary to others.

So, when the first rumors of old-age relief became certainty, everyone of the right age hastened to apply for his or her *pensión*, as it was popularly tagged. *Pensionistas* are an envied caste, which was established when soldiers' widows and disabled veterans of the World War received their adjusted compensation and insurance checks. They became symbols of economic independence and subject to the honor of being called upon to serve as godparents at innumerable christenings, weddings, and confirmations. Apart from the financial independence, there was the status of *pensionista*, and each became a person of importance in the family circle and in the village as a whole.

This caused a great flurry of trips to the central parish church for *fes de bautismo*. Oldsters who had only a hazy idea of their real age (perhaps determined by the year of the biggest flood in the river or that they were five years old when the D.&R.G.W.R.R. first puffed up the valley of the Rio Grande), for the sum of one dollar received certificates of baptism and for the first time knew for a certainty just how many summers and winters they had lived.

Receipt of the first check was a big event in each household. The schoolmaster, postmaster, or a war veteran was consulted as to the proper method of endorsing checks. If the recipient was unable to write his name, he made his mark with a symbolic cross, and the event took on the aspect of an important ceremony. The supply of indelible pencils in the local *tienda* ("store") was greatly depleted. Pen and ink were not favored because of the propensity of unaccustomed, time-gnarled hands to tremble and perhaps blot and irremediably spoil the check, with who knows what delays and possible loss as a consequence?

Clean shaven, with the ceremonial coat reserved for church-going, fiestas, weddings, and other important events worn over a clean and freshly ironed shirt, the *pensionista* is given the pencil to touch. His authority to sign thus symbolically transferred, his proxy signs his name. Then an X or cross is made by a shaking hand. The witnesses to the mark, of whom there must be two, have all this while been standing by silently. They are fully impressed with the importance of the ceremony and proud of the part they play in it. Grandchildren hover outside the door, having sensed the impor-tance of the occasion and expecting the gifts of *dulces* ("sweets") that nearly always accompany such events.

Freedom from economic care is not the only benefit these checks confer. Renewed importance in the home and community impart new life to the recipient. Again he is deferred to; his opinion and advice are sought and followed as of old. There is time for rest and leisurely conversation with his contemporaries with no loss of dignity or integrity. No longer need he saddle a burro with fumbling hands and take to the hills in search of wood to satisfy pride in accomplishment. And better yet, he would not have to listen to half-veiled references to mythical crows following his burro home, mistaking its load for their nest.

A group of four *pensionistas* gather every afternoon at the home of their senior member. They have been dubbed *Los Senadores* ("the Senators") by a wit of the village. They gather in the shade in summer and in winter seek the *resolana* or sunny side of their host's humble home.

The group is composed of two brothers, the elder eighty-seven, and two neighbors, one entirely blind yet mentally alert and in full possession of faculties that throughout his active life have earned him the title of *Pícaro*, a shameless rogue known for his double dealing. The fourth member of the group is entirely innocuous, tolerated because of his ability as a listener and a convenient witness to astonishing recitals.

An outsider drawing near the group cannot possibly receive the full flavor of their conversation if his presence is known. He is then the one questioned, and his views on affairs of the village as well as from outside are sought. The floor is given up to him entirely, perhaps to the satisfaction of his audience but not to himself. One must be a shameless eavesdropper to hear tales of the past related without restraint.

The old men live again the days of their youth, and many glimpses may be gained of a bygone day by implication contained in some chance remark or by direct relation of events of long ago. It is amusing to hear the rebuke administered by the oldest of this quartet to the *Pícaro* who happens to be his godson and therefore must take the rebuke with good grace. "*Pendejo, ¿qué sabes tú?*" ('Fool, what do you know?'). It was thus or thus." The godson is apparently as old as his *padrino* and blind besides. Perhaps this is fortunate, because his *padrino's* little blue eyes kindle to pinpoints of wrath as he rebukes this presumptuous one who dares question his statements concerning the duel between the *difuntos* ("deceased") Juan Antonio and Manuelito who fought on the Cuestecita, of the superiority of mules over horses, or that the Negro, Pata de Palo, was a much better schoolteacher than Simón.

The lowering sun disperses the meeting. *Pícaro's* meek and self-effacing wife comes to lead her lord and master home to his supper of *atole* and hot cornmeal. *Pícaro* attributes the fact that he has all his teeth and not a single gray hair to this repast. His blindness he regards as an act of God to which he has philosophically resigned himself, especially since it makes his check larger than those received by the other Senators. All his life he has endeavored to acquire a living with the least effort. Always the self-centered individualist, he accepts this physical disability as another instance of Providence manifesting itself on his behalf.

Los Senadores will doubtless continue to meet as long as they are physically able, until death, like *Pícaro's* black-shawled wife, comes to lead them home. (110)

> El que aguanta las velas bien puede aguantar
>   los cabitos.
> ("He who has survived the lighted candles can
>   wait out the guttering stubs.") (1)

*José Dolores López (1868-1937) was an imaginative and influential
resident of Cordova. Like many of his contemporaries, López was
disconcerted by the vision of his rapidly changing world. His
creative response signaled the birth of a cottage industry which
continues to contribute to Cordova's economy.*

To the right of the church door in the adobe-walled *campo santo*
there stands an elaborately carved cross. This grave marker shows
the final resting place of one of the best-known and most-beloved
characters of the village, Don José Dolores López.

When the United States entered the First World War, this loving
father of several grown sons felt his peaceful world tumbling about
his ears. Always a lover of peace and, more so than most, an
individual who believed in the unity of the home, he was now
confronted with an adversity that was hard to bear. His oldest son,
his best beloved son, and the one in whom all his hopes for the
future had been vested, must go to war. As the descendant of
pioneers, to whom the call of country was sacred when invasion
threatened, Don José could and would sacrifice everything in
defense of his country. But to send his son to another country far
across the seas to fight for an idea meaningless to him was beyond
his comprehension. Across the sea! To this inland man, the words *al
otro lado del mar* held a world of terror. Imagination stimulated by
mental anguish clothed the words with a dread of the many evils to
which his son would be subjected in crossing this vast expanse.

Don José brooded and mourned to such an extent that if he had
found no distraction his reason might have given way under the
burden of his grief. Mourning bitterly for his son, whom he counted
lost to him forever, Don José believed his own days to be
numbered, knew that he would soon die; all desire and incentive
for living had fled. It was with this morbid idea fixed firmly in his
mind that the grieving old gentleman set about to make a cross to
mark his grave.

At the outset, he intended only to fashion a cross similar to the
ones customarily employed for that purpose, nothing elaborate, just
a simple cross with the dates of his birth and death and inscribed
with a supplication for prayer to be said for the welfare of his soul.
Choosing his material with care, desirous of having something that
would withstand wind and weather for some time, Don José set

about his lugubrious task. In a spirit of experimentation, he carved a small cross on both ends of the horizontal arms. This led to a further embellishment with a design of delicately carved panels extending the length of the upright part of his cross. This design he extended to the arms. Intrigued and pleased with the results of his efforts with his penknife, he became interested in further decorating his cross. He added a fretwork design to the edges of the arms and the upright, spending long hours at night in what had become a fascinating hobby.

With the completion of the cross, a new lease on life came to him, especially after he had received a censored letter from his boy "somewhere in France." In the letter were several snapshots of his son in uniform and a glowing account of the eventful happenings he had witnessed. Don José, after proudly displaying both letters and snapshots to his admiring friends, bethought himself of his new hobby. He would make a fitting frame for these mementos which his son had sent him from so far away.

In the frame that he made for his son's pictures, he tried to give expression to an aroused sense of patriotism and pride in the fact that his son was a soldier in the army of the greatest country in the world. In the corners he carved stars, representative of those in the national flag. The rest of the frame was carved with bars, and the American eagle perched on the upper edge with outspread wings. The different parts of the whole were painted in their appropriate colors—red, white, and blue. This frame he hung above the fireplace mantle in his best room.

Gone was all thought of the immediate use of the cross; it was set aside, still to be used as intended, but on a day far in the future. Filled with hope and a certainty now that his son would come back to him, Don José Dolores, in the fullness of this new mood and on fire with his new hobby, began to share his handiwork with his friends and neighbors. Every married couple of his acquaintance received a clockshelf or lampstand, carved and brightly painted, with the initials of the couple conspicuously showing. The initials JDL, not so conspicuous, were to be found somewhere in the design if one looked carefully for them. After every couple with whom he was on friendly terms, and this included everyone in the village, had received some object or other of his handiwork, Don José made it a point to prepare articles as wedding gifts for every newly married pair in the village, so that a couple contemplating marriage could count on at least one article of furniture with which to start their married life.

From these useful yet gaudy articles for simple domestic uses, this village craftsman gradually evolved the type of work for which he later became famous. The first inspiration that caused him to change from making purely useful articles to those of ornamental value was, as he so often related, the antics of a chipmunk which he had partly tamed. This frisky creature lived in the little orchard belonging to Don José, which one sees just after rounding the curve of the grade that descends into the Cordova Valley. This was a favorite spot for serving *merienda* and the noonday lunch when he and his household were hoeing or otherwise employed in his lower fields below and to one side of the orchard.

Symbolic of the leisurely and seemingly indolent manner in which the people of Cordova accomplished their many tasks in the fields is the custom of having an afternoon luncheon served to them at the scene of their labors. This welcome pause is called *la merienda*, an opportunity to take one's ease while partaking of a repast in the shade of some friendly tree or the sunny side of some arroyo. This interruption is anticipated with eagerness not so much because tired or hungry bodies need rest or food, but mainly because it is a recognition that man should not take his work so seriously as to believe that he alone can accomplish a thing without the aid of Providence. This pause for lunch helps the worker to remember his Creator's share in every human endeavor and that man should not become completely absorbed in his own efforts. Around three o'clock in the afternoon women can be seen leaving their homes in the village with a basket or a pail or quite often a dishpan balanced on their head, a snowy cloth covering the whole. These women pass each other on the way as some hurry up the valley and others down to where their menfolk happen to be engaged in hoeing, irrigating, or harvesting their fields.

Don José Dolores López endowed this pause with special significance and charm for his family. At such times he was at his best. He delighted in being in their midst and never more than when he was with them around the little campfire built to heat the coffee under the trees of his orchard overlooking their fields. He seemed filled with a greater sense of satisfaction with himself and his family when he could look on growing plants or freshly turned earth and picture in his mind's eye the bounteous harvest to come.

This, coupled with his innate love of nature, which found expression in the little wooden figures of squirrels, birds, trees, and flowers he carved from blocks of wood, rendered his flow of genial wit more sparkling and his philosophic discourses more stimulating. His children and their spouses would sit around him enraptured. They all loved him, and these occasions seemed to draw them closer to him than at any other time.

And so with the other families of the village. These, for the most part wholly family, gatherings in the open enabled them to get together under the beneficent influence of a warm sun and open sky. Plans for the future made at this time were likely to be more successful because of the spirit of harmony and contentment that prevailed. With mind and body refreshed, work was resumed with a lightness of heart and spirit evidenced in the merry banter and snatches of song heard as the workers plied hoe or sickle according to the season. So long as this custom exists, life will hold less strain and tension. It is a wise provision which generations of New Mexican villagers have found sound and right.

After the noonday luncheon had been eaten, Don José would use the rest period that followed for whittling and carving a piece of chair or some other object. This chipmunk would scamper by, catching the old man's eye and highly amusing him. In a moment of inspiration he tried his hand at carving a figure of his little friend. The results of the skillful handling of his penknife were so pleasing and so truly captured the sprightliness of the subject that from that time on the hand of the carver turned out carved images of birds, mice, little pigs, and other animals. These added to Don José's fame and gave him a wide range of models to work with.

With these and his carved frames, furniture, and screen-door frames, he built up a thriving business in which most of the family engaged under his critical eye. His two sons George and Ricardo and his daughter Liria all seemed to inherit their father's skill. Of the three, the daughter excelled in the work, and in time her work developed individual characteristics as eagerly sought as those of her teacher. The López home became a mecca for tourists and artists who took great delight in the unique realism with which Don José imbued these little wooden figures. However, not only were people attracted to his home because of his display of woodcarving but also because of the personality of the man himself. The visitor was received with the courtliest of manners, not affected but genuine, with an ease and grace which charmed and made for him many friends who delighted to return for a visit with this unusual personality.

Don José was tall and slender, with the assurance and poise of the born gentleman. His were finely molded features with black, intensely compelling eyes surmounted by a high forehead above which his iron gray hair swept back in a thick and well-combed pompadour. The fine, sensitive mouth of the artist was framed by the points of a thin moustache. Long lines running from the sides of his aquiline nose to his chin accentuated the lean, tapering face. His complexion was a light brown from much exposure to the sun and rain. Lines at the corner of his eyes bespoke a man of understanding with a sense of humor.

As occasion required, Don José could and did speak with sincerity of things religious or of spiritual worth. Tales with a moral to suit any occasion he knew without number, and without being sententious would relate a tale with a fitting moral to help some seeker after advice in clearing up some domestic or other difficulty. These tales would be more effective than advice given in so direct a fashion as to antagonize the hearer. Also, Don José's fund of witty stories made him a popular and much-sought-after man at wakes or dances or other festivities when a lull in the attendant activities permitted time for conversation. Only a knowledge of Spanish could have enabled anyone to appreciate the many sides of this remarkable character.

The guiding and most compelling characteristic of his life was his love of his family and determination to keep them together as a unit. He had raised them in the old patriarchal style in which the father was the sole source of advice and guidance in any undertaking. His was the right to resolve any situation, and his instructions were carried out to the letter by his sons and daughter even after they were grown and had families of their own.

With a view toward keeping his family together, early in his married life he began to make provision for their future dwellings. He acquired and built additional rooms adjoining his ancestral home so that when his family married they could bring their wives to the virtual shelter of the same roof-tree. Thus he surrounded himself with those whom he most loved and who were the objects of all his planning. He was what might be called a benevolent tyrant in this respect, but this attitude was not resented in the least by his sons; they had been reared in the tradition of *los de cuando ay* ("those of other times"), by which all authority was vested in the father of a family to whom respect and obedience were due, a patriarchal system in the fullest meaning of the term.

True, this type of family management depended for its success on the character of the paternal head. In the case of the López family, they were blessed in having a father who was most understanding and patient, with unsurpassed tact in the manage-ment of his growing family. He succeeded in his aims with the exception of his eldest son, who did break away from the paternal home and marry a girl from another village, moving with her to her own home. Yet, even so, this son never failed to pay his father a respectful visit every weekend and always asked his advice. Another son who would not be drawn into the families' joint enterprise yet who, when married, chose to live within the family circle was a little wild and headstrong. Don José bore with him with loving understanding and tolerance, showing his affection by being ever ready to help him out of the many difficulties he incurred by reason of his headstrong tendencies.

It was a fine sight to see Don José set out with all of his family, with the exception of two of the women who must stay home and cook the meal. By an amicable arrangement all work in the fields was done cooperatively. The motto of the family could well have been "one for all and all for one." The women in the group carried earthen *ollas* full of cooked food for the noonday meal; these *ollas* were nicely balanced on their heads. The men carried the necessary tools. Arriving at the field to be worked that day, Don José would marshal his forces and assign to each one his or her particular task: so many rows to be hoed or so many to be weeded. Joking and laughing the whole group would fall to, making pleasure out of work. With such a spirit it is no wonder that the López family was accounted the best farmers in the valley.

A year of bountiful crops found the family with a larder and pantry crammed with a variety of foodstuffs preserved and dried, enough to take care of their wants through the ensuing winter. Under the skillful management of Don José each piece of land, regardless of ownership, was made to produce the crops for which it was best suited, in that way assuring a maximum yield. By so doing each family, since the rule was share-and-share-alike, was certain of a healthy variety of the best from each field. This cooperative plan was carried out even to the possession of only one team of horses, which was used in cultivation and other necessary phases of farming. The rest of the village was horse poor; each family must have a team to cultivate its fields, no matter how small, and thus much land must be planted to forage crops to feed the horses through the winter, curtailing the food production of the too-scant farming land. With the López family, however, one small portion of the total collective acreage raised enough alfalfa to feed the sole team while it was idle. The three sons with this one team would haul enough wood in a week's time to provide the entire family with fuel for the duration of cold weather.

With such a spirit, it is no wonder that the family prospered, acquiring more land and better implements until they were considered quite wealthy. With little food to buy, except essentials their own land could not produce—such as sugar, salt, and coffee—Don José and his family accumulated money for which they really had no use. This, however, was not spent foolishly; the sons remodeled their houses, bought furniture, and otherwise improved their homes. Don José, well satisfied with the comfort of his own home, was always willing to help a friend or neighbor with a loan, thus increasing his popularity in the village. For his own protection and the removal of temptation from the path of the borrower, he very shrewdly insisted on the pledging of the borrower's land as security for the payment of the borrowed sum. He well knew that if a piece of land were at stake, he would always get his money back. That his role as moneylender was not one he had adopted for the love of gain is shown by the fact that Don José did not charge any interest on the money he loaned.

The late Frank Applegate, Santa Fe artist and writer, was early attracted to Don José and the products of his penknife. He it was who first aroused the interest of others in this village craftsman and his works. Through him, Don José was induced to place some of his work on exhibition in Santa Fe, the excellence of his carving securing for him many orders for his handiwork and recognition of his artistry in his chosen field. His carved picture frames and screen doors adorned many homes in Santa Fe. His carved figures of birds, animals of every kind, and other interesting articles became the vogue, bringing an unending stream of visitors and buyers to his door.

Don José was a devout man, deeply religious and a faithful

practitioner of precepts laid down by his Master for the guidance of humanity. Charitable and tolerant toward all, he was greatly beloved by all with whom he came in contact. A faithful church member, he also belonged to the local Penitente *morada,* serving that lodge many times in the highest official capacities. Many visitors to Cordova during Lent saw his benign countenance during the religious observances of the Penitente order. It was his voice that proclaimed to the visitors from outside, as they waited in the church for the service of the *Tinieblas,* the high ideals of his Order, admonishing the villagers to be careful of the strangers in their midst, that everyone was equal in God's sight. It was he who sang the seemingly interminable verses of the *alabado,* the singing of each separate verse being the signal for pinching out the flame of one of the thirty candles left burning in the church. When the last flame expired, leaving the church in total darkness, it was his voice that was heard above the din and tumult of the *Tinieblas* service, coming from the closed door of the sacristy to which he had retired when the last candle flame expired.

Don José died from a lingering illness resulting from injuries suffered in a car accident while returning to Cordova from a trip to Santa Fe. He endured his last painful illness with sweet resignation, ever ready to greet visitors with a smile and cheerful conversation. Nearly twenty years after he had thought to use it, the cross which he had spent so many hours making was put to the use for which he had intended it. *Que en paz descanse.* [Unfortunately, this wooden cross was vandalized in 1945 and had to be replaced with a cement slab—Eds.] (125)

Perhaps more than anything else, the small churches and chapels of Hispano northern New Mexico symbolize the legacy of village life. These beautiful adobe structures provided the setting for community rituals and religious celebrations. Memories of times past and departed family and friends shared the sanctuary with the santos and devout worshippers. Brown senses the local church's importance in his careful description of Cordova's chapel of San Antonio.

In Cordova, one of the typical New Mexico villages, typical in that it retains more of the flavor of an earlier culture both in its physical appearance and in the characteristics of its inhabitants, there is a little adobe church which in itself and its appurtenances is one of the best examples of the early mission churches of Spain's North American frontier of the eighteenth century. This church, *La Capilla de Nuestro Señor San Antonio,* with its buttressed walls dominates the little village, whose houses cluster close to and around the small, open communal space in which the church stands. Made of adobe and plastered with the selfsame soil on which it rises, it might well be taken for a flat-topped mesa rising in the middle of the village, so naturally do its walls merge with the ground, melting into it with scarcely a sign of demarcation.

The interior is roughly sixty feet long by about thirty feet wide, but the structure covers much more space because the walls are three feet thick. These walls are unrelieved by any openings except the double doors of the front entrance and a three-foot window in the south wall placed high enough so that one cannot look into the church from the outside. Above the front entrance, which faces east, is a small, four-paned window directly under the bell tower, admitting light into the choir loft.

Entrance is gained to the graveyard *(campo santo)* through a small gate made of serrated pickets. This *campo santo,* which is in front of the church, is enclosed by an adobe wall or *tapia* higher than a man on the south side, slightly lower on the east, and only about two and a half to three feet high on the north or uphill side, which accounts for the several differences in the height of the wall. The floor of the burial ground is level, however, perhaps filled in with earth brought from the outside, accounting for the height of the south wall which acts as a retaining wall. The area of this enclosure is approximately thirty by forty feet.

There are six marked graves in the churchyard, the newest being less than a year old. However, the whole space is filled with graves long since obliterated, even graves on top of one another. About twelve years ago, when a grave was being dug for one of the patriarchs of the village, the mouldering bones of someone long buried were uncovered. With them were found scraps of blanket, but no traces of wood. According to some of the oldtimers standing by, the custom was to bury bodies thus, with no coffin or any other covering than the woolen folds of a blanket. A fall of earth from the sides of the newly opened grave dislodged with it a copper or brass-tipped shoe from some burial of a date later than the blanket-wrapped one.

Both the floor of the church itself and the *campo santo* are filled with graves, precluding any additions to the former and, with rare exceptions, to the latter. Only persons of importance or with the means to pay the fee charged are allowed interment in the *campo santo;* yet a worthy citizen, one whose life has been dedicated to the community, also receives this recognition. In recent years there have been only eight burials: Don Matías Córdova and his wife, great-grandson of the donor of the bell which hangs in the tower above his grave; Don Antonio Trujillo, who served as *rezador* or lay reader, always willing and ready with his services for the dead or the dying; and Don José Dolores López, whose grave is marked by the cross which he himself carved, the cross that started him on his career of wood carving. These four graves hold the remains of as many types representative of the best to be found in the village. The other visible graves perhaps do also, but the writer is not acquainted with the history of those remains.

Don Matías carried out the tradition of his family, the *ricos* and leaders of the community, with dignity and honor. He served as the village schoolmaster, *alcalde* (justice of the peace), merchant, and political and economic mentor of his neighbors for many years and was laid to rest with his ancestors, earning the same esteem of his fellow men as they had. He had lived in a tradition and had passed it on to his sons.

Doña Andrellita, wife of Don Matías, was for many years the *curandera* ("healer") and *partera* ("midwife") of the village. She was most faithful in the discharge of both offices, never refusing anyone the benefit of her ministrations. She was greatly beloved because of the sweetness of her nature and the infinite wisdom with which her years of experience had endowed her.

The cross that marks Don José Dolores's last resting place really dates from the year 1917, although he died early in 1937. . . .

Approximately in the center of the *campo santo* is a large wooden cross mounted on a pyramid-shaped earthen base. This cross is made simply and gives evidence of having been there for a long time. The cross arm fits into a slot in the upright and is further secured by wooden pegs. A small transversal piece, bearing the carved letters INRI and faint decorative designs as well, is affixed to the top of the upright.

From the center of the graveyard, one gets a good view of the bell tower and the clapperless bell of ancient make that hangs therein. The tower itself is made of two adobe columns about two feet thick and four feet high. These are not solid, each having a triangular opening at the base, and each slopes from base to top. About four feet apart, they are bridged by thick, adzed planks, and from these planks hangs the bell. It is a small bell, about a foot in diameter at the base and fifteen inches high, with comparatively thick sides, despite which it has a very sweet and carrying tone. When it was cast, a quantity of gold and silver as well as other metals went into its make-up. It was cast in Cordova in the patio of its donor, Don Pedro Córdova, long dead. In the sunlight, its sides gleam and glisten where the stones grasped by the bell ringer strike, bringing forth the clear tones which the sheepherder can often hear three miles away on the Llano de los Quemadeños.

Duly christened, when its sponsors gave it the name of María Antonia, the bell was carried in procession around the church and then secured in place. It tolled the slow, sad note of death or a staccato alarm, when Indian raids were common; it was also heard on joyous occasions. Short as the bell tower is, it is the most salient point in the village, rising as it does from the flat dirt roof of the church, and, although the church itself is not high, its forty-foot walls overshadow the comparatively low houses which cluster around it.

The double doors leading into the church are of recent construction. On each door there are four panels, the bottom panels longer than those on top. The panel divisions are painted green against the white of the rest of the door, thus forming an appropriate green cross on each door.

Inside the church it is cool and dark. To the right of the door is the ancient pulpit from which the visiting priest addressed his flock. At one time it stood within the altar rail, on the right. Since it has been in disuse, it was fixed where it now stands, a fortunate preservation. In the same corner stands a bier which has likewise fallen into disuse, a tapering, coffin-like box with four end handles something like a stretcher. Made of rough, hewn planks, it is about eight feet long overall. Holes gouged in the edges of the frame are burned and scorched. In these holes, to which still cling drops of ancient wax, candles were placed. In this bier the dead were kept throughout the long wakes held over their remains before interment. The bier was also used as a stretcher for the bringing in of wounded from the hills, victims of falls, encounters with bears or Indians, or other mishaps.

The pulpit is the ingenious creation of some skilled craftsman patently limited as to tools; it is made entirely without nails. It resembles a large tulip with convolute stem. This stem or base, on which the pulpit proper rests, is about a foot thick and three feet high and is embedded in the earthen floor. The chalice-like top in which the priest stood to address his congregation has a circular floor from which six panels rise to form the sides, leaving an opening at the rear large enough to admit a person. These panels, much like barrel staves only wider and three feet high, are quite uniform in their carving, concave in shape and confined in grooves, closely spaced and deep, incised on its inner surface. With the exception of its carved base, the pulpit has no ornamentation elsewhere but from age has acquired a mellow, light brown patina.

Immediately overhead as one steps in the door is what seems to be a low roof composed of nine beams embedded in the east wall of the church just above the door. The other ends of these beams rest on a large square timber *(viga)* which extends the width of the church from the south to the north walls, the ends given the added support of a carved corbel. This is the floor of the choir loft to which a huge, crude ladder in the southeast corner gives access through an aperture cut in the rough-hewn, heavy planks. The ladder consists of two hand-hewn planks, four by six inches in thickness with seven holes cut in each plank. Tough oaken staves thrust through these from the rounds of the ladder.

The choir loft is not used today, and if used in other days must have been very uncomfortable, for it is quite low and receives only the faint light which enters through the little window just below the bell tower. A railing about two feet high guards the choir loft from the floor of the church below. This is of decoratively notched palings topped by a hand rail.

From the choir loft one gets a closer view of the roof of the church and of the twenty-four large *vigas* which support its expanse. Each *viga* is supported at both ends by a *can* or corbel carved in three short steps, a bell narrowing down to a neck then flaring to a square width of about fifteen inches where the corbel emerges from the wall. The succession of *vigas* with their supporting corbels are quite impressive viewed from this vantage point as they follow the contour of the walls, which narrow slightly toward the west end of the church where the altar stands.

The church has a wooden floor of recent date. The fact that bodies are buried beneath is not so apparent as when the mud floor had not been covered over. Immediately overhead is a *bambalete*, a candelabrum made of two crossed sticks supported at their junction by an upright secured to the beam above. From the extremity of each crossarm an S-shaped support curves upward to the upright, and the four of them meeting form an open canopy. A carved wooden dove with outstretched wings hovers above on the tip of the upright. Boards connecting the crossarm tips have two holes in each for candles. The eight candles in this *bambalete*, together with the candles lighted on the altar and before individual figures of the saints, constitute the only light in the church during vespers. A hanging lamp, oil-burning, is suspended from one of the *vigas* in the middle of the church and down near the altar railing. It is fairly modern, of the chain-suspension type, permitting lowering or raising by the four chains which secure it. It is seldom if ever lighted, its value apparently being purely decorative.

On the right, about four feet from the northeast corner of this edifice, an earthen *banco* ("bench" or "buttress") three feet high and a foot and a half wide on top runs the length of the north wall to within three feet of the railing which separates the altar from the floor of the church. Too high to be used as a bench, this *banco* must serve as an inside buttress or to absorb moisture from seepage, a condition common to the north walls of most dwellings in the village. Covered with successive layers of *tierra amarilla*, a micaceous yellow earth, with its metallic luster and hard-drying quality, the *banco* gives the impression that it is made of some light metal. At its eastern end, near the door, a low column built against the *banco*, yet not quite as high and covered with the same decorative earth, holds a copper kettle. This kettle, which nestles in a hollow atop the column, is the fount for the holy water.

About midway between both south and north walls of the church are placed two paneled wooden screens composed of *retablos*, pictures of the saints painted on a series of wooden panels. They are held in a framework consisting of two supporting timbers each eight inches wide by about four thick with crosspieces of similar kind closing top and bottom, making a frame eight feet wide by seven feet high supported by the extension of the side pieces—legs which hold the whole and raise the bottom of the heavy frame three feet from the floor of the church. Each is surmounted by an ornamental cutout figure in the shape of a half sunburst, each having the figure of a dove painted thereon.

Each reredos has a series of panels across the top, each separated by a grooved framework. In each panel is a painting of some saint or group of saints; there are two panels below these, flanking a *nicho* or recess in the lower tier. This *nicho* is the highest and central of three *nichos* which form the lower row or tier of each reredos. Long ago these stood upright against the wall with their supporting planks embedded in the earthen floor. In time they rotted, and it was necessary for the safety of the congregation to cut them loose and lean them against their respective walls. Each one is approximately fifteen feet high.

On the north reredos there are three panels across the top. In the left panel is a painting of Christ on the cross, a militant Christ depicted in what is obviously a military uniform with a sword in its scabbard hanging from His side. Below, grouped in heraldic fashion, are spears, pennants, and lances and one object, hourglass in shape, which might be a drum. [An appended correction notes that "subsequent research has established that" this and a similar figure mentioned below "were not representations of the Cristo but of San Acacio, Cappadocian centurion, who, when he was cited to appear before the Roman governor, 'loudly declared himself a Christian.' From Thrace where he had been stationed he was sent to Byzantium 'loaded with chains,' and in that place he was tortured and suspended from a walnut tree, suffering flagellation before being decapitated in 303 or 305. There is no mention of his having been crucified. His bones were removed to Cuenca, Spain, whence his devotion spread to New Mexico via Mexico. He is honored as a saint by both Roman and Greek churches. Representations of San Acacio crucified are doubtless local distortions of tradition or a substitution of the cross for the walnut tree by a people who call the Cross *el arbol de la Cruz.*"—EDS.]

The central panel figure is that of Our Lady of Mount Carmel holding the Christ Child in her arms with two cherubim on each side holding back drapes which disclose Her to the view of a group of adoring figures below, who are gazing upward. The right-hand panel depicts The Holy Family *(La Sagrada Familia)*. The panel on the left of the high *nicho* in the lower tier depicts San Rafael, patron saint of fishermen. He is shown with a string of fish in his right hand. This figure is so faded that it is impossible to identify the object he holds in his left hand. Saint Joseph with his staff of flowers flanks the *nicho* on the right.

The central *nicho*, the highest one, holds a most excellent and well preserved *bulto*, the figure of Saint Peter carved in wood. It is about thirty inches high and imposingly dressed in black and yellow. There is a damask cincture around his waist with a lace cross sewed on it in the center. San Pedro has a beautifully modeled head with large expressive eyes. His hair and beard are neatly painted in black and look very natural—the beard, a Van Dyke, giving emphasis to a pointed face. He holds in his right hand a wooden key and in his left a book. Instead of the traditional triple tiara, one of his attributes, this figure wears a very jaunty velvet turban—perhaps red at one time—with a curling plume curving around its crown. The robe that is painted on his figure is green with a pointed, knotted cord hanging from the waist. The hem of the robe is decorated with a plume design.

In the smaller *nicho* to the right of San Pedro is a group carving representing *El Niño Escondido* ("The Hidden Child") with the figures of Joseph and Mary kneeling on either side of a little glass-doored cell. From this cell the Hidden Child peers out. His white face and rather pathetic figure is a unique presentation. The three figures are carved of wood in a branching, somewhat shell-like form stemming from a pedestal which supports the three. The whole group stands only about nine inches high, the figures themselves being only five inches. The door of *El Niño Escondido's* cell is secured with knotted buckskin strings or thongs.

On the left of San Pedro is the black-robed figure of a female saint twenty-one inches high. Judging from the knotted cord painted over her robe, she is probably one of the many nuns who have been canonized. What sets this figure apart is that she possesses a bountiful head of human hair twelve inches long, quite thick and affixed very naturally. She has a pensive face despite a sharp nose. Her hair is gathered in a beaded, snood-like headdress, from which it flows loose to her waist. This image is dressed in a white robe and veil with an embroidered jacket also.

Across the top on the south reredos are four panels which are the same size as those on the north. The first figure on the left depicts a booted angel with knotted cords held in one hand. The fourth and last figure on the top row is another representation of a militant

Christ on the Cross. The military uniform makes it similar to the one on the north. [This figure is San Acacio; see correction noted above.—EDS.]

The two side panels which flank the tall center *nicho* of the lower tier have the following figures painted on them: on the left, a female figure holding a babe in the left arm with her right arm extended in a seeming effort to rescue another babe from the jaws of a fierce-looking animal. This is undoubtedly *Nuestra Señora del Perpetuo Socorro* who is depicted thus in most paintings. The figure on the right is that of a bearded man in priest's robes holding a cross in his right hand and a staff in the other.

The central figure in the large *nicho* is a four-foot crucifix, the figure of the expiring Christ portrayed in all anguish. This figure is well carved and well preserved, with the exception of the feet, which have been broken at the instep just below the traditional red lines painted above the ankles which all these crucifixes have, although there is no Biblical account of Christ's feet having been broken at that point. A blue robe clothes this figure, whose outstretched arms span three feet.

In the smaller *nicho* on the left is a beautifully carved figure of *Nuestra Señora de Guadalupe.* Carved entirely of wood, she stands on an upturned crescent which has a large eye painted on its face. Her gown is blue, and there are little crosses marked on her veil which may represent stars. The traditional aura surrounding this figure terminates, in this instance, in a small wooden crown over which there has been placed a copper crown with round mirrors set in. The Virgin's cloth robes are very sumptuous, and she has many adornments in the way of necklaces; in particular, a small mirror pendant on a cord around her neck. The face of the image is rather full and has a proud, haughty look, while her eyes, although open, give the impression of being heavy-lidded. Upholding the crescent on which the Virgin stands is a winged cherub who, however, has lost one wing. This cherub has an oddly Egyptian appearance and might have been painted on one of the Egyptian tombs.

The figure on the right is a very appropriately carved *María Santísima.* In this figure of the Blessed Mary, the *santero* achieved a very happy result, for this image has a very sweet face wholly in keeping with the mother of Christ. In every detail it is well proportioned. Her hands are clasped and she is voluminously clothed in four petticoats and an elaborate silk dress, all white. Over this she wears a white veil with bouquets of white flowers affixed to her veil and clasped under her arms. Only the bust is carved, the rest of the figure being merely four thin wooden supports extending from the waist to the supporting pedestal.

There are four small crucifixes, faces draped in white veils, all of a very similar pattern, hanging two to a wall between the reredos and the altar railing. The figures on these crucifixes are all about fourteen inches long, carved in the round, blood gouted in a painfully realistic manner. One of these is decorated with two bands of inset wheat straw near the base of the cross; another has a pedestal attached so that it could be placed upright on a table. With the exception of these minor details, they are all very much alike, obviously very old and choice examples.

Scattered before the altar railing on the floor of the church are many low candle holders of many types. Among these are several pottery holders made in Cordova from the clay found nearby. They are very crude, consisting of short cylinders with flat bases.

The altar and the space directly in front of it are separated from the floor of the church by a railing about thirty inches high. This is made of upright palings secured top and bottom by a hand rail. Palings are spaced about two inches apart and each is decorated with a cutout design of a Maltese cross and a star. The whole of the railing is painted blue and white. There still remains embedded in the floor the foot-piece of the original railing. This piece is pierced at regular intervals and no doubt held round oak staves, perhaps carved rounds such as are seen in some of the old furniture, although this is mere conjecture.

From the railing, two broad, low platforms lead to the altar proper. The base is a massive bench a little over three and a half feet high, on which are figures of saints, the Holy of Holies, and the rest of the adornments that embellish the altar. This bench is covered entirely with embroidered altar cloths, one over the other, concealing it from the congregation.

The central figure on the altar, placed slightly above the top of this bench, is the figure of San Antonio de Padua, patron saint of Cordova. He stands on a pedestal decorated with many flowers, holding the figure of the Christ Child in his arms. Both San Antonio and the Christ Child have pronouncedly white faces and contrastingly black hair. Their eyes are large and quite strikingly outlined with black paint. They both repose in a blue and white *nicho* made and decorated by the late José Dolores López in 1921.

San Antonio is flanked by two figures of angels, both dressed in white gowns with close-fitting collars resembling Chinese robes. Each angel has an insignia in one hand, and the one on the left has the carved figure of what might be a dove at his feet, but it bears more resemblance to a duck or a goose. The angels seem to have been made by the same *santero* who made San Antonio and the babe.

Just below San Antonio there is a three-sided recess about ten inches deep paneled into the reredos which forms the background of the altar. This recess must have been originally intended for the housing of San Antonio, but the village patron saint is seen to better advantage where he is now. San Antonio as well as the babe are dressed in blue silk gowns edged in lace. Under his gown, San Antonio, tonsured, has a priest's robe painted on his figure, a knotted cord hanging from his waist. His figure stands about twenty-eight inches high.

Rows of candlesticks stand on the altar, which has beautifully embroidered scarves laid across it, each scarf and altar covering bearing the donor's name prominently embroidered in it. To the left and right of the altar are two tables, likewise covered with embroidered cloths and scarves. On each of these are four or five figures of the saints *(bultos)*, choice specimens of the *santero's* art, as are all the images found in this little church. These tables are set at an angle to the altar, following the curve of the walls, which narrow slightly from the altar railing to just the width of the altar with its reredos in the background.

The most interesting figure on the north table, which holds four large *bultos,* is that of San Miguel. This figure of the popular saint is about twenty-eight inches high, beautifully executed, but with rather an effeminate face for so militant a saint. His silken robes heighten this impression of effeminacy, but underneath these robes is a masterpiece. The figure is painted in what resembles the war attire of a Roman centurion, with all parts of the armor carved on the figure in relief and painted in contrasting colors. The corselet, the short skirt flaring below the corselet, and the shin guards or jambs are treated thus. The feet are bare, however. Saint Michael's wings hang down his sides and are covered by his cloth robes. His arms emerge through the robes with a sword held high in the left hand. Unfortunately, his left hand has been broken, and the broken piece, as well as the sword it once held, are suspended from the wrist by a string. On his head is a crown beneath which shows a generous growth of long black hair painted on in a very realistic manner. Beneath the pedestal on which he stands is a small drawer that fits into a box, the top of which is formed by the pedestal. On the face of the drawer is carved an animal's head somewhat resembling a lion's, with a mane and open jaws. This head, carved in relief, depicts the vanquished Satan.

Over this table on the yeso-white wall hangs an old tin *nicho*, itself a fine example of the tinsmith's art. It consists of a tin framework connected at the corners with built-in rosettes of tin also, the whole neatly decorated with a punchwork design with scalloped edges. A tin-edged glass cell or *nicho* is attached to the center of the frame. In this cell is a little *bulto* of *El Santo Niño de Atocha*, quite small, since the cell itself is only three by five inches; and from this *nicho* he peers out in surprise with his big black eyes painted into a chalk-white face. The mate to this tin frame or *nicho*, in perfect condition, hangs on the opposite wall. There is also on the table another *Santo Niño de Atocha* resembling the one in the *nicho*, only this one is seated in a little rocking chair and has blue eyebrows. A tiny Chimayo rug covers the back of the chair.

This side of the room is well supplied with *Santos Niños de Atocha*. The next figure of this beloved little saint is found in the arms of his mother, *Nuestra Señora de Atocha*. She is the central *bulto* on the earth table and is arrayed in four gowns and two capes and has a wooden crown balanced on her head. Much adorned with necklaces, she must also bear the weight of her Son, who, despite His rather old-looking face, seems to enjoy the security of his mother's arms. The *Niño's* figure, about seven inches high, is carved in a sitting posture. He is much adorned and wears a full-length gown, but his crowning glory is an arresting headpiece, somewhat resembling a shako, made of black silk cords whose downstreaming ends lend an imposing air to the little figure. Beneath her gowns, *Nuestra Señora de Atocha* has a harmoniously painted attire. Her flaring robe is decorated with intertwined flowers in brown, red, and orange. A yellow apron would seem to indicate that she is a good housekeeper and quite domestic. On the hem of her original robe are painted these words: *"El Santísimo Niño de Atocha de Nuestra Señora de Atocha."*

San José, foster-father of Our Lord, stands next to *Nuestra Señora de Atocha*. This figure, about thirty inches high, is that of a very distinguished gentleman with a sharp pointed face, large eyes, and an aquiline nose under a crown. He has a neatly pointed black Van Dyke beard, which is joined by sideburns to the hair of his head. Underneath his garments is painted a long, green black-striped robe from which his bare feet show. On the whole, the figure is very well proportioned and in an excellent state of preservation. In one hand he holds a flowered staff and in the other a bouquet.

On the south table are two crucifixes on pedestals. Both have small heads, or perhaps this is an illusion created by the voluminous robes in which they have been enveloped. The full robes extend beyond and cover the feet. These figures are carved in the round *(bultos)* and on each face is the anguished expression of the expiring Christ common to most of the crucifixes.

Next to these are two figures of *Nuestro Padre Jesús*, the tortured and thorn-crowned Christ of the Via Dolorosa on the way to Calvary. They are both robed in dark blue silk gowns with lace trimming. The smaller one, about twenty-two inches high, is carved in the round, naked except for a carved representation of a loin cloth. The body shows the traditional blood gouts, the pierced hands, feet, and the broken ankles. The larger figure is dressed in a painted red robe with feet showing. Beneath a plaited, removable crown, scraggly wisps of real hair give it an untidy appearance. Both arms are broken, perhaps accidentally, but both arms have been confined in the sleeves of the gown and tied in front. This figure of *Nuestro Padre Jesús* is about twenty-eight inches high. A cross has been tied to his back over his cloth robes. Both figures of *Nuestro Padre Jesús* have knotted cords tied around their bodies ending in fringed crocheted tassels.

Our Lady of Sorrows, *Nuestra Señora de Dolores*, fittingly stands beside the images of *Nuestro Padre Jesús*. She is a stately lady about three feet tall, having a beautifully modeled face, a little large perhaps, but with a beautiful pair of large eyes. Her black hair is depicted with an economy of paint which gives an impression of baldness. It is possible that this figure at one time may have worn a crown or headpiece whose close fit would account for so little hair. Her flaring skirt is strikingly painted with seven medallions down its center from her breast to the hem of her gown. These medallions, each exactly alike, are the size of a silver dollar and consist of the portrait of a man's head in profile, outlined in black paint. It is not known what their significance is. The body of the skirt is painted green. Each medallion is connected with the edge of the skirt with looping lines of red. Other decorative motifs are worked out in yellow. The devout have clothed this figure in beautiful robes of silk with the usual addition of jewelry and paper and cloth flowers.

Nuestra Señora de los Remedios, as imposing in height as Our Lady of Sorrows beside her, is one of the most exquisitely executed of the feminine figures in this mission. She has a very sweet face with well-defined features and large, pensive eyes. A nicely turned, fluted wooden crown gives her a queenly appearance in keeping with the elaborate and harmonious garb she wears. She has a white chiffon underskirt trimmed with lace over which she wears a pink dress trimmed in rich gold lace. Over her shoulders is a white cape and around her neck several strings of beads and a rosary. Her hands are nicely modeled, showing tapering fingers in good proportion with the rest of her body. In one hand she holds a bouquet and a figure of the Christ Child in her arm. The figure of the Child is not so well executed; his head is too large, his nose too sharp, his eyes too large for the face, and he has a receding chin. His appearance suffers in contrast with the beauty of his mother.

On the mother's skirts are pinned three pouches of different colored silks containing herbs, an attribute to Our Lady of Healing. Additional pins are affixed to her skirts for the convenience of anyone wishing to fasten more herb pouches to them. As is the case with most of the figures in this church, the real beauty lies hidden under the clothing with which devotees have adorned them. This is more true of this figure of *Nuestra Señora de los Remedios* than most of the others. The skirt which the *santero* painted on her is one of the most pleasing in design and color combination; it flares out at the hem to a width of about fifteen inches. The skirt itself is blue with three single flowers painted along each outside edge. These flowers, somewhat resembling chrysanthemums, are executed in red, gold, and green. In the center is a delicately drawn design of flowers gracefully linked and intertwined with flowing lines.

The reredos back of the altar contains a unique group of saints. It is larger than the side ones already described. A very substantial framework of handhewn planks and boards confines the panels that make up the group of thirteen saints and religious symbols painted on as many panels. There are two rows of these panels, with seven figures above and six below. On the upper edge the reredos is surmounted with decorative wooden half-circles at each end. Each of these has a sunburst design in blue, white, and red. An S-shaped decoration, also carved of wood, connects both of these end pieces with a larger and central half-circle, a wooden plaque with the figure of a descending dove, branch in beak, carved on it and outlined in blue and white.

Panels in the first or upper row are each approximately two by three feet. They are painted in black, red, green, and brown and depict various saints both feminine and masculine. They defy identification with the exception of the central one, which depicts the crossed arms of the Franciscan Order, one black and the other white, superimposed over a cross. The framework joining the different panels is decorated with scroll designs in blue and red.

In the lower row some of the figures could be identified. The first figure on the left is San Rafael with wings and a fish in his arms, one of his attributes. The wings show him to be one of the seven archangels. Next to him is San Miguel. The next panel contains a crowned female figure, perhaps Our Lady of Light. The central panel, as noted before, takes the form of a triangular recess or *nicho*, doubtless the appointed place for the patron saint (San Antonio) in other days. Right of center is the same female figure seen left of center and tentatively identified as Our Lady of Light. Next to her is San Rafael again. This time he holds a string of fish in his hand. In the last panel on the right is another San Miguel very similar to the one on the left. It is interesting that in this lower tier of panels there are two representations of each of three saints or holy figures.

Against the altar rail are to be seen the *enseñas* or holy standards carried in all religious processions. There are two of these mounted on five-foot poles; they have been recently decorated with blue and white paint. Held upright by the railing and in the corner where the old pulpit used to stand, close to the door leading to the sacristy, stands a curious pennant. This pennant is an oblong, swallow-tailed one. Some twelve years ago it was faced with parchment with the same metal ornaments on either side still visible. The parchment, which had become worn, was removed and replaced with the silk which covers it today. One of the metal ornaments resembles a seal lying on its side with a half halo showing over his head and holding in its mouth a pennant very similar to the one we are describing. This figure of the seal is enclosed in a metal circle about three inches in diameter. On the other side, a similar circle encloses a figure of the sun with rays extending beyond a cross in its center. The sun is in the upper portion of the circle and below it is a wavy line with the capital letter N below. This pennant has a ball and cross affixed to the staff on which it is mounted. The metal ornaments seem to be of foreign make, perhaps Spanish. They have all the semblance of heraldic markings or symbols.

At the right of the altar a low door, which is somewhat below the level of the altar floor, leads into the sacristy. This is a low-ceilinged room with a fireplace of native make in the southeast corner. A large chest of drawers with a covering embroidered in black on white stands against the west wall. In it are kept supplies of candles, extra altar cloths, and surplus supplies of dresses and robes for the images of the saints. The chest is quite crudely made with no decorative carving. It stands about forty-four inches high supported on four legs given stability by connecting dove-tailed rounds. The chest proper is approximately twenty inches wide by the same in depth and about four feet long, four deep drawers in its side holding the articles mentioned above. The whole chest is of mortise-and-tenon construction with no nails employed originally in its making, although it has since been reinforced with them.

The church censer, quite old and made of brass, hangs on the wall by the chest. It is a shallow brass bowl with a close-fitting lid with orifices to allow the incense to escape. The bowl is suspended in four chains, eighteen inches long, ending in a handhold by which it is swung.

In the sacristy reposes the original spindle door which at one time hung between the altar and the sacristy. This door is a very fine example of its type. Since it has been removed and preserved with its accompanying door jambs, it is easy to study the method of construction and its operation. It consists of one central beveled panel secured by a grooved frame mortised and further secured by wooden pegs at the corners. The rear member of this framework is elongated top and bottom into two spindles. These spindles fit into holes bored into the door jambs and on these the door turns to open and shut. The door jambs are four heavy pieces of handhewn planks mortised to form the supporting framework of the door. The top jamb is no longer than the lower one and serves as a lintel in the support it gives to the wall above. The height of the whole door, frame and all, is not much over four feet, making the actual entrance into the sacristy from the church a scant three and a half feet.

The low ceiling of this room is of the *raja* ("split wood") type, but it is usually covered with a tightly stretched ceiling cloth of white muslin. The walls are whitewashed with decorative bands of *tierra amarilla* at the base and protecting part of the fireplace. A small window opens to the south and a door gives outside entrance on the east. Near the window is the confessional, which is merely a screen between two kneeling boards or rests for the suppliants' and the confessor's knees. (67)

> Lo que no se puede remediar se ha de aguantar.
> ("That which cannot be remedied must be endured.")
>
> Tiene más Dios que darnos que nosotros que pedirle.
> ("God's bounty is beyond our selfish dreams.")
>
> El que a buen árbol se arrima buena sombra lo cobija.
> ("He who chooses a leafy tree is sure of a protecting shade.")
> (100)

Death too was accepted as a natural and all too familiar companion. The dying chose their own rituals of departure, and their final wishes and last words were willingly enacted and cherished by the survivors. A comic anecdote from Cordova deals lightly with this important rite of passage.

The hillside on which I walked was strewn with round boulders, stones large and small, like pumpkins in a pumpkin patch at harvest time. *Lágrimas de San Pedro* they were called locally. St. Peter must have shed many bitter tears, and here they were turned to stone, a hard evidence of his grief and remorse. The dim trail that ran the length of the hillside led to an upland plateau which showed the outlines of humble adobe houses with a scattering of plum bushes and junipers limned against the majesty of the Truchas Peaks.

I heard drumming hoofbeats coming from a dip in the trail which momentarily screened the source of the commotion. But not for long. I had just stepped aside when a whirlwind of accelerated motion swept by me. I had just time to catch a glimpse of a honey-colored burro racing by at full tilt with a very busy lad trying valiantly to keep his seat on the sleek back of his onrushing mount.

The burro was carrying a double load. Strapped to the lad's waist was another figure almost as tall as he, yet of strange aspect. Faintly glimpsed it was not a live figure, yet it twisted behind its captor in an erratic manner, jouncing and swaying to the motion of the harassed beast beneath him. It had articulated legs which, free of any restraint, repeatedly came in contact with the burro's quivering flanks.

Now a burro's flanks are his most ticklish points, next to the *cruz*, that is. The *cruz* or cross on a burro is that point where his shoulders join his withers. This place is outlined by the darker points athwart his shoulders, delineating a perfect cross. Prick this cross with the point of a stick and you provoke a bucking, whirling tornado which nine times out of ten leaves you spread-eagled on the ground. This mark found on all burros gave rise to an old conundrum which is an institution in the folklore of the villages: "*En el llano está Mariano, tiene cruz pero no es Cristiano.*" ("In the fields you'll find Mariano; he carries a cross yet he's not a Christian.") The answer being obvious, I'll not divulge it.

However, if you tickle a burro's flanks you bring on frenzied and swift flight, the animal's instant response to being visited with this, to him, the supreme indignity, outrageous and not to be tolerated. Hence, his instinct for sudden and precipitate flight to get rid of or ride out from under the malicious tormentor.

As I regained the trail and pointed my steps in the same direction as the fleeing trio, I evaluated and sorted out the kaleidoscopic images I had seen go by. The face of the figure in the rear had been turned to me for a brief instant. I recalled a long, mournful visage surmounted by a crown of thorns with gouts of red paint on the brow and cheeks. Also a cadaverous chest with one side of the rib case having its touch of red paint also. Below a loin cloth dangled long legs, jointed at the knees and perhaps at the hips as well.

There! All the pieces were falling into place. I had both the boy's name and that of his burro. They were well known to me and to all of the village. And a worthy pair they were too. You seldom saw one without the other, for *El Melado* ("the honey-colored one") admitted of no other master than Pascual, who kept his pet mount sleek and fat with many a choice tidbit slipped away under his shirt from the table.

Now I was certain. It was a figure of the crucified Christ, a product of the *santeros'* art, made so that it could be taken off the cross by removing wooden pins which held it there. This realization also explained the wind-borne words Pascual had spoken as he tugged at the rope around the burro's neck: *"Tente tatita Dios, tente porque yo no te puedo ayudar."* ("Hang on little father God, for I cannot help you.") I had to laugh as I recalled the tense face of Pascual as he braced himself backwards holding onto that encircling rope to keep from pitching forward between *El Melado's* ears.

I was mystified about the why of this particular mission. Why was the *bulto* being transported in this fashion by only an irresponsible boy on an equally questionable burro?

Below me where the trail leveled off into a small plain, I saw that Pascual had calmed *El Melado's* pace. Then I saw them stop and the boy dismount. Still with the figure clinging to his back, Pascual came back over the trail in my direction and then shaking his head he returned to where *El Melado* stood. First fixing a noose around his burro's nose, a deterrent to further spurts of speed, Pascual gingerly remounted and set off at a sober pace.

As he rounded the outskirts of the village walls, I cut across fields and through fences to where ladders let me over a roof and down into the village square. This was a route that even *El Melado* with all his nimbleness could not negotiate. I made for a cluster of women at the door of one of the humbler homes of the village. Thanks to my shortcut I arrived just as Pascual brought his burro to a halt amid the clamor of questioning voices and outstretched hands.

Early that morning it had been evident to everybody in the village that Don Toribio was dying. And no one knew it better than Don Toribio himself. He had made his peace with God. He had repeated his oft-quoted saying, *"Lo que no sirve, al pozo."* ("To the pit with that which is of no more use.") On hearing this, those present knew that he was resigned, yet he asked for one more favor before he died: "Send someone for *Nuestro Señor de Buena Muerte.* Tell my *compadre* Vicente that I am dying. He cannot refuse me that comfort."

Now *Nuestro Señor de Buena Muerte* was housed in a private chapel on the high plateau I had glimpsed earlier in the morning. Its keeper was Don Vicente. This blessed figure was much in demand by those who desired its presence at their deathbed for it insured peaceful departure into the next world.

However, his request dismayed those who were charged with its fulfillment. "Who can we send? All our men are upriver cleaning out the *acequia madre*" (a yearly task from which no ablebodied male was exempt).

"There is Pascual and his *Melado,*" someone rather dubiously suggested.

"Ay Dios, that one is good to send for death itself; he would never get back with him. But for *Nuestro Señor de Buena Muerte,* no. *Es imposible.*" But search as they might for a substitute, they had to settle for the impossible one.

Pascual was within hearing, close herding some communal cows and the saddle stock of those men who had ridden in to do their share of the cleaning of the *acequia madre*. The *mayordomo* of the *acequia* had refused Pascual's services as a peon for one of the larger landowners. This had angered Pascual, the more so when he had been charged with his present task, one he esteemed far below him. He made some insulting remarks to the two girls who were sent out to replace him. Feeling a little better for this, he rode up sullenly to the one who had called out to him.

Pascual set out on his mission cheered by the thought of a fast ride on his beloved *Melado* and also with visions of a tasty meal of fresh goat cheese and wild honey at Don Vicente's home. Whether he enjoyed cheese and wild honey I know not, but he left Don Vicente's with his charge safely tied behind him and set out on the road home. He had never been known to accomplish an errand in so short a time.

As he turned to loosen the band which bound him to his fellow rider, he was greeted with exclamations of horror and dismay, for somewhere along the trail the blessed figure had lost its head. Handing down the headless figure, Pascual turned his mount back toward the upland trail to shouts and imprecations directed at his retreating figure.

Still muttering at Pascual and lamenting the mishap that *Nuestro Señor de Buena Muerte* had sustained, three of the women reverentially carried the hapless figure in to the old man's bedside.

"Here's the blessed figure you asked for. May it grant you a peaceful death."

They brought the figure close to Don Toribio's side, screening that part which was so sadly lacking. One wooden hand was carried to the dying man's lips. Kissing it with fervor, he murmured something, then fell back on his pillow. Two hands as gnarled as the many roots they had grubbed out of a stubborn soil feebly fingered a rosary. Suddenly the hands were stilled and Don Toribio had been granted the boon of the peaceful passing he had wished for.

That evening when the men returned home from their labors they listened to a recital of the day's happenings. They were prepared for Don Toribio's death for they had heard the tolling of the bell which signaled it for all to hear. But the good ladies were not prepared for the laughter they provoked when they repeated Pascual's words flung back at them as he rode back to look for the lost head: *"Santíguenlo con el cuerpo mientras vuelvo con la cabeza."* ("Comfort him with the body until I return with the head.")

The women were horrified that their men should be so amused at something which to them was terrible, even sacrilegious. But Pascual's words were repeated again and again to evident amusement and over the years became a *dicho* or folk saying: "Make do with what you have while I go for more." Thus are *dichos* born. (31)

Brown's descriptions of wakes, funerals, and burials were published as part of his Echoes of the Flute *(122, 126). The following* alabado, *transcribed from a Brother's* cuaderno, *was among those commonly sung at wakes for the dead:*

La encomendación del alma	For the welfare of a soul
No la dejen de pedir,	Never forget to plead,
Encomendársela a Dios	Recommend it to God
Que Dios la ha de recibir.	For God will surely receive it.
O Divino Redentor	Oh Divine Redeemer
Hijo del Eterno Padre,	Son of the Eternal Father,
A ti te encomiendo esta alma,	I recommend this soul to you
Que la cuides y la salves.	That You may guard and save it.
Santísimo Sacramento	Most Holy Sacrament
Que en la Hostia te recibimos	Which we receive in the Host,

A ti te encomiendo esta alma
Que la lleves a tu reino.

I recommend this soul to you,
Take it with you to heaven.

O Jesús dueño y querido
Hijo de José y María
Recibe esta alma con gozo
Y tenla en tu compañía.

Oh Jesus my beloved Master
Son of Joseph and Mary,
Accept this soul with joy
And keep it in your company.

O Madre de mi Jesús,
Madre de los pecadores,
Recibe esta alma en tu seno,
Y atender a mis clamores.

Oh Mother of my Jesus
Mother of all sinners,
Take this soul to your breast,
And listen to my pleas.

Misericordia, Señor,
Te pido, y vuelvo a rogar,
Llévate esta alma a tu Gloria
A que vaya a descansar.

Mercy! Oh my Lord,
I beg, and I entreat again,
Take this soul to your Glory
So that it may find repose.

Y como humilde te pido
Que esta alma tenga consuelo,
A que vaya a descansar
Allá en tu Sagrado Reino.

In all humility I ask
That this soul receive consolation,
That it may find repose
Within Your Sacred Kingdom.

O Sangre de mi Jesús
O Remedio Universal,
Llévate esta alma a tu Gloria
No la dejes extraviar.

Oh blood of my Jesus
The Universal Remedy,
Take this soul with you to Glory
Do not let it stray away.

San Pedro (San José?) dulce y amable
Fuiste de María esposo,
Llévate esta alma a tu Gloria
Que goce dulce reposo.

Sweet and lovable St. Peter (St. Joseph?)
You were Mary's spouse
Take this soul with you to Glory
That it may know sweet repose.

San Juan Bautista hermoso,
Pues tú anunciastes la luz,
Llévate esta alma con gozo
Y entriégasela a Jesús.

Handsome Saint John the Baptist,
You foretold the Light,
Take this soul rejoicing
And present it to Jesus.

O Vírgen Madre de Dios,
Madre de misericordia,
Ruégale a tu Hijo divino
Que esta alma goze en Gloria.

Oh Virgin Mother of God
Mother of all Mercy,
Plead with Your Divine Son
That this soul may rest in Glory.

Rogarle Madre amorosa,
Y te ruego Madre amada
Que vaya esta alma a los cielos
De ángeles acompañada.

Plead with Him, gentle Mother,
As I plead with you beloved Mother,
That this soul may go to heaven
Accompanied by angels.

Angeles y Querubines
Que la vengan a topar,
Y la lleven a los cielos
Que de Dios vaya a gozar.

May angels and cherubim
Come out to give it welcome,
And carry it to heaven
To rejoice in God's presence.

Santo Niño de Atocha
O pastor de ovejas,
Junta esta alma en tu rebaño
Y perdonadle sus quejas.

O San Vicente amoroso
Santo fino y agraciado,
A ti encomiendo esta alma
Que le sirvas de abogado.

O mi Dios Omnipotente,
Padre, Hijo, Espíritu Santo
Llévate esta alma a los cielos
A que cante, Santo, Santo.

Llévala a que cante, Santo,
Esa hermosa claridad,
Con todo el reino glorioso
Y toda la santidad.

O Divino Redentor
O Vírgen, Madre querida,
A tí te encomiendo esta alma
Que sea bien recibida.

Padre Nuestro, Ave María
Gloria al Padre y un Sudario
Por el amor de Dios les pido
Por la ánima del finado.

Rogando te estoy, Señor
Y a los santos también,
Que de Dios vaya a gozar,
Por siempre jamás Amén.

Saintly Babe of Atocha,
Shepherding your flock,
Gather this soul into your fold
And pardon all its sins.

Saint Vincent mild and gentle
Noble gracious Saint,
I recommend this soul to you
Please mediate for it.

Oh my Omnipotent God,
Father, Son, and Holy Ghost,
Take this soul to heaven
That it may sing, Holy, Holy.

Accept and permit it to sing, Holy,
Amongst the Glory of the Blessed,
With all the souls in heaven
And all of the hosts of saints.

Oh Divine Redeemer
Oh beloved Virgin Mother,
To you I recommend this soul
May it be well received.

A Hail Mary and Our Father,
Glory to the Father and a Sudarium,
For the love of God I ask
For the soul of the deceased.

I pray to You, My Lord,
And all the saints as well,
That with God it may rejoice
Forevermore, Amen. (13)

Wakes provide time for mourning and time for warm sociability with family and friends. The following chiste *("joke") recounts an amusing response to an otherwise familiar occasion:*

—¿Mamá, que no vamos al velorio del vecino Santiago?—le preguntó Antonia a su madre, la viejita Soledad.
("Mother, aren't we going to neighbor Santiago's wake?" Antonia asked her mother, the little old lady Soledad.)
—Sí hijita, pero poco tarde porque tengo que acabar de airar (airear) este trigo antes de que se abaje (baje) este vientecito. Vete apreviniendo.
("Yes, dear little daughter, but a little late because I have to finish

airing out this wheat before this nice breeze goes down. But you can start getting ready.")

Acabando de airar su trigo la viejita se encimó sus enaguas negras sobre su traje de todos los días y echándose su tapalo, salieron ella y su hijita para la casa de su vecino donde estaban velando al recién muerto.

(Having finished winnowing her wheat, the little old woman pulled her black skirt over her everyday clothes and, throwing a shawl over herself, she and her little daughter left for the house of their neighbor where the recently defunct was laid out.)

Llegando allí entraron al cuarto donde el cuerpo estaba tendido.

(Having arrived there they went into the room where the body was laid out.)

¡Cosa extraña! pero el cuerpo estaba solo. La gente estaba cenando quisá (quizá) porque ya eran esas horas. No más unas cuantas velas alumbraban el cuarto y las sombras eran muchas allí. A un lado del cuerpo estaba puesto un altarcito adelante (delante) del cual se hincó la viejita.

(Strange thing, but the body was alone. The company must have been supping, it being around that time. Only a few candles gave illumination and the shadows were quite thick. Beside the body there was a little altar in front of which the little old woman knelt.)

Esta viejita Soledad le tenía miedo a los difuntos y por eso se puso a rezar tan pronto sin pararse a mirarle el rostro al difunto como es la costumbre. Su hijita se hincó atrás de ella y dándole un jaloncito al tapalo de su madre le dice, media asustadita también—¿Mama, qué rezo yo, qué rezo yo?

(The little old woman Soledad was afraid of the dead, that being the reason she began praying without even taking one glance at the corpse as was the custom. Her little daughter knelt behind her and gently pulling at her shawl said, not a little frightened, "Mama, what shall I pray?" [which sounds like *¿Qué resolló?* "What is that breathing?"])

Ya con miedo la viejita pensaba que le preguntaba que si resollaba y pensando que tal vez el muerto era el que resollaba, pegó un grito y arrancó a huir del cuarto. Corriendo como iba la pobrecita dejó caer un trapo que usaba de paño. Viendo esto su hijita le grita—Mamá, la garra, la garra, mama.

(Being already frightened the little old woman thought that she was asking her whether or not the corpse was breathing. Letting out a scream she fled from the room. In her flight the poor little old thing dropped a piece of cloth she had been using as a handkerchief. Seeing it drop the little daughter screamed, "Mama, the rag, the rag!" [which sounds like *la agarra*, "It will grab you."])

Pobre vieja pensando que ya el difunto la alcanzaba y ya sintiendo sus manos frías sobre ella, pegó otro grito aclamando a todos los santos. Dejó caer su tapalo para mejor correr y con sus "chonguitos" bien parados no paro hasta llegar a su casita.

(Poor old lady, thinking that the corpse was behind her and about to seize her, she started to run, her hair standing on end, until she reached her house.)

La pobre de Antonia asustada al ver esto salió corriendo detrás de su madre, llorando y tropezando por lo obscuro de la noche. Pero por fin llegó a la casa poco después de su madre.

(Poor Antonia, frightened at seeing this, ran after her mother, weeping and stumbling in the dark. Finally she reached the house a little after her mother.)

No volvieron al velorio ni al entierro hallándose enfermas del rebato el siguiente día.

(They did not return to the wake, nor did they attend the funeral, being too ill from fright the following day.) (103)

The following morning, the coffin is carried to the church and then to the campo santo *for burial.*

The newcomer to New Mexico, as he travels through the byways and lanes of the more remote sections of the state in search of new scenic beauties and visiting the villages to be found along the way, will undoubtedly notice upon nearing one of these villages clusters of crosses by the wayside—wooden crosses, some new, others weatherbeaten and still others wholly fallen to the ground. If the wayfarer tries to explain this to himself, the usual assumption is that these crosses mark a burial ground. But, the traveler might wonder, why choose such a public place where the irreverent dust and glances from a public road settle on these reminders of what were once living mortals?

Although these mute symbols do have some relation to the passing of some mortal from this world, they do not mark his final resting place. They mark the place where his coffin rested on the earth for the last time before being committed to its depths.

After a *velorio* ("wake") lasting all night, the funeral procession leaves the house of mourning with the remains of the deceased. The coffin is carried by friends of the departed to the church for the final rites. From there it is borne to the *campo santo* ("graveyard") to the measured tolling of the church bell and the accompaniment of *alabados* sung by the mourners. But the graveyard is quite a ways off and the coffin grows heavy. What could be more fitting than to endow this physical need for rest with a religious significance? And so it is, for when the pallbearers ease their burden gently to the ground it is with the thought that this is the last time that the dweller within its narrow walls will rest on his native soil.

The procession halts and, as the sound of the singing of *alabados* dies, the bell can more plainly be heard accenting the passage of a soul from earth to heaven. Soon, however, there is a gentler accompaniment to the bell's mournful tones as the kneeling group joins in a prayer for the peace and spiritual welfare of the soul of the deceased. After the prayer the bearers resume their burden but not before some member or friend of the bereaved family has placed a small cross by the roadside to mark the site of the halt, at the base of which each mourner places a small stone.

This cross will have inscribed on it a supplication to the passerby to say a prayer for the rest and peace of the soul of the deceased. If the passerby is heedful he will comply with the request and add his stone to the others supporting the cross. In time several crosses will decorate the same site, for it is the natural resting place, being midway from church to graveyard. The word *descanso* means a short halt or stop for rest, hence the name by which these places are known.

One also encounters lone crosses in remote places in the forest, along riverbanks, and beside roads and highways. These crosses mark the site where some victim of lightning, drowning, or highway accident met his doom and ask the passerby to say a prayer for the unfortunate soul. (53)

This alabado *too is copied from a Brother's* cuaderno *and was likely sung during wakes sponsored by the Brotherhood:*

San Pedro me abra sus puertas	May St. Peter open his gates to me
Y me baño con su luz,	And bathe me in his light,

Soy esclavo de María	I am one of Mary's servants
Y devoto de Jesús.	And a follower of Jesus.
A San Pedro como un ángel	Saint Peter as an angel
Tengo esperanzas de ver,	I have hopes of seeing,
Para que me lleve al cielo	So that he may take me to heaven
Para compañia de él.	To keep him company.
Damos gracias a María	We give thanks to Mary
Y al divino Salvador,	And to the Saviour Divine,
Que del cielo nos alcanze	So that His divine radiance
Su divino resplandor.	May reach to us from heaven.
Es tan bello resplandor	It is a radiance so beautiful
Que del cielo da su luz	Which from heaven sheds its light,
Debemos darle gracias	That we should all give thanks
A nuestro Padre Jesús.	To Our Father Jesus.
Es Jesús tan bello y santo	Jesus is so beautiful and saintly
Tan bueno de corazón	So good of heart is He,
Tanto lo desagradamos	That for all the displeasure we cause Him
Siempre nos echa el perdón.	He is always ready to forgive.
Tengo esperanzas en Dios	I have trust in God
Que nos ha de conseguir,	That He will grant to us,
San Pedro subir al cielo	Saint Peter, entrance to heaven
Para poderle servir.	That we may serve Him there.
San Pedro con alabanzas	Saint Peter with hymns of praise
Y alegría incomparable,	And cheerfulness beyond compare,
Entonará para nosotros	Will sing hymns of praise for us
A Jesús su dulce padre.	To Jesus his sweet Father.
Al Señor debe pedirle	To the Lord you should address your pleas
Con un amor verdadero,	With a love sincere and true,
Porque él es el Padre	For He is truly our Father
En la tierra y en el cielo.	In heaven as well as on earth.
San Pedro como puertero	Saint Peter as the keeper
De la puerta más sagrada,	Of that most sacred gate
Le debemos de pedir	Is the one to whom we should apply
Que nos conceda la entrada.	For entrance into heaven.
A San Pedro siempre tengan	Always keep Saint Peter
Presente en su memoria,	Ever in your mind,
Pa'que nos sirva de guía	So that he may serve us as guide
Para subir a la gloria.	On the path to heaven.
Mi Jesús y Rey del cielo	My Jesus, King of heaven
Y del alto firmamento,	And of the firmament,
Tengo esperanzas en él	I put my trust in Him
Me ha de dar el Sacramento.	To offer me the Holy Sacrament.

Adios Jesús Nazareno,
De el cielo Padre bendito,
Nos lleva a su gloria
Por su poder infinito.

Adios San Pedro bendito
Padre de mi corazón,
Echanos su bendición
Y seremos perdonados.

Amén Jesús Nazareno
Padre de mi corazón
Guíanos por buen camino
Echanos tu bendición.

Farewell, Jesus of Nazareth,
Blessed Father of heaven,
Take us up to Glory
Through Your infinite power.

Farewell, Blessed Saint Peter,
Father of my heart,
Grant us now your blessing
And forgiveness we will find.

Amen, Jesus of Nazareth
Father of my heart,
Guide us upon the holy way,
Grant us Your blessing.

Fin Amén (18)

APPENDIX:

Notes on Federal Project Number One
and the Federal Writers' Project in New Mexico

I wish we lived in Kansas,
Where everything is flat—
No Peak to make the tourists point,
And say *"What's that?"*

But here in dear New Mexico,
A million humps an' hollers
Keep us sweating all the week
And spoil our clean White Collars!

And every mountain wears the name
Of Spanish Don or Lady,
Of outlaw, Saint, or Indian tribe—
All sanctified, or shady!

I think it would be simpler far
To call the CCC's,
And have them roll the country flat,
So we could take our ease!

—Alice Corbin Henderson, "Lines
Mumbled in Sleep," 30 July 1936,
in *Over the Turquoise Trail,*
vol. 1, no. 1, 1937, p. 3.

The New Mexico Federal Writers' Project of the Works Progress Administration was organized in October 1936. Ina Sizer Cassidy became the first State Director, serving until February 1939.[1] The initial staff of fifteen workers was increased to sixty in 1936, and reduced to forty-two in 1937.[2] Before mid-1939, the unit had completed a calendar and a mimeographed periodical, and work on the state's contribution to the American Guide Series was nearly finished. After September 1939 and before the end in 1943, workers on the reorganized project, the Work Projects Administration Writers' Program, produced a New Mexico handbook for the American Recreation Series and a collection of Spanish-American songs and games, began to assemble materials for a "History of Grazing," and helped design a health almanac.

The Works Progress Administration (WPA) had been established by Executive Order No. 7034 on May 6, 1935, to coordinate and implement "the work relief program as a whole" and to develop "small useful projects designed to assure a maximum employment in all areas." In New Mexico, the WPA became known as *"El Diablo a pie,"* the Devil on foot. Roswell City Engineer and Water Superintendent and State Highway Commissioner Lea Rowland was appointed the state's first administrator on May 12, 1935. By January 1936, some 13,426 relief workers were employed on "public building projects such as schools, community buildings, city halls, fire-stations and libraries; farm-to-market roads, street grading, bridge, sidewalk and curb and gutter projects; reservoir, ditch improvement; flood control and irrigation projects, also water systems and sewage projects; projects to provide employment for women and white-collar workers and projects not classifiable under the above, such as excavation of ruins, telephone line construction, malaria control and sanitation, parks, playgrounds, stadia, cemeteries and air-ports."[3]

Federal Project Number One, the first of six WPA-sponsored white-collar projects, was officially announced on August 2, 1935. Directors appointed to head its four subprojects were Holger Cahill (art), Nicolai Sokoloff (music), Hallie Flanagan (theater), and Henry G. Alsberg (writers). President Franklin D. Roosevelt approved this program on September 12, 1935. A fifth subproject to survey state and local records was being planned, but the Historical Records Survey, initially directed by Luther H. Evans, did not receive approval until November 16, 1935. Generally known as Federal One, Federal Project Number One shortly became the "heart" of a government "supported and subsidized . . . arts program that in material size and cultural character was unprecedented in this or any other nation."[4] During its halcyon days (1935-39), each of the five subprojects undertook extensive and ambitious activities designed to employ as many artists and personnel associated with the arts as possible.

Although New Mexico never supported a unit of the Federal

Theater Project (FTP), it did boast active state divisions of the Federal Art Project (FAP), the Federal Music Project (FMP), and the Historical Records Survey (HRS), all three of which worked with the state Federal Writers' Project (FWP) on various endeavors. The New Mexico FAP began in October 1935. Artist Russell Vernon Hunter served as its director throughout, from 1935 until 1942. Because Taos and Santa Fe had become known as art colonies by the late 1920s, the state had a large number of artists who acutely felt the effects of the Depression. The FAP employed 206 persons between 1935 and 1939. Established artists were allowed to create in any medium, and many were also chosen to paint murals in public buildings and educational institutions. Various art education activities were undertaken, with art centers opened at Gallup, Melrose, and Roswell.[5] Although "in general the Federal Art Project discouraged handicraft units as beneath its artistic dignity, in New Mexico, where the artistic qualities of handicrafts were superior, it not only permitted but fostered their development."[6] Taos woodcarver Patrocinio Barela was among those discovered and encouraged by the Art Project.[7]

A New Mexico plan to record Spanish Colonial *santos* anticipated the FAP and was eventually finished under the WPA as part of the Index of American Design. Two hundred copies of an experimental (and apparently unauthorized) "Portfolio of Spanish Colonial Design in New Mexico," completed on August 1, 1938, were hand-printed and colored by FAP members.[8] This rare document contains fifty plates illustrating *santos*, other religious objects, and household objects, an introduction by regional adviser Donald J. Bear, historical background, a bibliography, and a glossary. It constitutes a valuable record which was eventually incorporated into the Index of American Design.

Music education activities rather than concerts were paramount in the New Mexico FMP. Some performers were paid for community programs, but the greatest attention seems to have been devoted to music instruction in rural areas and in various state institutions. For example, the 1937 Report claims:

> In Taos County, no music instruction has ever been available. Here an interested class of rural teachers is receiving instruction from an employee who, in turn, visits the rural school herself to give demonstration lessons. Much 'appreciation'

work is done. The children are taught to tune glasses or bottles to pitch and these are a great help in the rooms where no piano or other instruments are available.[9]

In two years, the FMP "offered instruction to nearly 10,000 people, and 736 free public concerts."[10]

New Mexico FMP Director Helen Chandler Ryan, working with Arthur L. Campa of the Spanish Department at the University of New Mexico, encouraged the collection of Spanish-American folksongs. FMP Unit No. 1 was a mimeographed collection of thirteen "Spanish-American Folk Songs of New Mexico" (1936-37), while Unit No. 2, with the same title and dates, contained eighteen songs plus descriptive notes in English. A mimeographed publication with nine songs, "Guitar method with guitar arrangements of Spanish-American folk songs of New Mexico," appeared in 1939. The 1940 compilation, FMP Unit No. 3, "Spanish-American Singing Games of New Mexico," was incorporated into a joint 1942 volume, *The Spanish-American Song and Game Book,* with the New Mexico FWP. "Spanish-American Dance Tunes of New Mexico," FMP Unit No. 4, also mimeographed, was produced in 1942.[11] New Mexico's song collection and music education projects apparently impressed national folk festivals director Sarah Gertrude Knott, who in 1939 claimed that "there is in New Mexico a finer integration of music project activities with the life of the people than in any other part of the United States that I have visited."[12]

The New Mexico Historical Records Survey was headed variously by historian George P. Hammond, Herbert O. Brayer, and G. Robert Massey. In April 1938, national director Luther H. Evans reported that New Mexico was among those states where he had experienced difficulty finding "competent certified workers, particularly of supervisory caliber."[13] By 1939, however, the New Mexico unit had produced mimeographed records inventories of Bernalillo, Colfax, Eddy, Otero, Sandoval, and Torrance counties. Doña Ana, Grant, Hidalgo, Luna, Mora, San Miguel, Sierra, Union, and Valencia counties had been added by 1942, when the HRS work was being completed by the War Services Program of the WPA Education Projects.

Various federal records in the state were also inventoried in 1940 and 1941. In addition, three useful mimeographed publications came out of the Survey's Work Projects Administration phase: the "Directory of Churches and Religious Organizations in New Mexico, 1940" (July 1940); the "Guide to Public Vital Statistics Records in New Mexico" (March 1942), both sponsored by the University of New Mexico; and the "Index to Final Report of Investigations Among the Indians of the Southwestern United States [1890, 1892], by A. F. Bandelier" (June 1942), sponsored by the Historical Society of New Mexico. A pamphlet, "The Price of Free World Victory," containing excerpts from an address by Vice President Henry A. Wallace was mimeographed in November 1942.[14]

A Translators' Project involving certain Spanish Archives then belonging to the New Mexico Historical Society was the first undertaken by the fledgling FWP in the state. Paul Farron served as supervisor, Claribel Fischer Walker as editor for English, Ireneo Chaves as editor for Spanish, and Rosario O. Hinojos, M. Baca, and J. M. Martínez, as translators.[15] National FWP director Henry G. Alsberg was not pleased with this activity. In a letter of January 6, 1936, he wrote to New Mexico WPA official Mary B. Perry that:

> I am rather alarmed by the number of writers apparently at work, the amount of material that apparently is being turned out on the undertaking, and the very little information I have about any work being done on the American Guide. However valuable the Translation Project may be, the Guide and Reporting Projects take precedence.[16]

Nevertheless the Translators Project was continued, and all workers temporarily or permanently assigned to the division uncovered useful historical data, provided translation services, and acted as a local review board for various Spanish-English, English-Spanish (no Indian languages apparently) translations.

Work on the New Mexico Guide was in full swing by 1936, but this undertaking did not yield tangible results until 1937, when Rydal Press in Santa Fe published a thirty-two-page *Calendar of Events,* compiled and written by members of the Federal Writers' Project, illustrated by members of the Federal Art Project, and sponsored by the Santa Fe Civic League and Chamber of Commerce. On March 1 of that year, the New Mexico FWP also finished a "Narrative Report on Historic Sites" at Alsberg's request. By September 1938, they had prepared a list of historic sites in Santa Fe County, research which, like the *Calendar,* was eventually incorporated into the New Mexico Guide.

In the spring of 1937, the Santa Fe office responded to a Washington suggestion to start an FWP magazine. Reports submitted for the state Guide formed the basis of this mimeographed periodical. According to the first page, its title, *Over the Turquoise Trail,* "was suggested by Alice Corbin Henderson's *The Turquoise Trail,* an Anthology of New Mexico Poetry [1928], to which acknowledgment is herewith made." Thirteen different writers, identified by initials only, are represented in the first number, which was acknowledged by Paul A. F. Walter in June 1937.[17] Volume 1, number 2, also undated, contains contributions categorized as Place Name Legends, Spanish Folk Ways, Cowboy Songs, One Lost Mine, The Signal Glass, and Told Around the Campfire, by nine different writers. Another number of volume 1, presently not on file in Santa Fe, is dated 1938.

Ina Sizer Cassidy's introductory "Facts about the Writers' Project" in the first number of *Over the Turquoise Trail* contains a claim that the New Mexico Guide was nearly ready for publication. The director states that the workers have "been gathering and compiling material for the New Mexico section of the American Guide, a federally sponsored *Travel Guide* of five or six volumes covering the entire United States, and the State Guide, of approximately two hundred thousand words of history and description of the State and its attractions for the use of schools, libraries, and travelers." She also notes that "the gathering of Folk Tales, myths, legends and pioneer stories, and place names, has been carried on simultaneously, resulting in material enough for the compilation of several extra volumes of valuable information." Except for the games book in 1942, these collections never materialized, although the place names project was continued by the New Mexico Folklore Society after 1948.[18]

Folklore collection was considered an important part of the federal arts projects, but it was generally subordinated to other goals in both the national and the state programs. Several guides to folklore materials and methods of collecting and sample folklore essays were sent from Washington to the state FWP units in 1936. National FWP director Alsberg also enlisted pioneer American folksong collector John A. Lomax to read and review manuscripts submitted to the Washington office. "From June 25, 1936, to October 23, 1937 (with a ninety-day furlough beginning July 24, 1937), John A. Lomax, honorary curator of the archives of American folksong in the Library of Congress, was national advisor on folklore and folkways, on the payroll of the Historical Records Survey."[19] Lomax's interests in folksong, the rural South, and Negro life influenced the Washington FWP during his tenure.

Presently extant documents indicate that Lomax was responsible for criticizing the folklore chapter of the New Mexico Guide.[20] The first version of this chapter, dated September 8, 1936, and entitled "Introductory Essay: New Mexican Spanish Folklore and Provincialisms," was written by Eustaquio García, a National Youth Administration student at the University of New Mexico. Dr. Arthur L. Campa of the University checked the 3,160-word essay, which included translations by Claribel Fischer Walker, and Alice Corbin edited it for submission to Washington on October 9, 1936.

The first prefinal revision of this chapter, dated January 30, 1937, apparently took a different tack. Entitled "Early Folklore Legends—Introductory Essay," it contained only thirteen-hundred words written by Robert Young of the University of New Mexico, checked by Dr. F. M. Kercheville and Dr. Arthur L. Campa, both of the University's Department of Modern Languages, and rewritten by Ina Sizer Cassidy. Lomax's criticism is dated February 24, 1937. He suggested a new title, a reorganization into sections on Indian, Spanish-American, and Anglo-American materials, more concrete examples, and a complete rewriting. Associate FWP director George Cronyn wrote Cassidy a covering letter which began: "I am returning the Folklore material with the comments of Mr. Lomax, who still is dissatisfied with the general structure and treatment of the essay. The material in your project work, and the character of it, was of such interest that we are very anxious to make this an outstanding essay."

Washington criticism of a second prefinal revision, seemingly still Lomax's work, was dated October 22, 1937. The review begins:

> The material included is excellent and shows the results of considerable research. There is however, a lack of balance in the essay. At the beginning, the three sources of folklore are cited: Indian, Spanish, Anglo-American. The contributions

from the first two of these are well presented, but those belonging in the third category are neglected. *Anglo-Americans* may be questioned, also, as a term to include the tales of Billy the Kid, of the early scouts, of the cattlemen, and others.

However, the term "Anglo-Americans" was retained in the published essay.

The third prefinal revision of the FWP folklore essay was submitted on February 18, 1938, after Lomax's departure. Its 4,491 words were checked by Dr. F. M. Kercheville and Dr. Arthur L. Campa. Washington criticism on March 29, 1938, claimed that it was: "Well written copy. Some notations are marked on text, which is print-ready." Alsberg's accompanying letter to Cassidy noted that *"Folklore* requires only a little revision to make it final copy and may be held in the State office until the whole guide is being made ready for press." The brief chapter that finally appeared in the 1940 Guide concentrates on Pueblo Indian tales, gives a short, comprehensive overview of Spanish lore, and covers Anglo-American buried treasure, hunting, outlaw, and cowboy tales and songs at greatest length.[21]

Ina Sizer Cassidy left the New Mexico FWP at the end of January 1939. Her assistant, Aileen Nusbaum, author of *Zuni Indian Tales* (New York: Putnam, 1926), served as Acting State Director until late fall of that year. When the Works Progress Administration became the Work Projects Administration on July 1, 1939, the Federal Writers' Project became the WPA Writers' Program. As a result of this change, Mrs. Nusbaum sent No. 403 termination notices to all workers, effective August 31. The new staff, which would include some former employees, was to be concentrated in Santa Fe and not spread out in the field.[22] The Coronado Cuarto Centennial Commission became the state-wide sponsors of the New Mexico Writers' Program with the University of New Mexico assisting them in sponsoring the state Guide.

At least three outside writers are known to have come to New Mexico to help with the preparation of the Guide. Poet Norman Macleod, who had earlier graduated from the University of New Mexico, was a casualty of the political turmoil in the New York City Writers' Project, but Director Orrick Johns got him a position with the New Mexico FWP.

The director . . . was Mrs. Inez [sic] Cassidy, a woman of matriarchal temperament with whom he got along famously. On one occasion when he wound up in jail after a drinking spree, she came to his rescue and had him released. "The first time you go to jail," she told him, "we get you out. The next time we let you rot." Despite his love for Santa Fe, he missed his friends in the East. Quitting his job, he returned to New York and began writing a novel about his experiences on the two writers' projects entitled *You Get What You Ask For,* which was published in 1939.[23]

Jacob Scher, a young Chicago writer connected with the FWP both in that city and in New Orleans, also spent about a year in Santa Fe with the New Mexico Project, probably in 1938.[24] Finally, the state director responsible for producing the first state guide, novelist Vardis Fisher, came from Idaho to help Aileen Nusbaum finish the New Mexico Guide during the summer of 1939.[25] According to Brown's recollection:

Vardis Fisher would show up at the office, peruse finished material submitted for his inspection, make revisions of same, or offer suggestions as to deletion or expansion. After a short verbal discussion on other aspects of the work in progress, he would then retire from the office and take refuge in the city park in Santa Fe. Here he would spend the rest of the afternoon writing furiously in a notebook. The many publications issued in his name attest to his capacity for work.[26]

Charles Ethrige Minton was appointed State Supervisor of the WPA Writers' Program in the late fall of 1939, but "most of the credit for the completion of the work belongs to Aileen Nusbaum, former director of the project, who wrote some of the essays and worked mightily under great handicaps to assemble the materials."[27] In keeping with a policy of relative anonymity, Minton's preface to the New Mexico Guide concludes with an acknowledgment that "all of this would not have produced the book without the labors of the anonymous workers on this project who did the research and gathered the material, typed it, and prepared it for publication." A majority of these writers are named in the following alphabetical list with their "home territory" noted in parentheses wherever possible[28]:

Hartley Alexander
Mrs. Myrtle Andrews
Aureliano Armendáriz (La Mesilla)
Mary Helen Armijo
Malaquías Baca
Elliott Barker
Lou Sage Batchen (Las Placitas)
Manuel Berg (Albuquerque)
Charles Bergmann
T. F. Bledsoe
Carlota Brent
Dora Johnson Brauning
Lorin W. Brown (Taos and Cordova)
James A. Burns
Allen A. Carter
Marie Carter
F. M. Casey
Elliott Cassidy
Beaudien Chapin
Genevieve Chapin
I. L. Chaves
J. B. Cisneros (Questa?)
Anna Nolan Clark
Charles F. Coan
Frank B. Coe
H. P. Collier
Lula Mae Collins
Mrs. John J. Cowman
Edith L. Crawford
Alice M. Crook
William Dean
Mrs. Eleanor De Long
Thelma James Dohrer
Frederic H. Douglas
E. L. Drake
William M. Emery (northeastern New Mexico)
Erna Fergusson (Albuquerque)
Louis W. Fisher
Mary Fulganzi
Vicente Gallegos

Eustaquio García (NYA student, University of New Mexico)
José Gonzáles
Alice Bell Gordon
Blanche C. Grant (Taos)
Helmut Gusdorf (Taos)
Muriel Haskell (Taos)
Sanford W. Hassell
Rosario O. Hinojos
W. F. Hodge
Carrie L. Hodges
Joyce Hunter (Roswell)
Mildred Jordan
Belle Kilgore
Tom Kromer
Margaret Lane
John Looney
Elisa Lucero
Philip Lucero
Aurora Lucero-White (San Miguel County)
Bright Lynn (Las Vegas)
Louisa Martínez
Luis Martínez
Reyes N. Martínez (Arroyo Hondo)
John E. McClue
Harold Mehrins
Grace Meredith
Samuel Montoya
May Price (Mrs. Benton) Moseley (Lovington)
Charles C. Onion
Nina Otero-Warren
Raymond Otis (Santa Fe)
William Leigh Patterson (Alamogordo)
Robert Pfanner
William Pillin
Lolita Huning Pooler (Albuquerque)
Henry Purmort
Moisés Rael
Katherine Ragsdale (Artesia)
Lester F. Raines (Las Vegas)
Bill Rawles

Georgia B. Redfield (Roswell)
Betty Reich
B. A. Reuter (Pecos)
Olive Rush
Frances Ruth Russell
Henry Schmeltzer
Mela Sedillo
José D. Sena
D. D. Sharp
Jacques Simons
Mrs. R. T. F. Simpson (Farmington)
Ann Smith
Janet Smith (also listed as Janet Smith Kromer)
J. Vernon Smithson (Clovis)
Helen S. Speaker
Lova Stovall
Simeón Tejada (Taos)
N. Howard Thorp (Alameda)
Mrs. Frances E. Totty (Silver City)
Don Antonio de Trueba
José and Rafaelita Trujillo (El Llano?)
Eulogio F. Ulibarrí (Tierra Amarilla)
Clay W. Vaden
Claribel Fischer Walker
W. E. Wheeler ("Pecos Valley of New Mexico since 1923")
G. N. White (Portales)
Goldie Wright

Ina Sizer Cassidy, Aileen Nusbaum, Paul Farron, Alice Corbin Henderson, Russell Vernon Hunter of the Federal Art Project, and Brice Sewall of the Vocational Trade and Industrial Education Program also submitted contributions.

Charles Ethrige Minton supervised the final years of the New Mexico WPA Writers' Program.[29] In 1940 and 1941, the "History of Grazing" project occupied many of the writers on the reduced staff. A circular from the WPA Technical Services (Community Service Circular no. 4, Writers' Program no. 2), dated June 6, 1940, offered suggestions for sources of information and appropriate questions to ask informants. The proposed volume was never published, but the New Mexico group did considerable work toward their share of the undertaking.

In 1941, *New Mexico* (Northport, New York: Bacon & Wieck) became No. 30 in the American Recreation Series. Remaining workers on the FWP compiled this recreational handbook. A memorandum of July 31, 1941, also suggested that the state programs prepare health almanacs similar to the *Alabama Health Almanac*, "an effective vehicle for health information in rural areas." A dummy version of such an almanac for New Mexico, dated 1943(44), remains in the WPA Administration Files together with a letter of December 1, 1942, addressed to Miss Mamie Meadors, Assistant State Supervisor for WPA Education Projects. The almanac, which includes historical notes and sayings in addition to health information, begins with an appropriately patriotic section on Francis Scott Key and "The Star Spangled Banner."

By 1942, the remaining WPA programs were nearly interchangeable and largely geared toward defense. A mimeographed booklet entitled "Folk Songs of the Spanish Southwest" was compiled by the Education Project, War Services Program, Work Projects Administration, State of New Mexico. State Supervisor of Education Projects Nina Otero-Warren wrote an introduction to the forty-two Spanish texts in November 1942.

The Spanish-American Song and Game Book (New York: A. S. Barnes & Co., 1942) was compiled by Workers of the Writers' Program, Music Program, and Art Program of the Work Projects Administration in the State of New Mexico. The Coronado Cuarto Centennial Commission of New Mexico copyrighted this illustrated volume, which was sponsored by the University of New Mexico and the State Superintendent of Public Instruction of New Mexico. Aileen Nusbaum wrote the introduction. Charles E. Minton's foreword notes that he, Mrs. Helen Chandler Ryan (Music Program), Russell Vernon Hunter (Art Program) and their staffs were "assisted by Dr. Arthur L. Campa, Professor of Spanish-American Folklore of the University of New Mexico, and Sr. Edmundo Lassalle of the Division for Intellectual Cooperation of the Pan American Union, who gave generously of their time in checking the manuscript and establishing the authenticity of the games; also by Sr. Pedro A. Ortiz, who assisted with the musical arrangement."[30]

Lorin W. Brown contributed nine games to this collection. Other collectors named in the table of contents are Aureliano Armendáriz, Reyes N. Martínez, José Gonzáles, Rosario O. Hinojos, Eulogio

F. Ulibarrí, Vicente Gallegos, Guadalupe Gallegos, Mary Elba C.
De Baca, and Lou Sage Batchen. In his foreword, Minton also
states that "special acknowledgment is due Mr. Aureliano Armendáriz, who collected most of the singing games and in addition
made the original arrangements and most of the transcriptions; and
to Mr. Lorin W. Brown, who, in addition to collecting many of the
other games, translated most of them." This eighty-seven-page
volume marks a small end to the waning programs, but it
nonetheless remains a useful collection.

The New Mexico programs were subject to the same new
regulations and suffered the same fate as WPA programs in the
other states. When Federal One was abolished by the Emergency
Relief Appropriation Act of 1939, the reorganized Works Progress
Administration became the Work Projects Administration. This
agency was prohibited from the sole sponsorship of any arts project
after August 31. State administrators were "requested to cooperate
with the State, Regional and Washington staffs of Federal Project
Number One for the continuation of the Art, Music, Writers' and
Historical Records Survey activities as statewide projects; [so that]
insofar as possible the work now in progress shall be carried
on. . . ."[31] The Theatre Project was terminated. Of the WPA
Community Service Projects, the Art, Music, and Writers'
Programs were grouped under public activities, while the Historical Records Survey was administered under research and records
programs. Welfare programs constituted a third category of the
Community Service Division.

Fiscal and administrative difficulties soon engulfed the reorganized projects, especially in managing the sponsorship require-
ments. These problems, coupled with prewar and wartime tensions,
vitiated all the arts programs. A few projects were completed, but
most lapsed in the overall defense efforts. Nevertheless, many WPA
publications appeared after 1940, and incalculable amounts of
valuable data still remain in archives throughout the country—a
tribute to the industry and imagination of numerous artists,
administrators, and culturally active citizens.[32]

NOTES

Part I: Lorin W. Brown in Taos and Cordova: A Biographical and Ethnohistorical Sketch

1. Charles D. Carroll, "Miguel Aragón, a Great Santero," *El Palacio* 50 (1943):60.

2. T. M. Pearce, ed., *New Mexico Place Names: a Geographical Dictionary* (Albuquerque: University of New Mexico Press, 1965), p. 51.

3. A number of lengthy quotations from Lorin W. Brown, Jr., will be incorporated into this introduction without individual references as to source. These are drawn from transcriptions of interviews with him, as well as from letters and personal comments on earlier drafts of this part.

4. Porter A. Stratton, *The Territorial Press of New Mexico, 1834–1912* (Albuquerque: University of New Mexico Press, 1969), p. 265. See also appropriate references in Pearce S. Grove, Becky J. Barnett, and Sandra J. Hansen, eds., *New Mexico Newspapers: a Comprehensive Guide to Bibliographical Entries and Locations* (Albuquerque: University of New Mexico Press with Eastern New Mexico University, 1975).

5. Stratton, *The Territorial Press*, pp. 282, 292–93.

6. F. Stanley (Rev. Stanley F. L. Crocchiola), *The Red River, New Mexico Story* (Dallas, Texas: n.p., 1962), pp. 9–10.

7. Richard Rudisill, *Photographers of the New Mexico Territory, 1854–1912* (Santa Fe: Museum of New Mexico Press, 1973), p. 16. Brown also served two appointments as postmaster in Taos, worked in that County Clerk's office, and taught bookkeeping to various young men of Taos and vicinity.

8. *Red River New Mexico Prospector*, 2 January 1902.

9. Brown, writing as Lorenzo de Córdova, has provided additional information on the Martínez school and its influence on his grandfather in his *Echoes of the Flute* (Santa Fe: Ancient City Press, 1972), p. 18. Also see the section on Martínez in Weigle's notes to the text, p. 52. A more recent booklet of family legends and reminiscences by a descendant of Martínez, Dora Ortiz Vásquez, *Enchanted Temples of Taos: My Story of Rosario* (Santa Fe, New Mexico: The Rydal Press, 1975), is an interesting comparison to Brown's family stories. Brown notes that he also consulted Pedro Sánchez's *Memorias del Padre Antonio José Martínez* (Santa Fe, 1903) in compiling his sketch (89, p. 1).

10. See Brown (24) for an oral historical sketch of the Alto Huachin.

11. Sheldon Holland Dike, *The Territorial Post Offices of New Mexico* (Albuquerque: Author, 1958), no pagination.

12. The earlier of the two dates, 1725, is suggested by the fact that a 1725 land grant to the neighboring settlement of Cundiyo does not refer to any occupation of the Cordova area (Spanish Archives of New Mexico I, no. 104, New Mexico State Records Center and Archives, Santa Fe). This grant was revoked, and the lands were reassigned as the Santo Domingo de Cundiyo Grant in 1743 (Spanish Archives of New Mexico I, no. 211). This later document indicates that Cordova constituted the northern boundary of the Cundiyo grant.

13. The document itself (Spanish Archives of New Mexico I, no. 718) has been summarized by Dr. Myra Ellen Jenkins in an unpublished manuscript, "Documentation Concerning Settlement of Pueblo Quemado (Córdova)" in her possession at the New Mexico

State Records Center and Archives, Santa Fe. Her generous assistance in uncovering the early history of Cordova is gratefully acknowledged.

14. E. Boyd, *Popular Arts of Spanish New Mexico* (Santa Fe: Museum of New Mexico Press, 1974), p. 341.

15. The fact that the Cordova chapel was built after 1776 is supported by Fray Francisco Atanasio Domínguez's failure to mention any such building in the village during his visitation (Eleanor B. Adams and Fray Angelico Chavez, eds., *The Missions of New Mexico, 1776* [Albuquerque: University of New Mexico Press, 1956], p. 83). The first reference to the chapel in the Archives of the Archdiocese of Santa Fe is an inventory taken by two Quemado citizens for taxation purposes. Although it bears no date, Fray Angelico Chavez dated it internally as 1821 in his *Archives of the Archdiocese of Santa Fe, 1678–1900* (Washington, D.C.: Academy of American Franciscan History, 1957), p. 88. A letter from Bishop Zubiría of Durango to Father Alcino of Santa Cruz parish, 17 April 1832, acknowledges receipt of licenses for three chapels: El Señor de Esquípulas (Chimayo), Nuestra Señora del Rosario (Las Truchas), and San Antonio de Padua (Cordova), the latter listed as being near completion (ibid, p. 103). This construction might have been an enlargement of the original chapel, however.

16. Cf. Boyd, *Popular Arts*, p. 406.

17. Prior to 1892, lands in the public domain, including the headwaters of the Rito Quemado and nearby streams and stretching to the Truchas Peaks, were open to the villagers for grazing their livestock. By Presidential Proclamation of 11 January 1892, these lands became part of the Pecos River Forest Reserve. Effects of the change were apparently minimal. However, by an Executive Order of 6 April 1915, the Pecos National Forest and the Jemez National Forest were merged into one unit known and administered as the Santa Fe National Forest. The Secretary of Agriculture had been given the authority to manage the range resources on Forest Service lands under the Organic Act of June 4, 1897. Changes in grazing regulations eventually deprived Cordovans of nearly all the subsistence they formerly derived from grazing livestock. Official rationalization for this action cited the erosive dangers of overgrazing, which indeed posed a substantial threat. A limited number of grazing permits were issued, and, although "local people who were depending on these lands for livestock use were given priority in permit issuance" (Zamora, written communication, 1974), the benefits of this policy were minimal for most Hispano villagers. Permits were issued on the basis of prior use, and commercial operators had established a virtual monopoly of grazing lands before this time (Allan G. Harper, Andrew R. Cordova, and Kalervo Oberg, *Man and Resources in the Middle Rio Grande Valley* [Albuquerque: University of New Mexico Press, 1943], p. 63).

18. A number of sources have reported this situation, notably, the Soil Conservation Service and other agencies listed in Marta Weigle, ed., *Hispanic Villages of Northern New Mexico* (Santa Fe, New Mexico: The Lightning Tree, 1975), pp. 250–54. Also see Harper, et al., *Man and Resources*, and Bernard J. Seigel, "Some Structure Implications for Change in Pueblo and Spanish New Mexico," in Verne F. Ray, ed., *Intermediate Societies, Social Mobility and Communication* (Seattle: American Ethnological Society, 1959), p. 38.

19. Harper, et al., *Man and Resources*, p. 77.

20. See especially "The Deep Village" (52).

21. Harper, et al., *Man and Resources*, p. 77.

22. Soil Conservation Service, U.S. Department of Agriculture, "Village Livelihood in the Upper Rio Grande Area and a Note on the Level of Village Livelihood in the Upper Rio Grande Area," Regional Bulletin No. 44, Conservation Economics Series No. 171 (Albuquerque, 1937), p. 5.

23. Jimmy Carl Diecker, "Culture Change in Córdova, New Mexico," master's thesis, University of Oklahoma, 1971, pp. 33–36.

24. This information was provided by Charles Hart (personal communication, 1973) on

the basis of a "Public Voucher for Work Performed under Provisions of the Federal Highways Acts, as Amended," which was filed with the New Mexico State Highway Commission in 1955.

25. See Marc Simmons, "Settlement Patterns and Village Plans in Colonial New Mexico," *Journal of the West* 8 (1969):7–21, for additional information on the *plaza-rancho* distinction and its historical context.

26. Ernest L. Blumenschein, "Origin of the Taos Art Colony," *El Palacio* 20 (1926):190.

27. De Córdova, *Echoes of the Flute*, p. 9.

28. Brown's major FWP manuscripts on the Brotherhood are reprinted with a 1971 essay of reminiscences in his *Echoes of the Flute*. See also Marta Weigle, *Brothers of Light, Brothers of Blood: the Penitentes of the Southwest* (Albuquerque: University of New Mexico Press, 1976), for an extensive history and description.

29. De Córdova, *Echoes of the Flute*, pp. 9–10.

30. Elizabeth Sage Hare, "The Wood Carver of Córdova," *Travel* 81 (1943):21. See also Charles L. Briggs, "What is a Modern 'Santo'?" *El Palacio* 79, no. 4 (1974):40–49; idem, "To Sell a Saint: The Manipulation of Religious Symbols in the Evolution of a Sacred Art," *Papers in Anthropology* 17 (1976):201–21; and idem, "To Talk in Different Tongues: The 'Discovery' and 'Encouragement' of Hispano Woodcarvers by Santa Fe Patrons, 1919–1945," in *Hispanic Crafts of the Southwest*, ed. William Wroth (Colorado Springs, Colorado: The Taylor Museum of the Colorado Springs Fine Arts Center, 1977), pp. 37–51.

31. See, e.g.: E. E. Maes, "The Labor Movement in New Mexico," *New Mexico Business* 4 (1953):137–40; Philip Stevenson, "Deporting Jesus," *Nation* 143 (18 July 1936):67–69.

32. Such community vocational schools were located in Taos, Galisteo, Los Lunas, Roswell, Costilla, Peñasco, Anton Chico, Española, Santa Cruz, Chupadero, San Jose, Grants, Atarque, Mora, Cundiyo, Cerrillos, Cienega, and Agua Fria. Public schools such as the Normal at El Rito adopted the program as well. See Mary W. Coan, "Handicraft Arts Revived," *New Mexico Magazine*, February 1934, p. 14; Wayne Mauzy, "Santa Fe's Native Market," *El Palacio* 40 (1936):66; Brice H. Sewell, "A New Type of School," *New Mexico School Review* 15, no. 2 (1935):49–50.

33. Brown's urge to return to his spiritual homeland after death parallels his mother's orientation as well. Cassandra López became quite ill while living in Santa Fe, and her sense of imminent death moved her to strengthen her bonds to Hispano New Mexico. By returning to the Catholic Church she reaffirmed the faith of her childhood, and by asking to be buried in Cordova she expressed her love for that community and its residents. Her Cordovan neighbors, relatives and pupils of two decades reciprocated her affection following her death in 1941. The members of the local *Cofradía* took responsibility for her wake, funeral services, and burial, as Brown has so eloquently described (*Echoes of the Flute*, p. 34). Teachers were highly esteemed individuals in Cordova in the first half of this century, and Cassandra Brown López evidently occupied a position of unusual reverence in the community.

34. Diecker, "Culture Change in Córdova," pp. 53–54.

Appendix: Federal Project Number One and the Federal Writers' Project in New Mexico

1. Ina Sizer Cassidy was born on March 4, 1869, in Bent County, Colorado, where her pioneer parents were homesteaders on the Purgatoire River. Her first marriage, to John B. Davis, took her to Detroit. When Davis died, she returned to Denver and became a secretary. In 1912, she married artist Gerald Cassidy (1879–1934), and the couple made their first trip to Santa Fe. They purchased a home on Canyon Road in 1915, and Cassidy gave up commercial art for "serious art." His eventual success allowed them to tour Europe in 1926, and they became an influential part of the Santa Fe arts scene. In 1931, Mrs. Cassidy began

writing a longstanding column, "Art and Artists of New Mexico," for *New Mexico Magazine.*
She remained actively involved in the arts, folklore, and historic preservation throughout her
long life. According to her obituary of September 9, 1965, she was a member of the Old
Santa Fe Association, Santa Fe Garden Club, Mayflower Club, D.A.R., New Mexico and
National Press Women's Associations, New Mexico Historical Society, Spanish Colonial Arts
Society, New Mexico Association on Indian Affairs, and other groups. See, e.g., "Ina Sizer
Cassidy—Lady of Contrasts," *The Santa Fe Scene,* 13 December 1958, pp. 6–9; Edna
Robertson and Sara Nestor, *Artists of the Canyons and Caminos: Santa Fe, the Early Years*
(n.p.: Peregrine Smith, 1976).

2. Ina Sizer Cassidy, "Facts about the Writers' Project," *Over the Turquoise Trail* 1, no. 1
(1937):4.

3. Mrs. Elizabeth F. Gonzales, Secretary of State, ed., *The New Mexico Blue Book: State
Official Register, 1935–1936* (Las Vegas, New Mexico: Smith-Hursh Printing, 1936), pp.
71–72.

4. William F. McDonald, *Federal Relief Administration and the Arts* (Columbus: Ohio
State University Press, 1969), p. ix.

5. Workers of the Writers' Program of the Work Projects Administration in the State of
New Mexico, comps., *New Mexico: a Guide to the Colorful State* (New York: Hastings House,
1940), pp. 169–70. For discussion of the artists and their relationship to the FAP, see e.g.:
Van Deren Coke, *Taos and Santa Fe: the Artist's Environment, 1882–1942* (Albuquerque:
University of New Mexico Press, 1963), pp. 97–98; Robertson and Nestor, *Artists of the
Canyons and Caminos,* pp. 129–52. For additional details on the national project, see e.g.:
McDonald, *Federal Relief Administration,* pp. 341–482; and Richard D. McKenzie, *The New
Deal for Artists* (Princeton, New Jersey: Princeton University Press, 1973).

6. McDonald, *Federal Relief Administration,* p. 385.

7. Ibid., p. 432. The October 1936 issue of the WPA newspaper, *The Sunshine State
Builder,* contains an article about Barela. See also Mildred Crews, Wendell Anderson, and
Judson Crews, *Patrocinio Barela: Taos Woodcarver* (Taos, New Mexico: Taos Recordings and
Publications, 1962).

8. There is a copy of the "Portfolio of Spanish Colonial Design in New Mexico: 1938" in
the History Library, Museum of New Mexico, Santa Fe. See references to it in McDonald,
Federal Relief Administration, pp. 442–43, 456. Also see an undated (1960s?) catalogue for
the exhibit sponsored by the United States-Mexico Commission for Border Development and
Friendship entitled *The Art of the Spanish Southwest: an Exhibition of Water-Color
Renderings from The Index of American Design,* National Gallery of Art, Washington, D.C.

9. Quoted in McDonald, *Federal Relief Administration,* p. 629.

10. *New Mexico: a Guide,* p. 147.

11. Marjorie F. Tully and Juan B. Rael, *An Annotated Bibliography of Spanish Folklore in
New Mexico and Southern Colorado* (Albuquerque: University of New Mexico Press, 1950), p.
117; Wilma Loy Shelton, *Checklist of New Mexico Publications, 1850–1953* (Albuquerque:
University of New Mexico Press, 1954), p. 83.

12. Quoted in McDonald, *Federal Relief Administration,* p. 639.

13. Ibid., p. 778.

14. Shelton, *Checklist of New Mexico Publications,* pp. 83–84; J. B. Hover to Nina
Otero-Warren, 3 December 1942, WPA Files, Administration, New Mexico State Records
Center and Archives, Santa Fe.

15. Booklet of photographs, Translators Project, WPA Project 65-1700-B, 21 December
1935, WPA Files, Administration, Santa Fe.

16. Quoted in McDonald, *Federal Relief Administration,* p. 659.

17. Walter to Cassidy, 11 June 1937, WPA Files, Administration, Santa Fe.

18. For a brief history of the Place Names Project, see T. M. Pearce, ed., with Ina Sizer
Cassidy and Helen S. Pearce, *New Mexico Place Names: a Geographical Dictionary*
(Albuquerque: University of New Mexico Press, 1965), p. vii.

19. McDonald, *Federal Relief Administration*, p. 704. Lomax was succeeded as folklore consultant by Dr. Benjamin A. Botkin on May 2, 1938. Botkin reorganized the FWP folklore section and issued a detailed *Manual for Folklore Studies* in September 1938, several months after the New Mexico folklore chapter in the state Guide had been approved. For a discussion of the relationship between the discipline of folklore and the federal arts projects, see Susan Dwyer-Shick, "The Development of Folklore and Folklife Research in the Federal Writers' Project, 1935–1943," *Keystone Folklore* 20 (1975):5–31; and idem, "Review Essay: Folklore and Government Support," *Journal of American Folklore* 89 (1976):476–86. Also see Perdue's introduction to Charles L. Perdue, Jr., Thomas E. Barden, and Robert K. Phillips, comps. and eds., *Weevils in the Wheat: Interviews with Virginia Ex-Slaves* (Charlottesville: University Press of Virginia, 1976).

20. These documents are not complete, and thus all references in this and following paragraphs are tentatively based on the Administration section of the WPA Files in the New Mexico State Records Center and Archives, Santa Fe.

21. *New Mexico: a Guide*, pp. 98–106.

22. Charles E. Minton to N. Howard Thorp, 19 September 1939, WPA Files, Administration.

23. Jerre Mangione, *The Dream and The Deal: The Federal Writers' Project, 1935–1943* (Boston: Little, Brown and Co., 1972), p. 178.

24. Margaret Lohlker, "The Santa Fean's Writers," *The Santa Fean*, July 1940, p. 22. Back in Chicago by that time, Scher contributed a short story, "The Dark Pool," to this inaugural issue and another, "The Big Nigger," to the issue of February 1941.

25. For an account of Fisher's difficulties with *Idaho: a Guide in Word and Pictures* (Caldwell, Idaho: Caxton Printers, 1937), see Mangione, *The Dream and the Deal*, pp. 78–79, 201–8. Fisher finally resigned in 1939 (ibid., p. 370).

26. Brown also notes that "in later years I was employed in Idaho with many of Vardis Fisher's ex-schoolmates. They generally acknowledged him to be a sissy with his head stuck in a book all the time. During recess or after school, he would never join them in school sports or activities, nor would he share with them the many surreptitious pursuits indulged in after school was dismissed: drinking whiskey, chewing tobacco, smoking cigarettes, or other diversions of like nature. So that it must have been the nature of the man, and his success is a tribute to the persistence with which he followed his true inclinations."

27. From Minton's preface to *New Mexico: a Guide*, p. viii. A second edition was published by the University of New Mexico Press, Albuquerque, in 1945. Hastings House published a revised edition, edited by Joseph Miller and Henry G. Alsberg, in 1953 and 1962.

28. The FWP Files now in Santa Fe at the History Library, Museum of New Mexico, and the New Mexico State Records Center and Archives have not yet been fully coordinated. No single source is an adequate guide to the local holdings. The most complete listing is the excellent card catalogue prepared by Stephany Eger at the History Library. There is also a folder containing biographical and bibliographical information on some workers in the WPA Files, Administration, State Records Center. Additional information may be found in two published bibliographies: Lyle Saunders, comp. *A Guide to Materials Bearing on Cultural Relations in New Mexico*, Inter-Americana Bibliographies, III (Albuquerque: University of New Mexico Press, 1944); and Gilberto Benito Córdova, comp., *Bibliography of Unpublished Materials Pertaining to Hispanic Culture in the New Mexico WPA Writers' Files* (Santa Fe: New Mexico State Department of Education, December 1972), a preliminary compilation.

29. Charles Ethrige Minton (1893–1976) taught and practiced law in St. Louis, Missouri, before coming to Santa Fe in 1930. He founded the Santa Fe Country Day School and served as its headmaster from 1931 to 1935. Later, he was instrumental in establishing the New Mexico Boys Ranch. In the 1950s and 1960s, he was especially active in Indian affairs, founding the New Mexico Indian Club (later the Southwestern Association on Indian Affairs) and the New Mexico Indian Youth Council and serving as the first executive director of the

New Mexico State Commission on Indian Affairs. In 1973, he published an ethnohistorical novel, *Juan of Santo Niño: an Authentic Account of Pioneer Life in New Mexico, 1863–1864* (Santa Fe, New Mexico: Sunstone Press), based on material from the FWP Files. Most of this had been submitted by Lou Sage Batchen from Las Placitas, the "Tía Lou" of the dedication. However, Brown has identified at least one of his own 1937 manuscripts (41) on pp. 36–39. According to Brown: "This incident occurred on the Staked Plains where El Capitán Vigil had accompanied a group of villagers on a trading trip to a Comanche *rancheria* on the plains. I wished to preserve an incident in the life of this doughty pioneer and Indian fighter, patriarch and founder of Cundiyo, New Mexico. This incident was related to me by an old gentleman, seventy-five years old at the time of interview, who had accompanied the expedition as a lad of twelve. . . . In Mr. Minton's book all historical significance was lost since he clothed his characters with names that had no value in that area. It was an encounter so unique that it could not have occurred in two different locales." Note that some of Lou Sage Batchen's materials were published under her name in *Las Placitas: Historical Facts and Legends* (Placitas, New Mexico: Tumbleweed Press, 1972).

30. A reorganized bilingual edition of this work, edited by Dolores Gonzáles, was published as *Canciones y Juegos de Nuevo México/Songs and Games of New Mexico* (South Brunswick and New York: A. S. Barnes & Co., 1974). A much more useful reprint edition was compiled by Richard B. Stark as *Juegos Infantiles Cantados en Nuevo México* (Santa Fe: Museum of New Mexico Press, 1973), based on the 1940 mimeographed FMP Unit No. 3. According to Stark's preface, he interviewed Dr. Campa at the University of Denver and discovered that the thirteen singing games "were collected in northern New Mexico in the summer of 1932 by Dr. Campa and his assistant, Aureliano Armendáriz, a musician from La Mesilla, New Mexico." Others "were supplied by Dr. Campa and Sr. Armendáriz from remembrances of singing games they played as children in Mexico." Notes to this revised bilingual edition with musical transcriptions include both Campa's and Armendáriz's recollections as well as occasional comparative references.

31. Quoted in McDonald, *Federal Relief Administration*, p. 314.

32. For a sound criticism of the FWP's accomplishments, see Daniel M. Fox, "The Achievement of the Federal Writers' Project," *American Quarterly* 13 (1961):3–19. Also see Monty Noam Penkower, *The Federal Writers' Project: a Study in Government Patronage of the Arts* (Urbana: University of Illinois Press, 1977), and the bibliography of sources cited in Mangione, *The Dream and The Deal*, pp. 397–403. Mangione includes a partial but useful listing by Arthur Scharf, "Selected Publications of the WPA Federal Writers' Project and the Writers' Program," pp. 375–96.

BIBLIOGRAPHY

I. Lorin W. Brown's Federal Writers' Project Manuscripts:
An Annotated List of the Basic Corpus

During his tenure with the New Mexico Federal Writers' Project, Lorin W. Brown wrote well over 150 manuscripts on a wide range of topics, locales, genres, and customs. Despite the lack of guidance and encouragement from and his incompatibility with most Federal Writers' Project administrators, Brown managed to record a vivid and useful picture of Hispano folklife in northern New Mexico. An accurate bibliography of this important work will probably never be possible. However, the following "basic corpus" is substantially representative. Only translations of others' submissions, obvious rewrites, or apparently incorrectly identified song texts—all of which comprise a very small portion of Brown's work—have been excluded.

The 125 manuscripts of the "basic corpus" clearly represent various stages of the editing process. Unfortunately, extant records and copies do not permit more than surmise as to which are Brown's originals. For example, Brown recalls being asked especially to contribute the elaborate piece on Basílico Garduño (28) for a nationwide book to be entitled "Men at Work" and to contain certain accounts of "typical occupations from each state." Neither this anthology nor the proposed "The Western Range: the Story of the Grasslands," also an appropiate volume for the essay, ever materialized, but Brown's manuscript, carefully typed and edited, remains in the New Mexico files. By contrast, many of his early manuscripts are either completely unretouched or covered with editorial blue-pencilings in several different hands.

Brown claims he was never specifically instructed to write for the New Mexico Guide, although he knew this project "was going on." However, "it was assumed that whatever material you sent in suitable to the Guide would be inserted . . . someplace." Three notes definitely written for a guidebook (35, 48, 49) indicate that he tried to satisfy some such requirement in 1937. He also contributed to the later project to collect games.

Page numbers and typefaces suggest that many of the Cordova materials were rewritten. Manuscripts numbered 36, 52, 75, 80, 88, 110, 116, and 125 together comprise a nearly complete document of more than 150 pages covering the major aspects of Cordova life and lore. Although only the twenty-three-page description of the Cordova church is entitled "Hands That Built America" (67), it may be that all this edited and retyped material was intended for inclusion in one of the six proposed regional guides of that title which were never completed in the early 1940s. These volumes were to have included plates from the Art Program's Index of American Design. Nevertheless, it is a tribute to Brown's abilities that his submissions and not Reyes N. Martínez's Arroyo Hondo manuscripts were apparently chosen to represent Hispano New Mexico.

A few of Brown's Federal Writers' Project manuscripts have been published; bibliographical details are given below following the appropriate entry. In addition, references to three more recent essays have been appended, bringing the total of the writings to an impressive 128 contributions. The Taos reminiscences (127, 128) are part of a work in progress, "Tales of Taos." The last, "Trompos are Trumps" (128), has been included in Part II above because it contains interesting new material not covered in the Federal Writers' Project manuscripts.

In the following listing, the original titles of Brown's manuscripts have been alphabetized and numbered consecutively. Each piece is characterized, e.g., as the text of a specific genre of folklore, a reminiscence, a narrative sketch, a description, and so on. An "S" indicates that the work is in Spanish only, an "E" that it is written in English, while an "S-E" designates a Spanish text with English translation. Except for the song texts, where the number of stanzas is noted, the number of typed pages in the original manuscript is then given. Finally, wherever possible, either the manuscript's date of completion or its date of reception in the Santa Fe Writers' Project office is included.

The Basic Corpus of Lorin W. Brown's Manuscripts

1. "Adages." 29 items. S-E. 2 pp. 4 August 1937. (Also: Same Spanish texts with E. F. Ulibarrí translations, 4 August 1937.)
2. "Adivinanzas." 6 riddles. S. 1 p. 4 August 193?.
3. "Adivinanzas." 7 riddles. S-E. 2 pp. 11 August 1937.
4. "Adivinanzas (Conundrums)." 2 theological questions. S-E. 1 p. 20 October 1937.
5. "Alabados" ("Adios Sangre de Cristo"). Hymn from Brother's notebook. S-E. 15 stanzas. n.d.
6. "Alabados" ("Al angel de guarda"). Hymn. S-E. 13 stanzas. n.d.
7. "Alabados" ("Ave María Purísima"). Hymn from Brother's notebook. S-E. 17 stanzas. n.d.
8. "Alabados" ("Ay de los tristes gemidos"). Hymn. S-E. 17 stanzas. n.d.
9. "Alabados" ("Ay mi Jesús Nazareno"). Hymn from Brother's notebook. S-E. 21 stanzas. n.d.
10. "Alabados" ("Bendito el Santo Madero"). Hymn. S-E. 8 stanzas. n.d.
11. "Alabados" ("Daremos gracias con fé . . . A Jesús, María, y José"). Hymn. S-E. 15 stanzas. n.d.
12. "Alabados" ("Dios te salve Dolorosa"). Hymn from Brother's notebook. S-E. 9 stanzas. n.d.
13. "Alabados" ("La encomendación del alma"). Hymn from Brother's notebook. S-E. 20 stanzas. n.d.
14. "Alabados" ("Niño pues vais a pagar"). Hymn from Brother's notebook. 20 stanzas. n.d.
15. "Alabados" ("O Jesús, por mis delitos"). Hymn from Brother's notebook. S-E. 6 stanzas. n.d.
16. "Alabados" ("Recuerda si estás dormido"). Hymn from Brother's notebook. S-E. 6 stanzas. n.d.
17. "Alabados" ("San Ignacio de Loyola"). Hymn from Brother's notebook. S-E. 11 stanzas. n.d.
18. "Alabados" ("San Pedro me abra sus puertas"). Hymn from Brother's notebook. S-E. 14 stanzas. n.d.
19. "Alabados" ("San Ysidro Labrador"). Hymn. S-E. 8 stanzas. n.d.
20. "Alabados" ("Santa Inés del Campo"). Hymn. S-E. 10 stanzas. n.d.
21. "Alabados" ("Si quieres alma tener"). Hymn. S-E. 22 stanzas. n.d.
22. "Alabados" ("Ven Pecador y verás"). Hymn from Brother's notebook. S-E. 23 stanzas. n.d.
23. "Alabados" ("Vuestro Cuerpo Sacrosanto"). Hymn. S-E. 7 stanzas. n.d.
Editors' note: Brown footnotes most of the alabado texts as "copied from the *cuaderno* (hymnal) of a member of the order of Penitentes and generously loaned by him to the writer." This Brother is identified only as a resident of Rio Arriba County, presumably from Cordova.
24. "Alto Huachin." History of Cordova. E. 3 pp. 9 September 1938.

25. "The Ambuscade." Personal reminiscence of Taos; stories of defense against Indian raids. E. 5 pp. 18 May 1937.

26. "Amor y Traición (Love and Its Betrayal)." Song from Federico Arellano, Santa Fe. S-E. 2 pp. 10 October 1938.

27. "La Ave María de los Borrachos (The Hail Mary of the Drunkards)." Song. S-E. 1 p. 4 August 1937. (Translated by Reyes N. Martínez.)

28. "Basílico Garduño, New Mexico Sheepherder." Descriptive sketch. E. 24 pp. n.d.

29. "El Bautismo (The Christening)." Description of customs. E. 3 pp. n.d.

30. "The Bell Marianna." Narrative sketch of Cordova bell christening. E. 4 pp. 3 May 1937.

31. "Birth of a *Dicho.*" Narrative sketch; origin of a local proverb. E. 6 pp. n.d.

32. "The Black Dog." Narrative sketch; personal reminiscence of a Taos *médica.* E. 5 pp. 2 July 1937.

33. "El Caballo de Siete Colores." Tale from Brown's mother. S. 6 pp. 14 March 1938.

34. "Canción de la Escoba (Broom Song)." Song from María Dolores Vigil, Talpa. S-E. 1 p. 10 October 1938.

35. "Chimayo and Potrero." Guidebook notes. E. 1 p. 15 April 1937.

36. "The Christening of the Bell." Description of associated customs and local Cordova traditions. E. 5 pp. n.d.

37. "Chueco or Pelota." Ball game. S-E. 4 pp. 8 December 1938.

38. "El Ciervo y La Oveja, Siendo Juez El Lobo (The Sheep and the Deer, with the Wolf as Judge)." Poem from Pedro Vigil, Talpa. S-E. 1 p. 23 September 1938.

39. "Los Comanches." Description of folk drama staged December 28, 1938, at El Rancho. E. 4 pp. 3 January 1939.

40. "Los Comanches." Folk drama from ms. of Martín Roybal, San Ildefonso. S-E. 10 pp. 14 August 1937.

41. "Los Comanches." Reminiscence about *Comancheros* from Vicente Romero, Cordova. E. 8 pp. 8 April 1937. Published as "'Los Comanches': The Narrative of Vicente Romero." In Rubén Darió Sálaz, *Cosmic: The La Raza Sketch Book.* Santa Fe, New Mexico: Blue Feather Press, 1975, pp. 77-82.

42. "Compadres y Comadres." Description of customs. E. 4 pp. 19 April 1937. Edited version published in *Over the Turquoise Trail* 1, no. 2 (1937):9-10.

43. "Comparison of 'Los Pastores'" (Agua Fria and San Rafael versions). Folk drama. E. 2 pp. 18 November 1938.

44. "Comparison of 'Los Pastores'" (Agua Fria and San Rafael versions). Folk drama. E. 34 pp. 29 November 1938.

45. "Comparison of 'Los Pastores'" (Agua Fria and Santa Fe versions). Folk drama. E. 2 pp. 4 December 1938.

46. "Comparison of 'Los Pastores'" (Galisteo and San Rafael versions). Folk drama. E. 3 pp. 23 November 1938.

47. "Comparison of 'Los Pastores'" (Taos and San Rafael versions). Folk drama. E. 2 pp. 23 November 1938.

Editors' note: The San Rafael, New Mexico, version used for comparison is in M. R. Cole, trans. and ed. *Los Pastores: a Mexican Play of the Nativity.* Memoirs of the American Folk-Lore Society, vol. 9. Boston and New York: Houghton Mifflin Co., 1907, pp. 211-34. Honora De Busk (Smith) witnessed the play and copied the manuscript in 1899.

48. "Cordova." Guidebook note. E. 1 p. n.d.

49. "Cordova." Guidebook note and clipping of José Dolores López's obituary, 17 May 1937. E. 1 p. n.d.

50. "Corrida de Gallo (Rooster Pull)." Description of Galisteo tradition. E. 1 p. 17 July 1939.

51. "Décima or poem in honor of San José patrón, of Galisteo." Dedication poem by Ramón B. Chávez, from Francisco S. Leyba, Leyba. S-E. 2 pp. 20 October 1937.

52. "The Deep Village." Folklife description. E. 10 pp. n.d.

53. "Descansos." Description. E. 2 pp. 29 October 1938.

54. "Despedidas (Farewell verses sung as the last part of the Pastores)." Song. S-E. 2 pp. 14 March 193?.

55. "Día de herejes." Origin of saying. E. 1 p. 9 January 1939.

56. "Día de los Inocentes." Narrative sketch; New Year's customs. E. 6 pp. 29 December 1937.

57. "Don Simón." Song. S-E. 3 pp. 9 May 1938.

58. "Doña Fortuna y Don Dinero." Tale from Pedro Vigil, Talpa. S. 5 pp. *(See* 116) n.d.

59. "Extraordinary Convention of the Beasts." Poem from Pedro Vigil, Talpa. S-E. 8 pp. n.d.

60. "El Filósofo y el Tecolote (The Philosopher and the Owl)." Song from Pedro Vigil, Talpa. S-E. 1 p. 23 September 1938.

61. "Flight to Mexico." Narrative sketch; legends told by Tía Lupe, Cordova. E. 5 pp. 26 April 1937.

62. "El Gallo." Ballad. S-E. 9 stanzas from Augustine Montoya, Galisteo; description. 6 pp. 11 October 1937.

63. "Gambusinos." Description of placer miners south of Santa Fe. E. 4 pp. 2 December 1938.

64. "Going for Wood." Description set in Cordova. E. 1 p. 19 April 1937. Edited version published in *Over the Turquoise Trail* 1, no. 1 (1937):28.

65. "The Golden Image." Reminiscences from Higinio Tórrez, Cordova. E. 6 pp. n.d.

66. "'Guashadas' or Tall Tales." Tall tale from José María ("Guashi") Tafoya, Taos. E. 5 pp. 18 May 1937.

67. "Hands That Built America." Description of Cordova church, plus "Correction on Cordova Mission" page. E. 23 pp. n.d. Several paragraphs quoted in Charles D. Carroll, "Miguel Aragon, a Great Santero," *El Palacio* 50 (1943):60, 62.

68. "Home-Made Furniture." Description. E. 4 pp. 31 August 1938.

69. "How San Cristóbal Got His Name." Tale from Tía Lupe, Cordova. *(See* 116) E. 2 pp. 17 May 1938.

70. "The Hunter's Stone." Narrative sketch; legend from Eusebio. E. 3 pp. 26 April 1937.

71. "Inditas." 2 songs from Francisco S. Leyba, Leyba. S-E. 3 pp. 1 November 1937.

72. "El Inocente." Description of Cordova village idiot. E. 6 pp. 20 September 1937.

73. "Jesu' Cristo a Caballo." Narrative sketch; origin of a saying. E. 4 pp. 22 November 1937. Published as "Santo a Caballo," *The Santa Fe New Mexico Sentinel,* 29 December 1937, p. 6.

74. "Juegos (Games)." Gallinita Ciega ("The Little Blind Hen") and El Florón ("The Large Flower"). S-E. 1 p. n.d.

Editors' note: Brown's name is on a number of the games collected by workers of the Writers', Music, and Art Programs. Their 1942 compilation has been reprinted in Dolores Gonzáles ed. *Canciones y Juegos de Nuevo México/*Songs and Games of New Mexico. South Brunswick and New York: A. S. Barnes & Co., 1974. Only the above representative page has been included here.

75. "Lent in Cordova." Description. E. 16 pp. n.d. Revised version published in Lorenzo de Córdova. *Echoes of the Flute.* Santa Fe, New Mexico: Ancient City Press, 1972, pp. 35-47.

76. "The Lion and the Man." Tale from Santiago S. Mata, Santa Fe. S-E. 8 pp. 12 September 1938.

77. "La Llegada de el Arzobispo Lamy a la ciudad de Santa Fe." Verses composed by Father Rómulo Rivera, from Francisco S. Leyba, Leyba. S-E. 8 stanzas. 30 September 1937.

78. "Lo Que Pasa." Poem from Francisco S. Leyba, Leyba. 1 December 1937.

79. "The Lost Juan Mondragón Mine." Narrative sketch; legends. E. 4 pp. n.d. Edited version published in *Over the Turquoise Trail* 1, no. 2 (1937):18-20.

80. "The Lost Treasure of Don Pedro Córdova." Legend from Cordova. E. 7 pp. n.d.

81. "Manuel Maes." Ballad. S-E. 19 stanzas. 11 October 1937.

82. "La Mujer (Woman)." Poem from Natividad Leyba, Leyba. S-E. 4 pp. 12 September 1938.

83. "El Negrito Poeta y el Maestro Vilmas." Song from Francisco S. Leyba, Leyba. S-E. 2 pp. 1 December 1937.

84. "Nichos." Description. E. 1 p. 31 August 1938.

85. "Noche Buena." Description of Christmas customs. E. 4 pp. n.d.

86. "Now I could be a broker." Untitled song from Ysidro Mares, Santa Fe. E. 1 p. 30 August 1937.

87. "Nuestra Señora de Dolores." Description, El Cañon de Taos customs. E. 2 pp. 23 January 1939.

88. "'Ollas de Barro' and 'Trojas'." Description of early pottery making at Cordova. E. 3 pp. n.d.

89. "Padre Martínez and the First College in New Mexico." History and personal reminiscence. E. 2 pp. 3 March 1939.

90. "Los Pastores" (Agua Fria version). Folk drama from ms. owned by Antonio Gallegos, Agua Fria; copied by Eliseo Trujillo, Santa Fe. S-E; musical transcriptions. 108 pp. n.d.

91. "Los Pastores" (Galisteo version). Folk drama from ms. owned by Gregorio Chávez, Leyba; copied from ms. of Pablo Madrid, Duran. S. 40 pp. 17 January 1938.

92. "Los Pastores" (Santa Fe version). Folk drama from ms. owned by Ysidro Mares, Santa Fe; originally copied by Nasario Rivera. S-E. 78 pp. 30 August 1937.

93. "Los Pastores" (Taos version). Folk drama. E. translation from ms. submitted by Reyes N. Martínez. 39 pp. 16 April 1938.

94. "Los Pastores and Other Plays Brought to New Mexico by the Spaniards and Presented at Different Seasons." Descriptions. E. 3 pp. 8 May 1939.

95. "Los Perros (The Dogs)." Song from Pedro Vigil, Talpa. S-E. 3 pp. 10 October 1938.

96. "The Pet Magpie." Family legend from grandmother. E. 2 pp. 30 January 1939.

97. "The Priest's Cats." Tale. *(See* 116) E. 4 pp. 2 July 1937.

98. "Problema." 2 conundrums from Pedro Vigil, Talpa. S-E. 1 p. 19 September 1938.

99. "The Proverb." Narrative sketch; use of gestured proverb. E. 2 pp. 16 November 1938. Rewritten as "Not All the Fingers of One's Hand," *The Santa Fean*, July 1940, p. 16.

100. "Proverbs (Dichos)." 51 items. S-E. 3 pp. 26 May 1938.

101. "Refranes." 14 items. S-E. 1 p. 3 August 1937. (Also: Spanish text only, 4 August 1937; Spanish text with translations by E. F. Ulibarrí, 4 August 1937.)

102. "Refranes (Descriptive Phrases and Sayings)." 77 items. S-E. 3 pp. 26 May 1938.

103. "Revato en un velorio (Occurrence at a Wake)." Humorous anecdote. S-E. 3 pp. n.d. (Translated by Aurora Lucero White.)

104. "La Rubia." Reminiscence of an old veteran of the battle of Val Verde, Miguel Archuleta. E. 7 pp. 2 July 1937.

105. "San Luis Gonzaga." Description. E. 1 p. 23 January 1939.

106. "San Ysidro Labrador." Personal reminiscence from Valdez. E. 2 pp. 1 September 1938.

107. "Santa Inés del Campo." Description. E. 1 p. 30 January 1939.

108. "Santa Persíngula." Description; Arroyo Hondo. E. 1 p. 30 January 1939.

109. "Se volcó la olla." Origin of saying. E. 2 pp. 1 September 1938.

110. "Los Senadores." Description; old people of Cordova. E. 5 pp. n.d.

111. "On Setting a Hen." Tale. E. 3 pp. *(See* 116) 22 November 1937.

112. "La Severiana." Song from Taos area. S-E. 2 pp. 1 September 1938.

113. "A Synopsis of 'Los Pastores'." Folk drama adapted for school use. E. 12 pp. 27 January 1939.

114. "A Tale about Santa Rita." Saint's legend from Amalia Kahn, Santa Fe. S-E. 4 pp. 8 October 1938.

115. "Tales of the Moccasin Maker of Cordova." Narrative sketch; witch stories told by Manuel Trujillo. E. 4 pp. 3 May 1937.

116. "Tía Lupe." Description of Cordova "character"; with five "Stories that Tía Lupe Told." E. 21 pp. n.d.

117. "Tía Lupe." Narrative sketch. E. 2 pp. 22 March 1937. Edited version published in *Over the Turquoise Trail* 1, no. 1 (1937):31-32.

118. "Trovo de el Viejo Vilmas." Song from Augustine Montoya, Galisteo. S. 4 pp. 11 October 1937.

119. "El Trovo del Viejo Vilmas." Song from Francisco S. Leyba, Leyba. S-E. 5 pp. n.d.

120. "Two Folk Songs." El Triste Corazón ("The Sorrowing Heart") and El Camarón ("The Shrimp") from Zoraida V. Montoya, Taos, S-E. 1 p. 19 September 1938.

121. "Villancico." Song from Desiderio Chaves. S-E. 1 p. 30 August 1937.

122. "The Wake." Description. E. 4 pp. 9 April 1937. Revised version published in De Córdova, *Echoes of the Flute*, pp. 48-50.

123. "The Witch Doctor." Narrative sketch; reminiscences about Indian encounters, told by Juan José Gonzáles, from near Corrales. E. 3 pp. n.d.

124. "A Witch Story." Narrative told by Melitón Trujillo, Truchas. E. 2 pp. 10 January 1939.

125. "The Woodcarver of Cordova: Don José Dolores López." Biography. E. 10 pp. n.d.

Addenda: Recent Writings

126. "Echoes of the Flute." Personal reminiscences about the Brotherhood, written in 1971. Published in De Córdova, *Echoes of the Flute,* pp. 5-34. This booklet includes illustrations by Eliseo Rodríguez and a section of "Notes, Place Names, and Glossary" by Marta Weigle.

127. "Noche Buena in Taos—Circa 1913." Personal reminiscences. E. 9 pp. n.d.

128. "Trompos are Trumps." Reminiscences about an entrepreneur and about gambling with tops in Taos. E. 11 pp. n.d.

Note: An anonymous article on "San Ysidro's Day in Cordova," also including mention of San Juan Day observances, was undoubtedly written by Brown, although no manuscript can be found at present. This article is part of the published Writers' Program compilation "Fiestas in New Mexico," *El Palacio* 48 (1941):239-42.

II. Hispano Folklife in New Mexico:
A Selected, Supplemental Compilation

The following list of *selected* folklore and folklife studies on Hispano New Mexico provides a larger context for the collection assembled by workers of the Federal Writers' Project (later Program) in New Mexico. More comprehensive bibliographies are also cited. Some published New Mexico FWP materials are given, as are certain publications by FWP personnel and contributors before, during, and after their association with the Project. The experience these contributors brought to their FWP work and the FWP's influence on them may thus be suggested. Other published folklore collections and pertinent folklife studies contemporary with the FWP (1935–43) have been included to indicate the state of both scholarly and more popular folkloristic and sociocultural studies at the time. Finally, because Lorin W. Brown, his "Santa Fe friends," and most FWP workers were largely oriented toward literature rather than social science per se, a short list of fiction published between 1930 and 1945 and dealing primarily with Hispano folklife concludes this compilation.

Bibliographies

Bratcher, James T. *Analytical Index to Publications of the Texas Folklore Society, Volumes 1–36.* Dallas: Southern Methodist University Press, 1973.

Córdova, Gilbert Benito. *Bibliography of Unpublished Materials Pertaining to Hispanic Culture in the New Mexico WPA Writers' Files.* Santa Fe: New Mexico State Department of Education, December 1972.

Heisley, Michael, comp. *An Annotated Bibliography of Chicano Folklore from the Southwestern United States.* Los Angeles: Center for the Study of Comparative Folklore and Mythology, University of California, 1977.

Major, Mabel, and Pearce, T. M. *Southwest Heritage: a Literary History with Bibliographies.* 3d ed. Albuquerque: University of New Mexico Press, 1972.

Saunders, Lyle, comp. *A Guide to Materials Bearing on Cultural Relations in New Mexico.* Inter-Americana Bibliographies, III. Albuquerque: University of New Mexico Press, 1944.

Tully, Marjorie F., and Rael, Juan B., comps. *An Annotated Bibliography of Spanish Folklore in New Mexico and Southern Colorado.* University of New Mexico Publications in Language and Literature, no. 3. Albuquerque, 1950.

Weigle, Marta, comp. "Part II: Bibliography." In *Hispanic Villages of Northern New Mexico: a Reprint of Volume II of The 1935 Tewa Basin Study, with Supplementary Materials,* edited by Marta Weigle, pp. 242–78. Santa Fe, New Mexico: The Lightning Tree-Jene Lyon, Publisher, 1975.

————, comp. *A Penitente Bibliography.* Albuquerque: University of New Mexico Press, 1976.

Published New Mexico FWP Materials

Batchen, Lou Sage. *Las Placitas: Historical Facts and Legends.* Placitas, New Mexico: Tumbleweed Press, 1972.

————. "Three Tales from Las Placitas." *Western Folklore* 15 (1956):89–92.

Calendar of Events. Santa Fe, New Mexico: Rydal Press, 1937.

Córdova, Lorenzo de [Lorin W. Brown]. *Echoes of the Flute.* Santa Fe, New Mexico: Ancient City Press, 1972.

"Fiestas in New Mexico." *El Palacio* 48 (1941):239–45.

Gonzáles, Dolores, ed. *Canciones y Juegos de Nuevo México/Songs and Games of New Mexico.* South Brunswick and New York: A. S. Barnes & Co., 1974.

New Mexico. American Recreation Series, no. 30. Northport, New York: Bacon and Wieck, 1941.

New Mexico: a Guide to the Colorful State. New York: Hastings House, 1940.

Pearce, T. M. *Stories of the Spanish Southwest/Cuentos de los niños chicanos: In English and Spanish,* trans. Catherine Delgado Espinosa. Albuquerque, New Mexico: Aiken Printing, 1973. (Two stories from Lou Sage Batchen FWP materials.)

————, ed., assisted by Ina Sizer Cassidy and Helen S. Pearce. *New Mexico Place Names: a Geographical Dictionary.* Albuquerque: University of New Mexico Press, 1965.

"Southwest Witchcraft." Special Issue of *El Palacio* 80, September 1974.

"Spanish-American Baptismal Customs." *El Palacio* 49 (1942):59–61.

The Spanish-American Song and Game Book. New York: A. S. Barnes & Co., 1942.

"Spanish-American Wedding Customs." *El Palacio* 49 (1942):1–6.

"Spanish Colonial Customs in New Mexico." *El Palacio* 81 (March 1975):2–30.

"Spanish Fiestas in New Mexico." *El Palacio* 51 (1944):101–6.

Stark, Richard B., ed. *Juegos Infantiles Cantados en Nuevo México.* Santa Fe: Museum of New Mexico Press, 1973.

Publications by New Mexico FWP Personnel and Contributors

Boyd, E. *Popular Arts of Spanish New Mexico.* Santa Fe: Museum of New Mexico Press, 1974.

Brewster, Mela Sedillo. *Mexican and New Mexican Folk-dances.* 2d ed. Albuquerque: University of New Mexico Press, 1938.

Campa, Arthur L. *A Bibliography of Spanish Folk-Lore in New Mexico.* University of New Mexico Bulletin, Language Series, vol. 2, no. 3. Albuquerque, September 1930.

———. "Chile in New Mexico." *New Mexico Business Review* 3 (1934):61–63.

———. "Cultural Differences that Cause Conflict and Misunderstanding in the Spanish Southwest." *Western Review* 9 (1972):23–30.

———. "Cultural Variations in the Anglo-Spanish Southwest." *Western Review* 7 (1970):3–9.

———. "El Origen y la Naturaleza del Drama Folklórico." *Folklore Americas* 20 (1960): 13–48.

———. *Los Comanches; a New Mexican Folk Drama.* University of New Mexico Bulletin, Language Series, vol. 7, no. 1. Albuquerque, April 1942.

———. "Mañana Is Today." *New Mexico Quarterly* 9 (1939):3–11.

———. "The New Mexican Spanish Folktheater." *Southern Folklore Quarterly* 5 (1941): 127–31.

———. "Piñon as an Economic and Social Factor." *New Mexico Business Review* 1 (1932):144–47.

———. "Religious Spanish Folk-Drama in New Mexico." *New Mexico Quarterly* 2 (1932): 3–13.

———. *Sayings and Riddles in New Mexico.* University of New Mexico Bulletin, Language Series, vol. 6, no. 2. Albuquerque, September 1937.

———. *Spanish Folk-Poetry in New Mexico.* Albuquerque: University of New Mexico Press, 1946.

———. *The Spanish Folksong in the Southwest.* University of New Mexico Bulletin, Language Series, vol. 4, no. 1. Albuquerque, 15 November 1933.

———. *Spanish Religious Folk Theatre in the Southwest (First Cycle).* University of New Mexico Bulletin, Language Series, vol. 5, no. 1. Albuquerque, 15 February 1934.

———. *Spanish Religious Folk Theatre in the Southwest (Second Cycle).* University of New Mexico Bulletin, Language Series, vol. 5, no. 2. Albuquerque, 15 June 1934.

———. "Spanish Traditional Tales in the Southwest." *Western Folklore* 6 (1947):322–34.

———. "Today's Troubadours." *New Mexico,* September 1936, pp. 16–17, 49–50.

———. *Treasure of the Sangre de Cristos: Tales and Traditions of the Spanish Southwest.* Norman: University of Oklahoma Press, 1963.

Cassidy, Ina Sizer. "Folklore in New Mexico." *New Mexico Folklore Record* 2 (1947–48):3–6.

———. "The Lost *Capitán* Is Found." *New Mexico Folklore Record* 1 (1946–47):11–14.

———. "A New Mexican Tale." *Western Folklore* 6 (1947):182–83.

———. "New Mexico in the First National Folk Festival." *New Mexico*, April 1934, pp. 24–25, 45.

———. "Spanish Colonial Art." *New Mexico*, April 1939, pp. 25, 40.

Clark, Anna Nolan. "Art of the Loom." *New Mexico*, November 1938, pp. 9–11, 35–36.

———. "The Circle of Seasons." *New Mexico*, January 1941, pp. 18–19, 43.

———. "Goodbye to Gloom." *New Mexico*, August 1937, pp. 11–13, 54.

Henderson, Alice Corbin. *Brothers of Light: the Penitentes of the Southwest*. New York: Harcourt, Brace & Co., 1937.

———. "Furniture for Colonial Spanish Homes." *House and Garden*, July 1928, pp. 62–63, 92, 106.

———. "New Mexico Folk-Songs." *Poetry* 16 (1920):254–63.

Crook, Alice M. "Old-Time New Mexican Usages." In *Puro Mexicano*, edited by J. Frank Dobie, pp. 184–89. Texas Folk-Lore Society Publications, vol. 12. Austin, 1935.

Knee, Ernest. *Santa Fe*. New York: Hastings House, 1942.

Lea, Aurora Lucero White. *Folk-Dances of the Spanish-Colonials of New Mexico*. Santa Fe, New Mexico: Examiner Publishing, 1940.

———. *The Folklore of New Mexico*. Volume I. Santa Fe, New Mexico: Seton Village Press, 1941.

———. "Folkways." *New Mexico*, February 1940, pp. 16–17, 38–39.

———. "Folkways and Fiestas." *New Mexico*, March 1940, pp. 18–19, 44.

———. *Juan Bobo, adapted from the Spanish Folktale Bertolo*. New York: Vantage Press, 1962.

———. *Literary Folklore of the Hispanic Southwest*. San Antonio, Texas: Naylor, 1953.

———. *Los Hispanos*. Denver, Colorado: Sage Books, 1947.

———. "More about the Matachines." *New Mexico Folklore Record* 11 (1963–64):7–10.

———. *New Mexico Folklore—Coloquio de los Pastores*. Santa Fe, New Mexico: Santa Fe Press, 1940.

———. "Our Treasury of Spanish Folklore." *New Mexico Folklore Record* 9 (1954–55):15–19.

———. "Wakes for the Dead and the Saints." *El Palacio* 52 (1945):255–58.

Minton, Charles Ethrige. *Juan of Santo Niño: an Authentic Account of Pioneer Life in New Mexico, 1863–1864*. Santa Fe, New Mexico: Sunstone Press, 1973.

Otero-Warren, Nina. "The Clown of San Cristóbal." *Survey Graphic* 24 (1935):16–18, 45–46.

———. *Old Spain in Our Southwest*. New York: Harcourt, Brace & Co., 1936.

Otis, Raymond. "Medievalism in America." *New Mexico Quarterly* 6 (1936):83–90.

Other Published Contemporary Accounts,
Collections and Studies, 1935–43

Agnew, Edith. "Rural Riddles." *New Mexico*, August 1943, p. 23.

Barker, S. Omar. "Sagebrush Spanish." *New Mexico*, December 1942, pp. 32–33.

Booth, Mary. "Pattern of the Centuries." *New Mexico*, April 1943, pp. 10–11, 32–33. (Taos County)

Carroll, Charles D. "Miguel Aragón, a Great Santero." *El Palacio* 50 (March 1943):49–64.

Casey, Pearle R. "Chimayó, the Ageless Village." *Southwestern Lore* 1 (1936):11–13.

Culbert, James I. "Distribution of Spanish-American Population in New Mexico." *Economic Geography* 19 (1943):171–76.

De Huff, Elizabeth Willis. "Day of the Innocents." *New Mexico*, December 1936, pp. 18–19.

———. "The Metamorphosis of a Folk Tale." In *Puro Mexicano*, edited by J. Frank Dobie, pp. 122–34. Texas Folk-Lore Society Publications, vol. 12. Austin, 1935.

———. "People of the Soil." *New Mexico*, June 1940, pp. 26–27, 44, 46, 48.

————. *Say the Bells of Old Missions.* St. Louis, Missouri: B. Herder Books, 1943.

Eggan, Fred, and Pijoán, Michel. "Some Problems in the Study of Food and Nutrition." *América Indígena* 3 (1943):9–22.

Englekirk, John E. "Notes on the Repertoire of the New Mexican Spanish Folktheatre." *Southern Folklore Quarterly* 4 (1940):227–37.

Espinosa, Aurelio M. "An Extraordinary Example of Spanish Ballad Tradition in New Mexico." *Stanford Studies in Language and Literature.* Stanford, Calif., 1941, pp. 23–34.

————. "Hispanic Versions of the Tale of the Corpse Many Times 'Killed.' " *Journal of American Folk-Lore* 49 (1936):181–93.

————. "New Mexican Spanish *Coplas Populares.*" *Hispania* 18 (1935):135–50.

————, and Espinosa, José Manuel. "The Texans: A New Mexican Folk Play of the Middle 19th Century." *New Mexico Quarterly Review* 13 (1943):299–308.

Espinosa, José Manuel. *Spanish Folk-Tales from New Mexico.* Memoirs of the American Folk-Lore Society, vol. 30. New York: G. E. Stechert, 1937.

Fergusson, Erna. *Our Southwest.* New York: Alfred A. Knopf, 1940.

Gilbert, Fabiola Cabeza de Baca. "New Mexican Diets." *Journal of Home Economics* 34 (1942):668–69.

Hare, Elizabeth Sage. "The Wood Carver of Córdova." *Travel,* May 1943, pp. 20–21, 32.

Harper, Allan G., Cordova, Andrew R., and Oberg, Kalervo. *Man and Resources in the Middle Rio Grande Valley.* Inter-Americana Studies, II. Albuquerque: University of New Mexico Press, 1943.

Hawley, Florence. "Beyond Taos." *New Mexico,* July 1941, pp. 14–15, 37–39.

Heller, Christine A. "Regional Patterns of Dietary Deficiency: The Spanish-Americans of New Mexico and Arizona." *Annals of The American Academy of Political and Social Science* 225 (1943):49–51.

Hurt, Wesley R., Jr. "Buffalo Hunters." *New Mexico,* November 1941, pp. 9, 35–36.

————. "Indian Influence at Manzano." *El Palacio* 46 (1939):245–54.

————. "Shadows of the Past." *New Mexico,* May 1940, pp. 21, 37–38. (Chililí)

————. "Spanish-American Superstitions." *El Palacio* 47 (1940):193–201.

————. "Witchcraft in New Mexico." *El Palacio* 47 (1940):73–83.

"The J. D. Robb Collection of Folk Music Recordings." *New Mexico Folklore Record* 7 (1952–53):6–20.

Jaramillo, Cleofas M. *Cuentos del hogar.* El Campo, Texas: Citizens Press, 1939.

————. *Shadows of the Past (Sombras del pasado).* Santa Fe, New Mexico: Seton Village Press, 1941.

Johansen, Sigurd. "Family Organization in a Spanish-American Culture Area." *Sociology and Social Research* 28 (1943):123–31.

————. *The Population of New Mexico: Its Composition and Changes.* Agricultural Experiment Station, New Mexico College of Agriculture and Mechanic Arts, Bulletin 273, June 1940.

————. "The Social Organization of Spanish-American Villages." *Southwestern Social Science Quarterly* 23 (1942):151–59.

Johnson, J. B. "The Allelujahs: A Religious Cult in Northern New Mexico." *Southwest Review* 22 (1937):131–39.

Johnson, James Wood. "Spanish-America in the Southwest." *Travel,* November 1942, pp. 13–17.

Kubler, George. *The Religious Architecture of New Mexico: In the Colonial Period and Since the American Occupation.* Colorado Springs, Colorado: The Taylor Museum, 1940.

Leonard, Olen E., and Loomis, Charles P. *Culture of a Contemporary Rural Community: El Cerrito, New Mexico.* U.S. Department of Agriculture, Bureau of Agricultural Economics, Rural Life Studies, no. 1. Washington, D.C.: Government Printing Office, November 1941.

Long, Haniel. *Piñon Country*. New York: Duell, Sloan & Pearce, 1941.

Loomis, Charles P. "Informal Groupings in a Spanish-American Village." *Sociometry* 4 (1941):36–51.

———. "Wartime Migration from the Rural Spanish Speaking Villages of New Mexico." *Rural Sociology* 7 (1942):384–95.

———, and Grisham, Glen. "The New Mexican Experiment in Village Rehabilitation," *Applied Anthropology* 2 (1943):13–37.

Lowe, Cosette Chávez. "Dos reales de ay!" *New Mexico*, August 1939, pp. 26, 35–37.

———. "Hallowed Ground." *New Mexico*, August 1941, pp. 24, 52.

———. "El Pelón." *New Mexico*, November 1938, pp. 40–42.

Maes, Ernest E. "The World and the People of Cundiyo." *Land Policy Review*, March 1941, pp. 8–14.

Oberg, Kalervo. "Cultural Factors and Land-Use Planning in Cuba Valley, New Mexico." *Rural Sociology* 5 (1940):438–48.

Pijoán, Michel. *Certain Factors Involved in the Struggle Against Malnutrition and Disease, with Special Reference to the Southwest of the United States and Latin America.* Inter-Americana Short Papers, no. 7. Albuquerque: University of New Mexico Press, 1943.

———. "Food Availability and Social Function." *New Mexico Quarterly Review* 12 (1942):418–23.

Rael, Juan B. "Cuentos españoles de Colorado y de Nuevo Méjico. (Primera serie)." *Journal of American Folk-Lore* 52 (1939):227–323.

———. "Cuentos españoles de Colorado y de Nuevo Méjico. (Segunda serie)." *Journal of American Folk-Lore* 55 (1942):1–93.

———. "Gathering of Linguistic Material, Folk Music and Other Forms of Folklore in Southern Colorado and Northern New Mexico." *Year Book of American Philosophical Society*, 1940, pp. 232–33.

———. "New Mexican Spanish Feasts." *California Folklore Quarterly* 1 (1942):83–90.

———. "New Mexican Wedding Songs." *Southern Folklore Quarterly* 4 (1940):55–72.

———. "The Theme of Theft of Food by Playing Godfather in New Mexican Folklore." *Hispania* 20 (1937):231–34.

Ross, P. "Village of Many Blessings: A Fragment of Colonial Spain in New Mexico." *Travel* 64 (1935):35–37, 46.

Rusinow, Irving. *A Camera Report on El Cerrito: a Typical Spanish-American Community in New Mexico.* United States Department of Agriculture, Bureau of Agricultural Economics, Miscellaneous Publication, no. 479. Washington, D.C.: Government Printing Office, January 1942.

Sánchez, George I. *Forgotten People: a Study of New Mexicans*. Albuquerque: University of New Mexico Press, 1940.

Stamm, Roy Allen. "October in Cordova." *New Mexico*, October 1935, pp. 14, 38.

Staples, Betty. "A Century of Mañanas." *New Mexico Quarterly* 5 (1935):161–69. (Questa)

Storm, Dan. "The Pastor and the Serpent." In *In the Shadow of History*, edited by J. Frank Dobie, pp. 122–33. Texas Folk-Lore Society Publications, vol. 15, Austin, 1939.

Taichert, Ruth Parker. *Santa Fe Songs and Dances*. New York: Mills Music, 1940.

Walter, Paul Alfred Francis, Jr. "Rural-Urban Migration in New Mexico." *New Mexico Business Review* 8 (1939):132–37.

———. "The Spanish-Speaking Community in New Mexico." *Sociology and Social Research* 24 (1939):150–57.

Wilder, Mitchell A., with Breitenbach, Edgar. *Santos: the Religious Folk Art of New Mexico.* Colorado: The Taylor Museum of The Colorado Springs Fine Arts Center, 1943.

Williams, Arthur D. *Spanish-Colonial Furniture*. Milwaukee, Wisconsin: Bruce Publishing, 1941.

Woods, Betty. "Timeless Town." *New Mexico*, August 1943, pp. 16–17, 38–39. (Cordova)

Zunser, Helen. "A New Mexican Village." *Journal of American Folk-Lore* 48 (1935):125–78. (Hot Springs)

Hispano Folklife in Literature, 1930–45

Applegate, Frank G. *Native Tales of New Mexico.* Philadelphia: J. B. Lippincott Co., 1932.
———. "New Mexican Sketches." *Yale Review,* n.s. 21 (1931):376–92.
Austin, Mary. *One-Smoke Stories.* Cambridge, Massachusetts: Riverside Press, 1934.
———. *Starry Adventure.* Boston: Houghton Mifflin Co., 1931.
Botkin, B. A., ed. "New Mexico Number." *Space,* vol. 1, no. 5 (September 1934).
Bright, Robert. *The Life and Death of Little Jo.* 1944. Reprint. Albuquerque: University of New Mexico Press, 1978. (Talpa)
Carr, Lorraine. *Mother of the Smiths.* New York: Macmillan Co., 1940. (Taos)
Chavez, Fray Angelico. *New Mexico Triptych.* Paterson, New Jersey: St. Anthony Guild Press, 1940.
Eyre, Alice. *Torture at Midnight: the Mystery of the Penitentes.* New York: House of Field, 1942. (Sandia Mountains)
Foster, O'Kane. *In the Night Did I Sing.* New York: Charles Scribner's Sons, 1942. (Taos Valley)
Hall, D. J. *Perilous Sanctuary.* New York: MacMillan Co., 1937. (Sandia Mountains)
Martin, Curtis. *The Hills of Home.* Cambridge, Massachusetts: Riverside Press, 1943.
Otis, Raymond. *Little Valley.* London: The Cresset Press, 1937. (Cundiyo)
———. *Miguel of the Bright Mountain.* 1936. Reprint ed., Albuquerque: University of New Mexico Press, 1977. (Truchas)
Stevenson, Philip. "At the Crossroads." In *Folk-Say: a Regional Miscellany,* edited by Benjamin A. Botkin, pp. 70–82. Norman: University of Oklahoma Press, 1931.
Sylvester, Harry. *Dayspring.* New York: D. Appleton-Century, 1945. (Taos)
Waters, Frank. *People of the Valley.* Denver, Colorado: Sage Books, 1941. (Mora)

INDEX

Abuelo ("bogeyman"), 175–76, 177

Acequia ("ditch"). *See* Irrigation

Adobe ("mud-straw" method of construction), 12, 97, 115. *See also* Banco; Chapel; House; Tierra amarilla

Agua Fria, N.M., 19, 22, 23, 174, 175, 255 n. 32

Alabados ("hymns"): *Al Angel de Guarda*, 38–39; *Daremos gracias con fe*, 179–80; *La encomendación del alma*, 230–32; mentioned, 80, 120, 185, 192; *Oh Jesús, por mis delitos*, 184; *San Pedro me abra sus puertas*, 235–37; *San Ysidro Labrador*, 185, 186–87; *Santa Inés del Campo*, 157–58; sung at feast day, 41; sung at funerals, 235; sung at Tenebrae, 210; sung at wakes, 78. *See also* Song; Wakes

Albuquerque, N.M., 10, 14, 31, 32, 50, 189

Alcalde (justice of the peace), 90, 147, 148, 212

Alcalde, N.M., 149, 174

Almarios (wall storage niches), 61, 62, 108

Almud (traditional "measure"), 59, 94, 95, 101, 105

Alsberg, Henry G. (FWP official), 240, 243, 244, 246

Alto Huachin (vicinity Cordova), 21, 55–56

American Guide Series (FWP), 239, 243, 244. *See also* New Mexico Guide

American Recreation Series, (FWP), 240, 251

Americanos: references to, 91–93, 98, 109–10, 112, 137, 195; troops, 63, 64–66. *See also* Hispanos

Angelitos ("little angels"). *See* Death and dying

Anton Chico, N.M., 255 n. 32

Apaches, 48, 55, 59, 64, 65, 104. *See also* Indians

Applegate, Frank (writer, patron of arts), 17, 18, 209

Aragón, José Rafael (Cordova *santero*), 12

Architecture. *See* Chapel; House

Archuleta, Miguel (informant, Taos resident), 81–85

Armendáriz, Aureliano (NMFWP collector, La Mesilla resident), 248, 251, 252, 258 n. 30

Arroyo Hondo, N.M., 5, 7, 27, 249

Arroyo Seco, N.M., 7

Artists (friends, contemporaries), 17, 33, 206, 209, 252, 255–56 n. 1. *See also* Cinco Pintores; Federal Art Project; New Mexico FAP

Atarque, N.M., 255 n. 32

Austin, Mary (writer), 17, 18

Bailes ("dances"), 66, 76, 82, 83, 86, 89, 104, 122–23, 124. *See also* Dances; Music

Bakos, Jozef (artist), 17, 27

Baptism: certificates of, 200; described, 116–19, 120; part of tall tale, 151–52

Barela, Patrocinio (Taos woodcarver), 241

Batchen, Lou Sage (NMFWP collector, Las Placitas resident), 26, 248, 252, 258 n. 29

Bear, Donald J. (FAP official), 241

Belen, N.M., 86

Beliefs and superstitions: chickens, 139–40; hunting, 155–56; protection from elements, 135–36, 137; weather prediction, 162, 163. *See also* Death and dying, beliefs about; Healing; Legends; Witchcraft

Bell: accompanies procession, 186; announces death, 147, 193, 230; Cordova chapel bell, casting and christening, 101–5, 212–13; for funeral processions, 235

Birthdays, 180–81

Bosque Redondo, N.M., 53

Botkin, Benjamin A. (FWP official), 257 n. 19

Boyd, E. (artist with NMFAP), 26, 28, 32

Brayer, Herbert O. (NMHRS official), 242

Brotherhood of Our Father Jesus ("Penitentes"), 17, 18, 31, 41, 57, 111–13, 121, 148–49, 184, 192, 210, 235, 255 n. 28, 255 n. 33

Brown, Amy Crawford (sister), 9, 31

Brown, Anna (daughter), 29, 31

Brown, Bascom Howell (brother), 9, 10, 31

Brown, Cassandra Martínez de (mother), 5, 6, 7, 10, 16, 17, 18, 255 n. 33

Brown, Floy Violet (sister), 9

Brown, Frances (daughter), 29, 31

Brown, Frances Juanita Gilson (wife), 28–29, 30, 33

Brown, Lorin William, Jr.: biography, 3–34 passim; *Echoes of the Flute*, 32, 184, 253 n. 9, 255 n. 33; games collecting, 251, 252

271